Software Development From A to Z

A Deep Dive into all the Roles Involved in the Creation of Software

Olga Filipova
Rui Vilão

Apress®

Software Development From A to Z

Olga Filipova
Berlin, Germany

Rui Vilão
Berlin, Germany

ISBN-13 (pbk): 978-1-4842-3944-5
https://doi.org/10.1007/978-1-4842-3945-2

ISBN-13 (electronic): 978-1-4842-3945-2

Library of Congress Control Number: 2018960193

Managing Director, Apress Media LLC: Welmoed Spahr
Acquisitions Editor: Louise Corrigan
Development Editor: James Markham
Coordinating Editor: Nancy Chen

Cover designed by eStudioCalamar

Cover image designed by Freepik (www.freepik.com)

Distributed to the book trade worldwide by Springer Science+Business Media New York, 233 Spring Street, 6th Floor, New York, NY 10013. Phone 1-800-SPRINGER, fax (201) 348-4505, e-mail orders-ny@springer-sbm.com, or visit www.springeronline.com. Apress Media, LLC is a California LLC and the sole member (owner) is Springer Science + Business Media Finance Inc (SSBM Finance Inc). SSBM Finance Inc is a **Delaware** corporation.

For information on translations, please e-mail rights@apress.com, or visit http://www.apress.com/rights-permissions.

Apress titles may be purchased in bulk for academic, corporate, or promotional use. eBook versions and licenses are also available for most titles. For more information, reference our Print and eBook Bulk Sales web page at http://www.apress.com/bulk-sales.

Any source code or other supplementary material referenced by the author in this book is available to readers on GitHub via the book's product page, located at www.apress.com/9781484239445. For more detailed information, please visit http://www.apress.com/source-code.

Printed on acid-free paper

We dedicate this book to our soon-to-be-born son Alex

Table of Contents

About the Authors

Olga Filipova was born in Kyiv, Ukraine. She grew up in a family of physicists, researchers, and professors. She studied applied mathematics at the National University of Ukraine Kyiv Polytechnic Institute. At the age of 20, she moved to Portugal, where she studied Informatics Engineering at the University of Coimbra. During her studies, she participated in the investigation projects at the research lab of her department and taught Operating Systems and Computer Graphic topics as an assistant teacher. After completing her Master's degree, she started working at Feedzai—a small startup at the time—with a small development team of four. At the time of this book writing, Feedzai has more than 300 employees and is considered one of the most successful tech companies in Portugal. After moving to Berlin in 2014, Olga immediately started working as a Lead Frontend Developer at an online advertising measurement company called Meetrics, and 2 years after, joined Optiopay as VP Engineering. Olga believes in the power of peopleware over software and hardware and in the energy of learning and knowledge-sharing.

Rui Vilão was born in Coimbra, Portugal. During his studies in Informatics Engineering at the University of Coimbra, he was a member of the Laboratory of Communications and Telematics research group, where he participated and contributed to two FP7 European Projects: EuQoS and WEIRD. Following his graduation in Informatics Engineering in 2009, he started working at Feedzai in early 2010, where he was one of the first four engineers to develop the company's core product, Feedzai Pulse. In 2014, he decided to move to Berlin along with his wife and step-daughter, where he started working at Gymondo, an online fitness company, and where he still works to the present day as Lead Software Engineer.

Olga and Rui studied together at the University of Coimbra and worked together at Feedzai. They got married and moved together to Berlin in 2014.

Both Olga and Rui are the technical co-founders of EdEra (`https://ed-era.com`), a non-profit online education project based in Ukraine. EdEra explores teaching and learning in the most innovative ways and positions itself as a bridge between the knowledge possessors and those who need this knowledge.

In Berlin, Olga and Rui live together with Olga's daughter Taíssa—a beautiful and smart teenager, two cats named Patuscas and Objectos, and two fluffy chinchillas named Cheburashka and Barabashka. They are expecting their son Alex to come really soon (could be any minute at the time of writing these lines).

About the Technical Reviewer

Yevhenii Moroz is a software engineer based in Berlin. He currently works at a company that develops software-related financial technologies for clients like Daimler and Volkswagen. He is passionate about his job, with about 5 years of experience in web development and everything around it. He is also interested in modern technologies, science fiction, and traveling. You can follow him on GitHub at github.com/eugene-moroz or Linkedin at www.linkedin.com/in/eugenemoroz.

Acknowledgments

We would like to thank Apress for the opportunity, especially Louise, Nancy, and Jim for their continuous support.

We would like to address a huge thank you to our parents for their love and investment in our education.

We would like to thank our friend and technical reviewer of this book, Evgeny. Evgeny's kind words and sincere admiration enhanced our believing in this product.

Thank you, EdEra team for the collaboration on this book—especially Ilia (Olga's brother) for the brainstorming and ideating, Alexandra (EdEra's designer) for the great illustrations and mockups, and Vasiliy (EdEra's head of motion-design and post-production) for our beautiful videos.

Thank you, Malu, for sharing your great experience as a UI/UX designer in such a deep detail with our readers.

Thank you, Safi, for the great brainstorming session to start with hand-drawn mockups. Thank you, Oleg, for transforming that hand-drawn work into Sketch mockups.

Thank you, Jan, for being there for the usability testing of the mockups and for giving us your awesome feedback!

Thank you, Natasha, for being our QA engineer and providing us with the output that enriched the book with more real examples.

Thank you, our colleagues and friends, for taking part in the interviews that helped to enrich this book with vivid experience—Sagar, Tomás, Olga, Stan, and Anderson.

Thank you, our friends and colleagues from OptioPay and Gymondo for your kind support and interest in this book.

Thank you, Taissa, for reviewing a couple of chapters and giving your invaluable feedback.

CHAPTER 1

I Have An Idea!

This morning I woke up in my bed, looked at the sunlight coming through the tiny gap in my curtains, and all of a sudden, this great idea came to my mind. I made a couple of calls to some investors, registered a startup and voilà! Here I am, all millionaire hipster with crypto-wallets in every pocket.

Last week I was taking my bath and enjoying salts and smell of essences when all of a sudden... "Eureka!" I came up with a new law of physics. I went immediately to a global conference with all the important physicists in the world, spoke in front of all the old and wise physicists, received a Nobel prize, and became a millionaire.

There are couple of similar points in these two different stories. First of all, in both of them, the idea comes "all of a sudden," second, the person immediately becomes a millionaire; and third, and most important, both of them are lies.

In this chapter, we are going to talk about ideas: how do they come to us, how they are transformed into something empirical, and why and how they bring success.

Introduction

First, I would like us to stay on the same page not only of this book but also of the concepts and notions. Let's define the word **idea** and establish the notion of the idea we are going to talk about in this book.

The easiest way is to Google it, right (Figure 1-1)?

© Olga Filipova and Rui Vilão 2018
O. Filipova and R. Vilão, *Software Development From A to Z*, https://doi.org/10.1007/978-1-4842-3945-2_1

Dictionary

idea   🔍

idea
/ʌɪˈdɪə/ ◄))

noun
noun: **idea**; plural noun: **ideas**; noun: **the idea**

1. a thought or suggestion as to a possible course of action.
   "recently, the idea of linking pay to performance has caught on"
   synonyms: plan, design, scheme, project, proposal, proposition, suggestion, recommendation, aim, intention, objective, object, purpose, end, goal, target
   "our idea is to open a new shop"

   - a mental impression.
     "our menu list will give you some idea of how interesting a low-fat diet can be"
     synonyms: concept, notion, conception, conceptualization, thought, image, mental picture, visualization, abstraction, perception; hypothesis, postulation
     "the idea of death scares her"

   - an opinion or belief.
     "nineteenth-century ideas about drinking"
     synonyms: thought, theory, view, viewpoint, opinion, feeling, outlook, belief, judgement, conclusion
     "Elizabeth had other ideas on the subject"

2. the aim or purpose.
   "I took a job with **the idea of** getting some money together"
   synonyms: purpose, point, aim, object, objective, goal, intention, end, end in view, design, reason, use, utility, sense, motive; value, advantage
   "the idea of the letter was to get patients to protest"

3. PHILOSOPHY
   (in Platonic thought) an eternally existing pattern of which individual things in any class are imperfect copies.

   - (in Kantian thought) a concept of pure reason, not empirically based in experience.

Origin

GREEK	GREEK	LATIN
idein	idea	idea
to see	form, pattern	*late Middle English*

late Middle English (in sense 3): via Latin from Greek *idea* 'form, pattern', from the base of *idein* 'to see'.

Figure 1-1. *The definition of* **idea**

For the matter of this book I will use the first definition as the base.

Idea is a thought or a suggestion that leads to a course of actions.

The synonyms that appear under the definition can totally be used as keywords to describe this book. Prepare to run into a lot of these words: *plan, design, project, goal.*

I also like the etymology—*"from the base of idein 'to see'"*. Everything that comes as an idea is a mental visualization of something. This something can be totally new or it can derive from existing things. The general law of humans is that everything that we can see we can build, so each and every visualization or imagination we have can actually be transformed into some product.

Thus, in this book we are going to talk about ideas that lead to carefully planned actions where the goal is to transform the idea into a product.

Now, let's define **product** in the context of this book. Again, my friend Google defines product as a result of an action or a process. All these words are equally and extremely important in that context.

Result, action, process. Without an action, your idea will remain just an idea forever. Without a clearly defined process of the implementation, you will never reach your goal. And of course, you expect results! You define the expected outcome of your idea and you establish a process to reach it.

A product is the outcome or result of a course of actions defined as necessary to implement the idea.

There are a lot of different types and categories of products. They can be business, consumer, or both; consumer products, in their turn, can be divided into four groups of shopping, convenience, specialty, and unsought products. The aim of this book is far from giving you insights into business and marketing. Therefore, I would like to categorize products into two types (Figure 1-2):

- Physical products: stapler, notebook, pen, cars, toys, etc.

- Digital products: software programs, movies, e-books, etc.

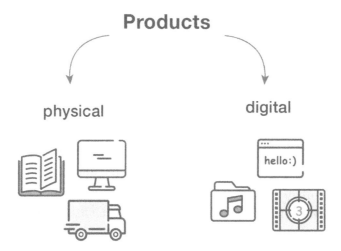

Figure 1-2. *The categorization of products*

As I already pointed out, we are not going to talk about all types of products in this book. The aim of this book is to show how software is created; therefore we are going to talk about a very particular subset of the digital products category: software products. Therefore, the ideas that we are going to talk about are those that lead to the creation of software.

Software Products and Ideas Behind Them

Probably the most widely used software products are operating systems. The Microsoft Windows operating system has gone on a huge journey since its first version in 1985 (Figure 1-3). The actual work on GUI in Microsoft started in 1981 when Microsoft decided to build a bit-mapped software interface. After, Bill Gates saw the demonstration of VisiOn (`https://en.wikipedia.org/wiki/Visi_On`), a GUI software for IBM-compatible computers. He also realized how sophisticated the Apple GUI was, and Microsoft has been working with Apple on applications with user interface for the new Apple Computer. Bill Gates decided the Microsoft's user interface should be different.

The first version of MS Windows had several applications such as calculator, calendar, Clock, Notepad, Paint, Reversi, Terminal, Cardfile, and Write. It looked like the what is shown in Figure 1-3.

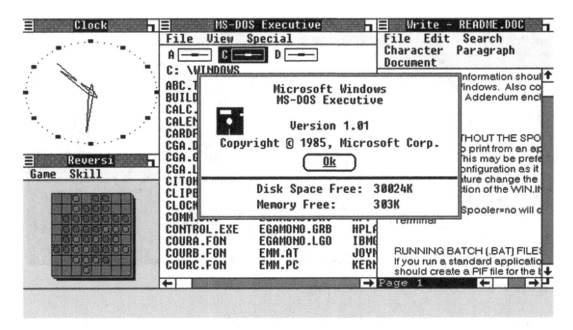

Figure 1-3. *Microsoft Windows first version in 1985*

It's hard to imagine how the modern version of MS windows actually evolved from this. It was not even considered an operating system: until its third version Windows was considered as an operating environment. The first version was code-named "Interface manager."

Over the years the program has been enhanced, improved, and polished. The latest version has nothing to do with its first predecessor.

It's very important to mention that despite big business opportunities, Microsoft had in its hands as one of the biggest corporations in the world and despite the harsh criticism that Windows 1.0 received, Bill Gates has always emphasized that Windows is the main Microsoft product that defines its whole direction and future.

By the way, if you want to prank your friends, especially Mac or Linux users, here's a very nice windows XP simulator: http://geekprank.com/.

Talking about Microsoft reminded me how expensive their services and products are, which in its turn reminded me about digital payment systems. Enough of Microsoft for now; let's talk about PayPal (Figure 1-4).

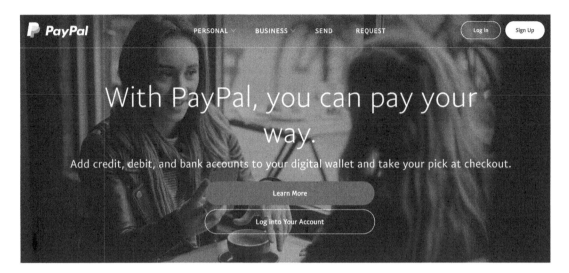

Figure 1-4. *Current PayPal's homepage*

A lot of people think that PayPal is one of Elon Musk's inventions that he sold to start playing with his crazy ideas. That's not entirely true. PayPal was a small part of a software called Confinity (`https://en.wikipedia.org/wiki/Confinity`). Its creators decided to concentrate only on this part after they realized that it solves a big pain to eBay users. The article found at `https://www.entrepreneur.com/article/228206` demonstrates in a very nice way how one should be flexible about their ideas and not be afraid to change the direction of a whole company after realizing that it might solve real customers' problems! What's Elon Musk's role in this? In this PayPal story, Elon Musk was in fact a big visionary, since after merging his company (X.com) with Confinity he decided to terminate all other development and focus only on the PayPal money service.

Since we've been googling quite a lot in this chapter, let's talk about Google!

Back in the '90s, two young PhD students from Stanford University, Larry Page and Sergey Brin, developed a search algorithm called BackRub. This algorithm soon became so popular at Stanford and began to consume so much of the Stanford servers' bandwidth that both geniuses dropped their PhD and decided to build a company around it. Why did BackRub transform into Google? At some point they decided that the name BackRub was not good enough and formed a brainstorming session. During this session Sean Anderson, graduate student at the time, came up with the name googolplex. Page liked it and proposed to shorten it to Googol. While searching on the domain name registry to determine whether the name Googol had been taken already, Sean made a mistake and typed "google.com." This domain was free, and everybody

loved the mistake. So it was immediately registered and has been well-known
by everyone ever since. Check out the short history behind Google's name here:
`https://graphics.stanford.edu/~dk/google_name_origin.html`. Nowadays we use
tons of google services besides the search engine: Google+, Google analytics, Google
cloud solutions, Gmail, etc.

As you can see, big software companies always start somewhere, and usually
this "somewhere" is someone's idea. Don't be afraid of your ideas, don't be afraid of
sharing them, and don't be afraid of moving forward with them. One in millions of
spermatozoids inevitably becomes a human being, the same way one of many ideas, if
properly pushed and planned enough, has the power of becoming another Google.

Different Models

Different companies build different products that serve different needs. Some products
serve needs of individual people (e.g., operating systems), whereas other products are
used for the business needs of other companies. For example, e-commerce platforms
that can be sold to different companies for their e-commerce needs.

Products that satisfy needs of individual customers are called B2C (business to
consumer) while those that satisfy needs of other businesses are called B2B
(business to business).

There are a lot of other forms of marketing—G2B (government to business), B2G
(business to government), even C2C (consumer to consumer). In this model the product
facilitates the customers to provide services or sell products to other customers.

How do you decide what your product should do and what type of needs it should
target in the first place? Run a research. Then develop. Let's talk about research and
development.

Research and Development

In the previous section, we discussed how ideas change existing corporations and how do they can originate new companies.

Of course, it's not as easy as someone just lying under a tree and waiting for an apple to fall on their head. In today's fast-changing and highly competitive technological world, there must be some organizational structure that leads to the generation of ideas for new products or even ideas to improve the existing ones, making them attractive in the market. In fact, some companies have quite big Research and Development departments.

There are different ways of saying "Research and Development." "R-and-D," "Rn'D," "R&D," "R+D," or even "RTD" (Research and Technological Development)—these terms are all the same.

It's quite tricky to give the right value to an R&D department within a company. The research for innovation and creativity usually aims at a long-term success; therefore it's not easy to evaluate its current value. Companies have to decide how much to invest into R&D. Usually, the more technological a company is, the more money is spent on R&D. For example, in the United States, a typical industrial company spends no more than 3% on R&D, whereas a highly technological company such as Ericsson invests 24% of its revenue on it (from Wikipedia: `https://en.wikipedia.org/wiki/Research_and_development`).

The amount (in percentage) of what a company invests in R&D is called **R&D intensity**.

Of course, investing more in R&D doesn't mean that your product will be the most innovative and the most creative one. However, some studies had proven that companies with stable R&D process outperform those where there's no investment in R&D at all.

How does the process look like? It's a cycle (Figure 1-5). Research, explore, prototype, develop, test, improve, research, explore… Repeat these actions forever because your product will never be perfect! The inevitable process left to us by our old Darwin works. The world evolves every day; people change as well as their needs. Things that are relevant today can be completely obsolete tomorrow. Software that we've been using and loving can seem outdated today. That's why R&D is important not only for creating new products but also to continuously improve the existing ones. Therefore, the diagram of this process is cyclic.

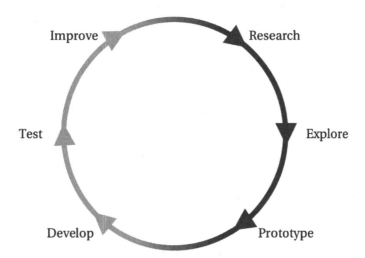

Figure 1-5. *Research and development process lifecycle*

Who should run the research? It might vary from company to company. In some companies, the research is being run by marketing, business development, and analytics experts; other companies handle the research tasks to the engineers; some companies don't have an R&D department at all but try to organize their working process in a way that R&D becomes part of a daily routine.

We've seen a lot of different things happening. At OptioPay (the company where I am currently working as a VP of engineering), R&D is run by business owners, product owners, analytics experts, and engineers. The analytics dashboard is built by business analysis experts on top of live metrics gathered from the running system in production. These metrics are being constantly discussed in weekly meetings by all the stakeholders. During these meetings, we think of possible solutions that will improve the number of existing metrics as we also come up with new metrics to measure our success. Based on these discussions, sometimes new ideas are born, opening a way to new business opportunities.

We also worked at a company where research was being conducted by engineers—they were checking huge data reports, comparing the numbers to the existing products from the competitors, thinking of the solutions to improve, and trying them right away because they knew how to write code. Very convenient, by the way.

At EdEra (an online education company that we represent as technical co-founders), R&D is run by a dedicated person. This person runs deep research on educational processes. Careful analysis of different educational tools, techniques, and platforms, such as Udemy, Khan academy, Coursera, EdX, Duolingo, etc., allows us to build an idea not only of what a modern contemporary person wants to learn but also how they want to do it. This is not only about how the cognitive process works; this is about how quickly society changes and how the technological progress plays a strong role in our perception of information. As a result, from these studies we got a huge amount of blog articles about gamification, adaptive learning, micro-learning, personalization, online learning, blended learning, mixed learning, etc. It's unbelievable how different the process of learning must be now from the one we learned from.

Actually, all the investigations we've been running during the last 3 years lead us to the idea of creating a new educational platform.

Knowledge Sharing Platform

Currently at EdEra we are using a third-party open-source platform (Figure 1-6) to host and share our online courses. This platform is called Open edX (`https://open.edx.org/`), and it was developed at MIT. The platform was created in 2012, and it's being developed by more than 300 contributors from around the world and offers a vast range of possibilities for creating and running MOOCs (Massive Open Online Courses). We are happy users of this platform, but...

There always has to be some but, right?

In 3 years of extensive use of the Open edX platform, we got stuck with a lot of different issues. The technology stack of the platform is scary. Different databases, message queues, programming languages, and technologies are bound together, offering a huge tightly coupled system difficult to scale horizontally, maintain, and upgrade. The system is so complex that you can find companies out there that offer services of installing, upgrading, and maintaining Open edX. These services are not cheap at all. So, either you spend a lot of time doing it yourself, or you pay a lot of money to those companies and they will do it for you. In each case, the free open source software is not as free in the end.

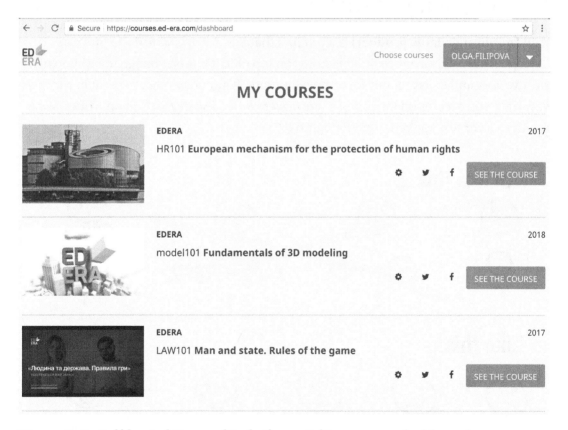

Figure 1-6. *Self-hosted Open edX platform: EdEra courses dashboard*

The idea of building a new in-house platform was born a long time ago. There was no R&D involved, no apple falling on our heads, no waking up in the morning with sudden enlightenment. Just struggling with an existing third-party platform lead to the idea of "Let's create our own!" You can't even imagine how many times we have talked about that. Now we've got plenty of structured research on top of this idea that can help us to build a nice learning platform. Of course, in the short term, we will not be able to build a platform with all those fancy characteristics of adaptive learning, micro-learning, augmented reality, gamification, and personalization, but we can try to build a solid system that will allow us to easily add different features and improve the existing functionality while being scalable and maintainable. For this we need to understand that we want to build a very basic first version of a product. In business, such a version is called an MVP.

Minimum Viable Product

MVP (minimum viable product) is a product that has enough features to prove its concept. It also allows one to build features on top of it. It's good enough to be shown to the investors and to ask money for its development. It's good enough to use it in a basic way. Have you ever heard the phrase, *"We need to build a skate first"*? People often say it exactly in a context applied to MVP (Figure 1-7).

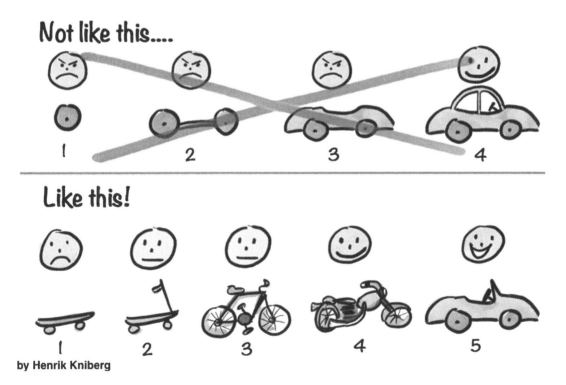

Figure 1-7. *Famous illustration by Henrik Kniberg about MVP*

What does it mean? If you want to build a car you could start by building a tire, then a wheel, then a carcass, and then come to the whole car, thus making the whole product usable only when it's totally built. MVP means that first you build a skate, then you build a kick scooter, then you build a bike, and then you build your car. This process is slower, but you have something working at every iteration.

In this book we are going to build our skate for our learning platform. What is an MVP for a learning platform? Well, the learning platform has to offer a way to... learn, right? Hence, we get to write a list of basic things required for someone to be able to learn. The online learning process usually consists of two simple stages—there's some material to consume the knowledge (it can be a video, or a book, or just a piece of text), and there's a way to check the acquired knowledge (it can be a quiz, a test, a list of questions or some peer-to-peer assessment in more complex environments). I would say that if we build something that will allow the user to read through some learning material or watch a learning video and then go through quizzes, then we will be good to go. We will define a more complete list of requirements in the later chapters. And we will build our MVP from scratch until its deployment. Do you know who will help us in doing this? You, our dear reader. You will help us from the very first version of the learning platform, and with this creation you will learn what is it like to get from an idea to a fully functional product.

Summary

In this chapter we discussed different ideas and we've seen how they are transformed into products. We've approached different types of products and different types of needs they can serve. We explained how we came to the idea we are going to implement in this book. We prepared you to work with us on this project. What will be your role? Or, maybe, let's put this question from a different perspective: what roles are required for building software? We are still talking about software, even though we were speaking about skates in this chapter. There are lots of different roles that can be involved in the path of taking your idea to the MVP stage. And you will experiment each and every important role during the course of this book. In the next chapter, we will talk about the roles whose hats we are going to wear throughout this book.

CHAPTER 2

Roles, Responsibilities, and Methodologies

Now that you have your idea, it's time to assemble your team. In general, it is never good to have one person taking care of everything. First, it is very unlikely that someone possesses all the skills to bring a product through all the stages to life; second, even if hypothetically such person exists, it's always good to have each person responsible for each part of the product so the same amount of attention is fairly distributed. Well... this is true if you are working in a well-established company where all the teams are already in place and settled, but of course it doesn't apply if you just had an idea and want to build a company out of it. In that case, you would have to be prepared in the beginning to do a bit of everything.

Imagine that you are searching for investment. It is common that when you do such a thing, you already have some demo or proof of concept in place, so you can show it to your possible investors. That means that at some point you and your partners had to come up with a set of features that you felt important to show in order to catch the attention of your possible investors along with some product design to make it appealing and some actual implementation to show some interaction, so they get a concrete feeling on what you want to accomplish. If you want your idea to come to life, the proof of concept and a running demo is of the utmost importance, as it will show to external people how serious and committed you are to the project.

In any case, this chapter approaches this topic as if you are working in a company where all the teams are already in place. We will guide you through the roles and responsibilities of each department as well as how to plan your project and all the processes involved.

© Olga Filipova and Rui Vilão 2018
O. Filipova and R. Vilão, *Software Development From A to Z*, https://doi.org/10.1007/978-1-4842-3945-2_2

Roles and Responsibilities

There are several roles that you can identify in most companies where software is a strong player. Most of the companies nowadays operate over the Internet, making them some sort of software companies as well, even if their primary business is not software-related. Imagine, for example, a company that has several bookstores deployed in a country. As the Internet started to become more prominent, these businesses had to reinvent themselves in order to survive, where the obvious response was to create online stores. A company as big as a bookstore chain already qualifies to have their own product and software departments with in-house solutions to overcome their challenges.

The idea here is to show that, in general, the roles we are about to describe do not only apply to software companies but to any company where software plays an important role in its business.

Figure 2-1 shows the cross functional team we are going to talk about (note, this set of people may vary a lot!).

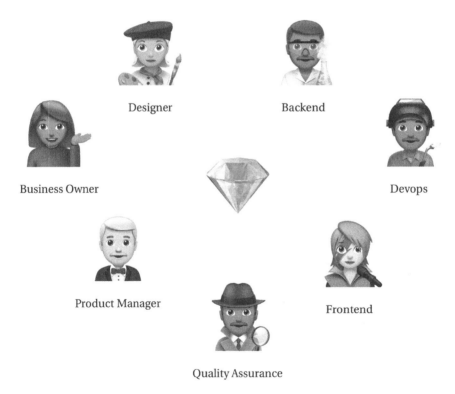

Figure 2-1. *The team around the product*

In the next sections we are going to describe each of these roles in more detail.

Business Owner

Sometimes people have a hard time differentiating between business owners and product managers (described in detail in the next section), which is understandable because not all the companies have the former. It is likely that smaller companies do not have it since in the beginning they tend to focus mainly on getting a product out on the market. During this time it is quite common that people running the company along with the product manager somehow cover most of the responsibilities of the business owner.

As a company grows and several other businesses come into play, it starts to become clearer that such positions must exist. Considering our online platform example, if we look at a first glance, the business model seems quite clear: we sell online courses to customers. This is the typical **business-to-consumer model (B2C)**.

But does it mean that's it? As companies become successful, they become a magnet for new businesses, especially with other companies. Everyone wants to hang out with the cool kids, right? This model is called **business-to-business (B2B)**. As you can see, now not only our platform needs to deal with their direct customers, but other companies are some sort of customers as well or, to be more politically correct, *partners*. In our opinion this is the turning point in a company, when one or more business owners start to be needed: when a company starts running several businesses in parallel or bringing in new partnerships that require further and dedicated software development.

The business owner can usually make decisions for the company and is responsible for identifying new possible businesses and partnerships. They are responsible also to make some sort of assessment and understand if such partnerships will bring value to the company. Value here doesn't mean revenue. Companies have several interests, and at some point, even if a cooperation doesn't bring any direct money, in the end it might still be a good partnership for the strategy of the company. A business owner is not a technical person. They will not define how things will be done. They work at an abstract business level by defining the problem, how it can be tackled, and how to measure the success.

Another responsibility of the business owner is to negotiate the terms of the partnership or establish the prices of a new product. Also, the viability of the new project itself is something that is usually run by the business owner. This also includes, for example, checking if the solution is legal and whether the company will face any judicial problems in the future because it violated some patent or committed some illegal market approach.

Often forgotten, but important, is to keep track of the business metrics and key performance indicators after the project is done. There is no perfect product. All of them have their flaws. It is important that the business owner keeps track of those metrics in order to improve the product and respond to possible market changes. This could be as simple as taking metrics on how people use filters in a website—this gives us insights on what people are actually looking for.

Business owners work closely with product managers in order to come up with a concept that can be further implemented by a technical team.

Product Manager

The product manager can be seen as the orchestrator between the business owners and the development teams. Common tasks of product managers include prioritization of tasks, supporting non-technical teams such as marketing and content, and gathering feedback, among other tasks.

The product manager role is important since they are responsible for translating ideas and concepts into products or features for the company. As they need to orchestrate between several teams in a company, it is often a stressful job. Every team in its own way thinks its requests are the most important for the success of the company and will push product managers hard until they get what they want.

A product manager needs to possess several skills in order to successfully fulfill the role. Soft skills are important since they need to deal with several different individuals but so are technical skills, as they will be the ones to define at some extent how things will be implemented and when. That doesn't mean they need to have a background in engineering of course, but they must possess a solid knowledge in technology in order to make quick assessments and provide fast answers to the stakeholders.

Preparing the roadmap of a product and making sure the product meets the users' needs are also responsibilities commonly assigned to product managers. It is important that this job is done properly so the development teams are occupied and producing value to the company. Understanding what technical debt is and how often the development teams have consolidation sprints/iterations is one of the key points of success between product managers and development teams. Don't worry if you don't understand some concepts such as technical debts or sprints/iterations, as they will be covered in detail later.

On a daily basis, product managers are responsible for writing user stories, which are brief descriptions of use cases usually centered around the users' needs. Along with that, the acceptance criteria are also commonly supplied by product managers. They basically state how a feature can be given as complete. Usually quality assurance (QA) teams rely on the acceptance criteria of a user story to check if the implementation is meeting the specified requirements. It is also common that in the end of the implementation and verification cycles, the product manager checks if the user stories are in fact meeting the requirements previously specified; in other cases, QA is fully responsible for the approval—depending on the maturity of the teams or even the company, these processes may vary from case to case.

Designers

Depending on the user stories or features that come from the product managers, design might be needed. Designers are important because they are not only responsible for creating the interfaces users will interact with, but also bringing some sort of identity to a product or even a company to make it consistent among all platforms. They are somehow the bridge that connects the users to the technology a product exposes. Understanding how users interact with the products and taking that into account in designing them is a responsibility assigned to design teams.

The interaction with a product includes how people will use or, if the product is already out, are using the product—what can be clicked, transitions, states, drag-and-drop functionalities, among others.

Consistency between elements is also something to consider; all clickable buttons share the same color or shape; some examples of elements where consistency is needed are a heart-shaped button as something that can be "liked," a plus sign adding some item to a list, and arrows navigating through multiple input forms.

Design teams work very closely with development teams in order to assess what is viable for implementation, how long it might take, whether some waiting animation is needed when server-side calls are made, etc.

Considering that nowadays every product is multi-platform—different browsers, mobile versions on different screen sizes, and mobile applications on different operating systems—it is sometimes a challenge to keep the product consistency, as design might go against the operating system guidelines, which can often result in applications being rejected by some vendors. That is something with which designers often struggle; it is part of the job so they just have to accept this fact and overcome those challenges in the best way possible and by being creative.

When talking about design, two major terms often appear: *UI* and *UX*. The former stands for **user interface** design and the latter stands for **user experience**. They are sometimes mixed and mistaken, but they are quite easy to explain. UX focuses mostly on the interaction the user has with a product (experience), what and when something can be clicked, feedback to the user when some action is finished, etc. UI focuses mostly on the appearance, branding, and consistency—hence, interface. Take it as some sort of vest or skin of a product. Depending on the size of the company, there might be different people doing each of them. From our experience, even midsize companies tend to hire people that have experience doing both, as there is often no place to have a dedicated person doing UX only.

Once the designs are finished for some user story, they are handed out to the product manager for approval. Several interactions will happen among the product management, design, and development teams during this process until a final decision is made and handed to the development teams for further implementation.

Backend

The backend is the entity of a software product that is responsible for receiving requests from the client applications and handling them by running on dedicated servers typically hosted on cloud services or server providers. Amazon web services, Google Cloud platform, and Microsoft Azure Cloud computing are just some examples of places you can host the backend of a product.

There are several types of backend web services (e.g., RESTful, WSDL, SOAP) that expose a set of operations that can be used by frontend applications or even integration services, but in this book, we will focus on RESTful. RESTful web services is nowadays one of the most popular because it typically relies solely on the HTTP protocol having no other complex layer, like WSDL and SOAP do, and it's very simple to understand and implement. More of that will be covered later in this book.

That said, backend teams focus on exposing operations, so the frontend applications can retrieve, store, modify, and delete data entities of an application. Going back to our online course platform, backend teams implementing it would come up with endpoints to list and filter courses (retrieve), start courses and do the quizzes (store or create), change their answers (modify), and remove previous answers (delete). These are just some rough examples on possible operations the backend of the application could do.

When product managers come up with new features or stories, usually the first implementation is done by backend teams, since they are required by the rest of the product to fulfill the story. In some cases, both frontend and backend implementations will start in parallel, since there are always tasks that can be done without the backend, such as the implementation of the screens, and later on connected.

Backend engineers are often challenged when implementing backend operations, mainly on performance. This is due to the fact that the backend needs to deal with a large number of requests at the same time, as all applications will be pointing at it. Optimization is a big topic when designing backend endpoints, how to fetch data, how to organize data, making them in a way so that they can easily cope with future changes, how to integrate with external services, caches, databases, etc.

Another topic that the backend has to take care of is authentication and authorization. Public versus private endpoints, user roles (what users can access or not), revocation of access, etc. must be carefully defined by product managers, as they are part of the product concept in general.

When the application exposes some sort of online shop or subscription-based services, the backend is also responsible for handling the payments with the Payment Service Providers or, also common nowadays, receiving receipts from the mobile stores (Apple, Google, Amazon), validating those receipts, and acting accordingly. This means that often backend services work along with other backend services. This is often referred to as server-side communication or server-to-server communication.

Having your backend ready, it's time to start implementing our frontend application, the one our users will directly interact with.

Frontend

The frontend application of a product is the one that is visible to the end-user. In general, when we refer to frontend we are thinking of a web application running on a browser. Even though that's true, any application that exposes a graphic interface or even command line interface can be considered a frontend application. In general, we can consider a frontend application a piece of software that runs on the client side; this includes not only web applications but also mobile and, more recently, TV applications. In the context of this book when we refer to frontend application, we'll be mentioning web applications running on browsers using *JavaScript, HTML, and CSS*.

We can split the frontend work in two main modules: representation and logic. Representation is what the user sees, the interface, how the elements are rendered, and how to interact with them. The logic is everything else that makes it an application, such as fetching data, transforming them to present it to the user, and handling requests, states, validation of data input, etc.

Depending on the size of the team or company, there might be people dedicated to a specific frontend task, such as people that are only doing representation using HTML and CSS as well as people only doing the coding in JavaScript. In startup companies this is very hard to find since there is usually not enough work for these positions to be separate. There are even some cases where you will find people doing frontend and backend altogether; usually people with such abilities are called full-stack engineers or full-stack programmers, depending on the experience or academic degree.

When a user story or feature arrives at a frontend engineer's desk, it's not completely clear if they should start with the logic or the design implementation. From our experience, and this is quite common in companies, the frontend implementation starts even when the design is not final. In such cases, frontend engineers tend to start with the logic. Nevertheless, there are no hard rules when it comes to this topic, it will always depend on the dynamic and experience of the team.

To summarize, frontend teams are responsible to implement the interfaces and the logic of the application that interacts with the users. Usually this is the last development step for most of the user stories or features. After implementation, the tickets are handed to QA for testing, where they can bounce back and forth until the acceptance criterias are met. It is also quite common that during this implementation step, further backend development is needed. Sometimes the clear picture can only be seen after things are actually implemented. Even though this is accepted, in general lessons must be learned from such experiences so they are mitigated in the future. As teams grow in experience by working together along with product management, backend changes during frontend development stop becoming a tendency.

Quality Assurance (QA)

The quality assurance (QA) department is responsible for making sure everything that gets to the end user meets the requirements and is working properly. While this can be the definition of QA, the quality in a product starts in early stages of development. During development, several types of tests will be written, such as unit tests, where components in general will be tested on an isolated manner; integration tests, where several components are tested to work together; and also, functional tests, to check if the requirements are met given the acceptance criteria.

The structure of QA departments also depends on the size of the company or even what they are doing. For example, there are companies where the development teams are fully responsible for the QA. In general, even for startups, it is quite normal to have dedicated people doing manual testing to make sure everything meets the requirements, especially if the product exposes graphic interfaces. Some QA teams, depending on the experience, also include people that can write automated tests. Those require more knowledge and programming skills, as the members of the QA teams need to write code to achieve the results.

After a feature is implemented, it is handed to QA for testing. This kind of testing is often manual testing. The QA member will pick up the ticket and make several tests to assert everything is implemented according to the acceptance criteria. Along with it and since several changes are often made release to release, QA teams will also focus on doing regression testing. Regression testing is basically making sure that a set of changes (the new version) is not damaging the system as a whole. Imagine a feature where now, instead of just paying with Visa and MasterCard, people can also pay with PayPal. Regression testing in this scope would be to verify that after introducing PayPal, people can still pay with the previous payment methods and not just verify that the new "paying with PayPal" feature is working. System testing is also the responsibility of QA teams; it is verifying the product works as expected on all target environments. This can be operating systems, in cases where software gets installed on premises, or, for example, checking if a web application can work with all the specified browsers.

There are also other types of testing, but from our experience they are not found within QA teams but rather within development and operations teams (DevOps). Some of them include (1) stress testing—making sure the system performs during heavy loads and anticipating how the system behaves if those occur; and (2) performance testing to check if the system is performing as expected and answering requests within accepted time frames.

It is quite normal that during the testing phase, QA will pick-up some issues with the feature—for example, something in the UI that is not optimal or some behavior that is 100% correct. In most of the cases, it is up to the product manager to decide what to do. Usually two possible outcomes can originate from that: either the feature gets rejected, and it's iterated from the beginning, passing by all the necessary stages; or the feature gets released as it is, but further development or optimizations will be considered in the next versions.

DevOps (development + operations)

DevOps teams are responsible for all the operational aspects of the development and infrastructure. This means they are responsible for building the continuous integration and continuous delivery pipelines, managing the servers, performing migrations, and doing the actual deployments. This is quite a technical role. In fact, in some companies the development teams are also responsible for the DevOps role. Again, it will always depend on the size of the company, how often they deploy, and how they operate in general.

As mentioned before, these teams are also responsible for making sure the current infrastructure can handle the expected load and that it still performs under it by not entering in denial of service.

This role is often mistaken with *System Administrators*. Though they seem the same, they differ quite a bit. Although in some companies the same people can perform both roles, DevOps are more focused on the development and delivery processes of software rather than making sure the systems, even unrelated to the product in general, are operating under normal conditions. System administrators also deal with the all the entities that keep the company running—for example, the office network and internal systems used on a daily basis.

It's Normal to be Confused About Roles!

If you feel confused right now and have mixed all the roles in your head, don't worry and don't feel bad about it. You're not alone. Actually, sometimes even people that work for quite a long time together don't know each other's roles and responsibilities. One of us (Olga) has been working in the company where people did not understand the role of a UI engineer. Some of them thought that he was a frontend developer (coding in JavaScript), and some of them thought that he was a designer. Remember, UI lies somewhere in between, but it's neither those two.

So, people who thought the guy was a designer tend to give the design tasks to him and would become a little bit frustrated if he would not deliver a perfect shiny design. At the same time, people who thought the guy was a frontend developer would ask him to perform complex programming tasks and would become angry to see that he couldn't deliver that either. Can you imagine that kind of situation? The guy is a real professional in HTML and CSS, so he can translate any design into a web interface that would look amazing in any browser and any device. No engineer in that company was able to do such magic. However, the miscommunication and misunderstanding regarding his role and responsibilities could actually cost him his job! The situation was solved by gathering a board meeting where I drew the sketch in Figure 2-2.

Figure 2-2. *Whiteboard sketch explaining UI engineering*

This picture shows that frontend development consists of three main parts: HTML, CSS, and JavaScript. While HTML is a simple markup language that defines a website's structure, CSS makes it beautiful and nice, and JavaScript makes it dynamic, as depicted in Figure 2-3.

Figure 2-3. *Frontend development for n00bs*

UI engineering is focused on the first two parts: defining a clear structure and dressing it up nicely so it can totally impress your target audience. UI engineering is not focused on making website dynamic or in drawing beautiful designs in Photoshop (Figure 2-4).

Figure 2-4. *UI engineering does not include the dynamic part of the frontend development*

After that meeting everyone was on the same page regarding this engineer's role, and the expectations were aligned but, remember, half a year had passed.

In this section we've indeed covered a lot of new terms and roles, but worry not, if you haven't fully understood all of them, we'll cover most of these items in more detail later in this book. The purpose of this chapter is for you to have a quick introduction on the roles you can typically find in a company and to get used to them. Now it's time to learn briefly about software development methodologies and how things are or can be done in a typical software company.

Methodologies

When we talk about methodologies, we talk about software development methodologies although most of them already existed before software development and were later applied to software development. There are two main well-known flavors when it comes to methodologies: *waterfall* and *agile*. This chapter will focus on *agile* development since it's the most popular and flexible nowadays, but we feel that is important to provide you with a rough comparison just for you to understand where both of them stand.

The waterfall model (Figure 2-5) was quite popular in the early days of software development. The waterfall model states that a project has several stages—**requirements, analysis, design, coding, testing, and maintenance**—and their implementation is sequential, meaning the next stage cannot be started before the previous one has been closed, documented, and approved.

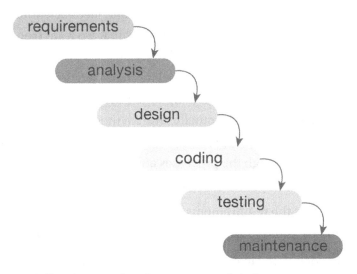

Figure 2-5. *Waterfall software development model, from requirements to maintenance*

This makes the methodology not very flexible, especially nowadays where requirements often change during the execution of a project. Even though the waterfall approach presents some downside, it doesn't mean that it is totally bad. It has been proven very effective for small projects that are not likely to change within their time of implementation. On the other hand, if some issue is discovered in a later state, let's say during testing, it is quite difficult to go back, and it might even be expensive to the whole project since the launch dates will be heavily affected by those changes. A big downside about it is that since the methodology is sequential and linear, it means that there's no actual implementation before all the previous stages are completed, meaning that the client or the owner of the project will never see a working version before the project reaches the implementation phase. One other thing that is quite a struggle is to gather all the possible requirements in the beginning of a project. It is almost inevitable that something will not be taken into consideration and only noticed during the implementation or even the testing phases. As we live in the world that is constantly changing, it makes it very hard to follow whatever requirements that were thought and accepted a long time ago, sometimes 6 months or even more.

The only thing that is constant is CHANGE. (Heraclitus)

As a matter of fact, agile relies exactly on that: everything always changes.

Requirements are not unchangeable; they can be altered at any time! If everything always changes, we can't afford building software without feedback until its testing phase.

Therefore, the most important principle of agile is that we want **frequent software deliveries**. The faster we ship software to production, the faster we get feedback and the faster changes can be applied if needed. Seems like chaos at a first glance: something is being implemented, then changed, then implemented... When does it end? When's the design phase, when do we test it? Actually, even in the agile approach, software development goes through all the important phases, because in the end we are building serious things, right? Even though the processes and phases of agile and waterfall seem similar at first, there are two main points that make all the difference:

- Agile states that the requirements can change at any phase of the project and be reiterated and refined as the project is ongoing.

- Agile starts delivering in early stages and this helps to identify possible issues and fix them while there is still time, hence minimizing the impact on the whole project.

In 2001, a group of 17 software engineers met at ski resort in Utah to discuss all these things, and as a result, the so-called Agile Manifesto was born: `http://agilemanifesto.org/`. Here are four main statements of agile:

Individuals and interactions over processes and tools

Working software over comprehensive documentation

Customer collaboration over contract negotiation

Responding to change over following a plan

In order to implement agile a **cross-functional** team is needed. Having a cross-functional team means that for that specific project, there's a team that is responsible for all the stages of the project: planning, analysis, design, implementation, and quality assurance. The roles and responsibilities of the cross-functional team members may vary according to the specifics of the project. All the members of this team work closely together and reiterate the project frequently to adapt to changes and act quickly if something isn't right. All the stages previously mentioned should be implemented in a time box approach, typically a few weeks where the main goal at the end of each iteration is to have a working version to show to the stakeholders for immediate feedback.

Scrum and **Kanban** are two widely popular frameworks that implement the aforementioned agile patterns. Even though they differ in the actual implementation, they share the same principles. The following subsections describe them in more detail. In the end you will see there's no silver bullet, but there are definitely tools that can be adapted for your purpose. We believe it will always depend on what you want to achieve, how you want to achieve it, and the nature of the project.

Scrum

If we would have to evaluate scrum framework from 0 to 5, where 0 means "Do whatever you want" and 5 means a "really strict process," we would give it a 4. Scrum prescribes very well-defined roles and strict rules. Implementing scrum "by the book" can be hard, complex, and an energy-consuming task. We've worked in different companies and we've been in several software development teams. We visited startups and big corporations, and we've talked to project managers and developers from all over the world. We have never seen a pure scrum implementation exactly as it is described in the books. Every team has to adapt the process to the needs of the team, to the business model, to the nature of the product, and to the culture of the company.

So, what is exactly that complex framework that is so difficult to use "by the book?" The main principles of scrum rely on:

- Cross-functional teams

- Time boxed iterations called sprints

- Product roadmap

- Product backlog

- Sprint planning meetings

- Retrospective meetings

- Daily standup meetings

- Tasks estimations

- Burndown chart analysis and velocity calculation

- Scrum master, product owner, and business owner roles

Cross-Functional Teams

A cross-functional team, as we already pointed out, has all the needed skills to complete the work. What are the needed skills? This depends on a project. For example, if the team is working on a web application, it needs a design, frontend application, and backend part. Thus, the cross-functional team for this kind of project would be composed by at least a designer and a frontend and a backend developer. If the business requires a mobile application, add a mobile developer to the team. You might also add a QA engineer, analytics specialists, product managers, security, and infrastructure engineers. The possibilities are endless, and there's no recipe for how to structure your cross-functional team.

An opposite to a cross-functional team would be a bunch of functional teams—a team of backend engineers, another team of frontend engineers, etc.

We've worked on such teams as well.

There can also be a mix. You might have some functional team—for example, the team of designers that are being used as a shared resource between several cross-functional teams. In the end, the process of team structuring is an ongoing evolutionary process.

For example, in one of the companies where Olga has worked, once there were several functional teams that were divided into four cross-functional teams, each of which was responsible for some specific company's KPI. It worked for a while and worked pretty well. After some time, the business direction started to change, which made small teams interact more and more with each other. At some point it was clear that three of small teams were actually working on the same product serving the same main purpose. Thus, the decision was made to unify those small teams into one big cross-functional team. And it worked well. Thus, your team will always be changing, and the changes should always respond to the type of the project, its budget, and its requirements.

Work

Where does the work for the teams come from? The work that needs to be done starts from business and priority discussions. Usually there is a product roadmap that results out of discussions regarding business priorities, the strategies of the company, budget, and needs. This roadmap is agreed among the business owner, the product owner, and the team. This is a high-level description of what needs to be done. It's up to the product owner to split the work into smaller chunks that can be implemented during the next iteration. All the work that needs to be done in scrum is put into the backlog. There are two types of backlog in scrum: product backlog and sprint backlog. Product backlog is a list of prioritized features to be implemented or bugs to be fixed in a product. Sprint backlog is an estimated list of features that are going to be worked on during the next working iteration. Typically, the features are described from the user's perspective. They are even called "**user stories**." Each of the stories starts like this: "*As a user, I would like to....*" For example, imagine that we are describing a user story for a feature of a door knob for a doctor's office. We would describe it as, "As a doctor, I would like to be able to open the door of my office to let my patients in." Then the basic requirements and the acceptance criteria would follow this summary. The product manager and the team have to prioritize the backlog items and decide when to do what.

Basically, it's all about **goals**, **planning**, and **priorities**. And of course, discipline—otherwise it doesn't work. The product owner has to plan and prioritize the backlog according to the business needs and goals. The team has to stick to the plan, be focused, and commit to it. How to keep focus? That's an exercise for everyone involved in the project, and that's a subject for a whole other book.

Just to sum up, in scrum the work that needs to be done lives in a product backlog, in the form of prioritized user stories. Every iteration, several stories from the list make it to the sprint backlog to be worked on during the next sprint.

Sprints

Chunks of work are distributed along the time box iterations called **sprints**. In the beginning of each sprint there is a **sprint planning meeting**. During this meeting, the team analyzes the tasks that will make it into the sprint, estimates them, and commits to them for the next 2 weeks (the length of the sprint may vary, but usually doesn't go longer than 4 weeks). In the end of the sprint there's a retrospective meeting where the scrum master analyzes the burndown chart, calculates the team's velocity, and the team discusses what went well during the sprint, what problems were encountered, and how to avoid them in future sprints. Every day, typically in the beginning of the day, a scrum meeting takes place. This meeting is usually moderated by a scrum master and held with everyone standing to make it fast and concise, and that is when each team member informs everyone what they did during the previous day, what will be done in the present day, and the impediments blocking their progress.

Wrapping it up, a sprint is a time boxed iteration during which some tasks are implemented and discussed every day during daily meetings and is planned in the beginning and analyzed in the end. That's pretty clear, right? But all this terminology—estimations, retrospective, meeting, velocity, burndown chart... What? Let's have a closer look at each of these concepts.

Estimations, Velocity, and Burndown Chart

We've pointed out that each task that makes it into the sprint has to be estimated. How does the **estimation** work? Actually, to answer this question, first we need to understand WHAT we are trying to estimate. Think about any task, it doesn't need to be related to software development. For example, cleaning the room can be considered as a task. How can you evaluate this task? You can tell that this is quite a difficult task (assessing its *complexity*), and you can also say that it would take you up to 2 days to complete it (assessing the task's *length in time*). The Scrum team can decide if it wants to estimate in time or in complexity. When the team estimates the sprint tasks in time, the team members must think in time units—typically days and hours—that the implementation of the tasks might take. If the team decides to estimate the complexity of the tasks, then the members of the team must think in different kinds of units. Usually these units are called *story points*. Why story points? Because we are analyzing user stories, remember? The number of story points that the team is able to complete during each sprint is called the team's *velocity*.

There's a huge battle between people who prefer story points (or some other complexity units—for example, T-shirt sizes) and those who prefer estimating in time. It is easier sometimes to assess the task's complexity rather than thinking about how long it would take to complete it. However, in the end, what business owners expect from us is telling WHEN the feature will be finished. With nice argumentation you can win this battle regardless of the side you take, so in the end it doesn't really matter. What really matters in agile is that the work is delivered and delivered fast. Any type of estimation, if well done, will give you a basic sense of predictability, which is not only very important for transparency but for the foundation for fast delivery. Estimate in elephants if it makes you happy, but be transparent and agile.

In order to be able to understand whether or not the sprint went well, the **burndown chart** (Figure 2-6) is analyzed in the end of each sprint. The burndown chart is a chart that establishes the relationship between the amount of committed and amount of completed work.

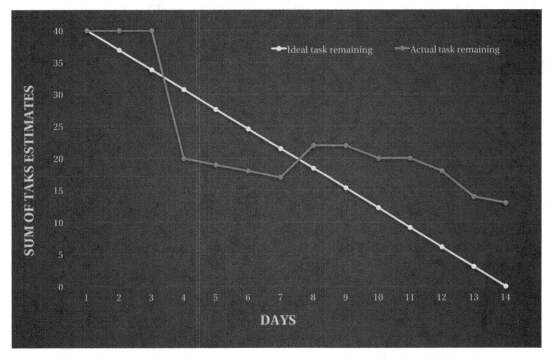

Figure 2-6. *Burndown chart*

The x-axis shows the number of days in a sprint—in this example, 14. The y-axis represents the number of estimated tasks—in this example, we assume that tasks have been estimated in story points and that there are 40 story points of tasks in the sprint.

The green line represents the scrum Nirvana; all the tasks that have been planned and estimated in the sprint planning have been finished until the end of the sprint with a well-balanced uniform pace. The red line represents the actual state of the sprint. Analyzing the chart in the end of the sprint gives you an idea of how the sprint went. In this example, we can guess that for the first 2 days nothing really happened (or developers forgot to update the state of their tasks), then all of a sudden the team went really productive on the third day, then there has been a constant pace during the next 3 days, then someone committed a crime and added some tasks to the sprint on the eighth day (adding tasks to a running sprint is a **NO-NO** in scrum!!!), and after that there was almost a constant pace until the end of the sprint but still some tasks remained unfinished.

They say that the more the red line is closer to the green, the more ideal the sprint is. We've never seen it happening. Teams that try to reach it sometimes end up trying to adjust their estimations and process to the chart, so it looks nice in the end. Don't do that. The process should help you to be productive, not to feel like you are productive while in fact you are not. If you want some Nirvana, here's a Spotify playlist for you: `http://spoti.fi/2tZJfgO`.

Meetings

As we already pointed out, scrum prescribes different types of meetings. Sprint planning, retrospective, demo-meeting, and daily scrum are the most popular ones. Besides those, we can think of the backlog grooming and backlog refinement meetings. Let's talk briefly about what each of those meetings means.

During the **sprint planning** meeting the team with the product owner decides what tasks will move from the product backlog to the sprint backlog. They also estimate the tasks and stop moving them when the amount of "units" reaches the average team's velocity. In order to keep the team focused, during this meeting the sprint goal is defined.

The sprint starts right after the planning session. The team works hard to achieve the goal and to complete all the stories to which they have committed. Every working day starts from the **daily scrum meeting**. During this meeting each team member talks about was done yesterday, what is planned to be done today, and what impediments there are. This morning exercise not only keeps the team synchronized and focused but also gives an opportunity for each team member to solve some impediment right in the morning before starting their workday.

Once the sprint is over, it is a good idea to analyze whether or not it has been successful and understand what made it like that. The **sprint retrospective meeting** exists exactly for this purpose. During this meeting the team reflects about three things:

- What they believe went well

- What they believe didn't go that well

- What can be done to keep the good things and prevent the not so good things

The retrospective meeting should end with several **action points**. These points must be visible to everyone, have a responsible person assigned, and idealy a deadline. During the next retrospective, the team will analyze the progress on the action points from the previous retrospective meeting.

Backlog grooming and **backlog refinement** are the types of meetings that aim at making the backlog clean. During the backlog grooming session, we are metaphorically grooming the backlog. With time its items become obsolete, so if you see something sitting there for quite a long time it might be a good candidate for deletion. Believe me, if something is really relevant for your business, it will end up reappearing again. With time the priorities and requirements change as well, so during this meeting the team can re-prioritize some items and move them to the top of the backlog. During the backlog refinement meetings, each task is carefully analyzed and redefined if needed. The team has to make sure that the requirements are clear and that the acceptance criteria is achievable. The tasks can also be broken into several subtasks, depending on the size and the needs.

Demo meetings might be public to the entire company, and their purpose is to show what has been done during the last iteration.

Scrum Board

Scrum board represents the state of both product backlog and sprint backlog. During the sprint the tasks can move from the "**To Do**" state to the "**Done**" state. Seems pretty straightforward: once the task is done, it's moved to the "**Done**" state, but when is the task actually done? Scrum answers this question by introducing the concept of **definition of done**.

Definition of done is a formal description of what criteria the task should meet to be considered done. For example, some teams might consider the task as done when the code is complete, while others might only consider the task done once the tests are passed. We think that it makes sense to consider the task done once it is already deployed and running in production. Between both "**To Do**" and "**Done**" states, the task might go through multiple stages—for example, *To Do–In Progress–Review–Testing–Ready to Deploy–Done*. Again, every team adapts the task stages to its needs. For some teams it might be enough to have only three states: *To Do–In Progress–Done*.

It is also worth mentioning that the sprint board has a limited number of tasks. The scrum teams limit the number of tasks per sprint according to the velocity of the team. Figure 2-7 shows how the scrum sprint board might look if the velocity of the team corresponds to 40 story points.

Scrum Product Backlog		Scrum Sprint Board					40
Task 8	13	**ToDo**		**InProgress**		**Done**	
Task 10	1						
Task 13		Task 3	3	Task 7	2	Task 1	1
Task 11		Task 5	5	Task 2	8	Task 4	8
Task 12	5						
Task 20		Task 6	13				
Task 19							
Task 18							

Figure 2-7. *Scrum sprint board*

The backlog contains prioritized items. Some of them are already estimated during the backlog grooming and/or refinement meetings. During the sprint planning meetings, the tasks are moved to the sprint board. The sprint board contains only estimated items. The sum of estimations of the sprint tasks cannot exceed the team's average velocity. No one can add tasks to the sprint board during the sprint because it will affect the velocity in the end. Sometimes there are some exceptions, and the team can agree on moving the tasks to the sprint if some other task of the same estimation is removed from it.

As you can see, even though scrum is agile and flexible, it still poses hard rules if you implement it by the book. Nevertheless, it's definitely a good software development framework to take consider when implementing your own processes since it provides a clear view and nice approaches to already known problems. In general, even if you think you are not, you will end up including some scrum features in your own custom processes.

Kanban

When we started discussing scrum, we evaluated it from **0** (*"Do whatever you want"*) to **5** (*"Really strict process"*) and gave it **4**. Kanban, in our opinion, deserves a **2** on this scale. There are no must-have meetings, no special roles, and no time boxed iterations in Kanban. There are no estimations and no velocity calculations. The only restriction that you can have in Kanban is the limit of tasks per task stage. For example, we can say that the column "**In Progress**" cannot have more than five tasks accumulated there at the same time. We can also limit the number of tasks in the "**To Do**" column. Actually, it is a pretty good idea, because in Kanban, everything that makes into the "To Do" column is expected to be delivered as fast as possible to guarantee that the knowledge about the requirements is still fresh.

Usually software that is used to design Kanban boards allows one to specify the limit of tasks per column.

Planning

Even though Kanban doesn't have sprints, such as sprint planning meetings, Kanban teams still do planning. Remember, he who doesn't plan doesn't know how to manage time. Hence, any process that is designed to help us in managing our time, so we are productive and efficient, at some point requires some planning. In Kanban, the team gathers for the planning session whenever there is capacity. The team might define regular planning meetings or planning on demand. During these meetings, the team analyzes the backlog and moves the tasks to the "**To Do**" column.

Cycle Time

Remember the **velocity** metric from scrum? Kanban also has a very important metric called **Cycle time**. Cycle time is the time that takes a task to move from the "**To Do**" to "**Done**" column. The smaller the average cycle time, the more efficient the team. This is how you decrease this metric:

- Learn how to break big tasks into small self-contained units

- Decrease dependencies between tasks

- Stay focused!

- Celebrate the tasks' completion :)

Actually, decreasing the cycle time also helps to increase the quality. Do you agree that it's way harder to make mistakes building something small that does not have dependencies from other tasks than something huge with several dependencies?

Even if this small piece will break your system, it's easier to remove it since it represents a self-contained feature.

Some studies also depict the metric called **lead time**. Lead time is the time between the creation of the task until it's actually done. Hence, it means that the lead time is basically the cycle time plus the time that takes task to be moved from the backlog to the "**To Do**" column. Reducing this metric also helps you to run your business smoothly. For example, in one of the companies where Olga worked, the CEO was complaining that he created a simple task that he really wanted to be worked on and it had been postponed repeatedly until it just remained permanently in standby. Two years had passed, and this task was still in the backlog! Something is definitely wrong with this. If you ever realize that your tasks are sitting in the backlog for such a long time, they either are not important for your business (then please delete them) or your business is suffering. Don't make your business suffer: prioritize your task, and move it into the "**To Do**" column immediately!

Kanban Board

Kanban board is very similar to the scrum board. Instead of limiting the number of tasks per board, it limits them per column. Figure 2-8 shows how Kanban boards may appear.

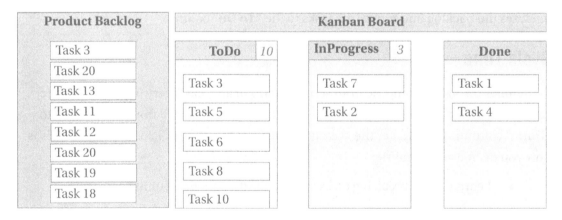

Figure 2-8. *Kanban board*

The tasks of higher priority live on the top of the backlog. The tasks from the top of the backlog are making it into the **To Do** column. The **To Do** column is limited to 10 tasks. The **In Progress** column is limited to 3 tasks. Once the limit is overreached, the team brainstorms on how to clean up the problematic column.

Limiting the number of tasks per column also helps to explain where the bottleneck is. Imagine that one of your columns is **Testing**. If the number of tasks in this column is overreaching the limit (considering that the limits are already adjusted to the number of team members) this means that the testing is the bottleneck of your development process. Based on this, you can make some important decisions like hiring new people or increasing the number of automation tests.

Ok, But What Should I Use?

We have introduced a lot of new terms and concepts. Let's sum them up.

- Scrum is full of different kinds of meetings, while Kanban does not require any of particular meetings besides a planning session, and even this one is not really strict in when, how, and where it is used.

- Scrum demands specific roles (product owner, business owner, scrum master), while there are no strict roles in Kanban.

- Scrum divides work into the time boxed iterations called **sprints**, while in Kanban there are no specific time limits on working iterations. The team starts planning next work chunks whenever it feels ready for that.

- Scrum limits the number of tasks on the board per sprint, while Kanban limits the number of tasks on board per column.

- Scrum relies on team's velocity, while Kanban respects the lead and cycle time metrics.

Even though we have discussed so many different things, we haven't explained when to use what. As many times noted in this chapter, it's up to the team to decide what to use. You don't need to use Scrum by the book nor Kanban. You can mix them both and use whatever applies to your business and your team needs. There's even a methodology called scrumban! Oh yes, software engineering is full of Michurins (`https://en.wikipedia.org/wiki/Ivan_Vladimirovich_Michurin`) that like to mix stuff together and get new ideas, processes, tools, and frameworks.

Adopting a software development framework or tool is usually a very natural process that evolves as the team grows and as the software is being developed. Your process is not something that you write once and follow afterward. Built on top of agile principles, your process will always be changing. That's because you change as well, don't you?

In the end, what really matters is that the team feels productive, knows the positive impact that it creates on the company, and feels the value that it brings to the business. Adopt your process, refine it, and play with it until you see every member of your team on the same page. Revise from time to time.

Different concepts from agile can be used not only for the software development process. For example, we used some of them while writing this book (Figure 2-9). We used, for example, the following concepts:

- **Definition of done**: We considered each chapter **done** when the text was finished and reviewed by both of us, when the illustrations were finished and when the full chapter was accepted by the technical reviewer and the main editor.

- **Cycle time**: We tried to divide each chapter into small achievable chunks of work, each of which didn't depend on others, so we could be efficient and productive.

- **Limiting number of "In Progress" items**: We tried to have no more than three items in progress. First, there were only two of us. Second, if there was some item that was being worked on by another person (e.g., we have a friend that helped us with the illustrations) and it was stuck in the "In Progress" column, then we would ping our friend and ask if she needed some help.

- **Retrospective meetings**: We talked about our success and reflected on our weaknesses. With each new chapter, we wanted to become better and better. Honestly, we found retrospectives such a good tool that helped in improving that we even advise you to use it for your personal growth!

- **Board**: We have a beautiful physical board that we enrich with new items every week. This is how it looks:

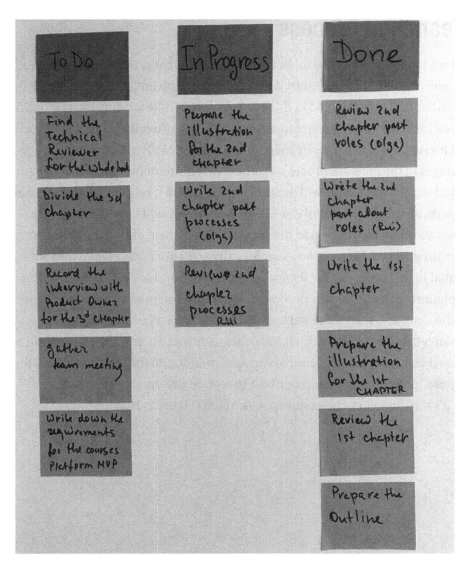

Figure 2-9. *Board for the tasks of this book*

As you can see, agile concepts can be applied to nearly everything. Let's see how we can apply them to the software creation process we are going to cover in this book. Also, let's finally meet the team!

Our Team and Process

Now that we have described the roles, teams, and different processes in software development, it's time to finally start developing our software. Almost all the roles we have described will be explained in this book in detail while we develop our online courses platform. To make it even more real, we have gathered a real team of real people, our good friends. They will happily help us to build the MVP while going through all the needed stages of the creation process—gathering requirements, design, development, testing, and deployment. How will the process look? Will it be the waterfall, scrum, kanban, scrumban, or something else? Well, it definitely will be something else; remember, we adapt the process to the specifics of the team and to the business goals.

Our main goal is to help you to learn how the software is developed and what roles are essential in this process. Our secondary goal is to build an MVP for the online courses platform. Therefore, our process followed a sequential approach because of the order of the chapters, with some back-and-forth iterations because we are agile, and things changed as we wrote this book. We obviously had planning meetings and we had our own task board, and of course we paid attention to the limit of tasks in the "**In Progress**" column and we did our best to reduce our cycle time.

Now it's time for you to meet our specific team (Figure 2-10)!

Figure 2-10. *Roles in our team*

Our team is a **cross-functional** team (even though we are not using pure scrum). Meet the team members:

- **Business owner**: Ilia. Ilia is a CEO of EdEra, the one who is pretty much interested in using the new EdEra platform on a daily basis.

- **Product manager**: Ivan. Ivan works with Olga, and he is a very talented engineer with entrepreneurial and management skills.

- **Designers**: Safi and Oleg. Safi comes from the computer science background, has a huge interest for UX research, and recently has successfully defended her master thesis in this field. Oleg is the magician in the UI engineering. He is able to transform any design into a responsive and adaptive web interface.

- **Backend**: Rui and Nadia. Rui is one of the authors of this book and a very experienced and pragmatic software engineer. Nadia is an amazing software engineer who is able to scale any system. Even the ones that are based on the technologies she has never worked on before!

- **DevOps**: Nadia and Olga. Olga is one of the authors of this book, and Nadia is the same amazing girl that will build the backend with Rui.

- **Frontend**: Olga and Eugene. Eugene is our very good full stack developer friend who is interested in technologies, processes, and education. Eugene, by the way, is the technical reviewer of this book.

- **Quality Assurance**: Maryna and Violetta. Both of these amazing girls are experienced in manual and automated software testing, and both of them work closely with product managers and developer teams to establish the bridge between requirements and software process to guarantee a reduced cycle time and increased quality.

The most important member of our team is you. Your role will vary across the book. We hope you'll enjoy each and every one of them.

Summary

In this chapter we discussed different roles in the software development process. We have also seen different tools and frameworks that are being used in the world of software creation. We have depicted the fact of every team's process being different from all other teams' processes because every team is so different and unique.

TEST YOURSELF

You already know a lot about different processes and different roles. It's time for you to check yourself.

- You want to build a web page for your online shop. You already know how to structure and organize it. Whom would you ask to draw a rough sketch of your thoughts?

    - Designer

    - Product manager

    - Frontend developer

- You are pretty good in Adobe products when it comes to design and illustrations. You can easily put business thoughts into rough sketches and low-fidelity and high-fidelity mockups. Who are you?

    - DevOps

    - Site reliability engineer

    - UX designer

- You already have a well-defined design of your system. Whom would you ask to create web interface out of it?

    - Backend engineer

    - Frontend engineer

    - Analytics expert

- During your development process, the requirements are constantly being changed and readjusted. What kind of software development framework would you use?

    - Waterfall

    - Agile

- In your board, you limit your "Testing" column to a maximum of 10 items. What kind of board are you using?

  - Kanban board

  - Scrum board

If you answered "Designer–UX designer–Frontend engineer–Agile–Kanban board," then you are good to go to the next chapter!

In the next chapter, we will start working on our software. We will wear the product manager's hat and define the requirements of our product, important milestones, and deadlines. Are you ready for managing your software product? We are! Let's go!

CHAPTER 3

Requirements, Commitment, and Deadlines

In the previous chapter we discussed different tools and frameworks that can be used for organizing the software development process. We also discussed the different roles that participate in the creation of software—from business owner to DevOps, and quality assurance engineer.

In this chapter we are going to start the process by defining the high-level requirements, product roadmap, different important milestones, and deadlines. The role of product manager is very important at this stage because they have to clearly understand all the business implications, pitfalls, and details. They are also responsible for analyzing risks and business value as well as for establishing the bridge between the business people and the development teams. Any small mistake at this stage can put at risk the whole project. On the other hand, smooth, clean, and a nicely kicked-off project leads itself to its very own success. Our project is meant to be successful, thus let us do everything to bootstrap it and charge it with positive energy.

Product Manager

In this chapter you will be a product manager, and you will kick-off the project. What does it mean to be a product manager? Why is it so important to have a person on the team who is responsible for managing a product? What exactly must a product manager do? We could talk a lot of theory around this position and point you to hundreds of articles on the Internet, but is there anything better than talking to a real person?

© Olga Filipova and Rui Vilão 2018
O. Filipova and R. Vilão, *Software Development From A to Z*, https://doi.org/10.1007/978-1-4842-3945-2_3

Interview With Product Manager

A big advantage of working in software companies is that we don't need to spend any time looking for real people to talk to. They surround us every day. For this book, Olga interviewed Sagar Datta, the product manager that is currently working with her at OptioPay. This interview took place between March and April 2018.

How People Become Product Managers and What They Deal With

Olga: What does your role mean exactly?

   Sagar: Currently at OptioPay, my role is a mixture of a product manager and a product owner. As a product manager I am responsible for achieving the business goals of my product, which involves defining a strategy to achieve "key product indicator" (KPI) goals. As a product owner I am responsible for managing the Product Backlog, which includes clearly expressing product backlog items, ordering the items in the product backlog, whilst optimizing the value of the work performed within the team.

   Olga: How long have you been working as a product manager?

   Sagar: I have been working as a product manager since 2012. Prior to this my title was game designer, which had some element of production role included. As a game designer I would devise concepts and bring them to life to form a playable experience. This lies at the bedrock of the production process, so naturally exposing me to a few product management tasks.

   Olga: What did you study?

   Sagar: I have a bachelor's degree in management studies and a master's degree in digital media. The goal of my master's degree curriculum was to make graduates work-ready with a flexible repertoire of skills, rather than a single specialization giving me exposure to various multiple career paths. The ones that stood out the most were production roles. During my masters, I found mentors who taught me and guided me in the path of what is today known as product management.

   Olga: How did you start your career as a product manager?

   Sagar: The transition was not as simple as this answer. My coworker decided to move on from the role of product manager. I naturally filled the gap and took over the role.

Olga: What are you enjoying the most in your day?

Sagar: Dealing with challenges and overcoming them along with the development team. There is nothing better than seeing all the hard work come to fulfillment and have proof that it's having a positive impact!

Olga: Do you have to deal with stress? Where does it come from?

Sagar: Sometimes yes, but it's almost always manageable. Most of the time this stress is self-brewed within my mind of the situations that have been witnessed in the past. These start to reinforce negative thoughts. Dealing with it is simple—accept that it's a normal part of life and it can and will be overcome. Keeping a cool in these situations is of utmost importance.

Differences Between Product Owner and Product Manager

Olga: We know about a role called product owner. What is the difference between product owner and product manager?

Sagar: To me the key difference between a product owner and product manager is what role the person plays within a scrum team versus the one that is responsible for achieving the business goals of the product. The product owner according to the scrum guide should be:

- Clearly expressing Product Backlog items;

- Ordering the items in the Product Backlog to best achieve goals and missions;

- Optimizing the value of the work the development team performs;

- Ensuring that the Product Backlog is visible, transparent, and clear to all and shows what the scrum team will work on next; and,

- Ensuring the development team understands the items in the Product Backlog to the level that is needed.

Whereas a product manager to me:

- Creates a strategy to achieve business goals;

- Represents the voice of the market and customers;

- Generates a long-term roadmap;

- Performs a pricing and competitor analysis; and

- Owns the product vision and takes a full responsibility for the drive of this vision with the rest of the stakeholders.

Involvement on the Path From Idea to Product

Olga: On the path from the idea to the working deployed product how much are you involved in the process?

Sagar: I am involved in almost every step of the process. If a new idea matches the business goals and the vision, then it goes through a process which involves me doing the following things:

- Most important thing is validating ideas! This is the least expensive time to think of whether your idea will work or not. Prototype it quickly as possible, test it, and, even better, sell it!

- If the idea proves to work, then define what is your MVP; make sure your stakeholders are aware of what the MVP entails;

- Next is to take this knowing what you and your team agrees on what to build first within your MVP;

- During development if there are any reasons such as new market insights, or new competitors that make a strong case to pivot, then being willing to make that happen; and

- At the end of it, making sure that the product is delivered to the right market at the right time to ultimately meet the business goals.

Olga: How do you get the ideas to put on the roadmap? Who are the stakeholders?

Sagar: Ideas come from lots of places. From every department and every function. Mostly from clients, customers, people working closely on the product and other similar product. I try to remind people involved that ideas are cheap, but what happens after can become really expensive. Therefore, the ideas are gathered and matched against the business goals and product vision. If there is a match, they go onto a specific ideas list, which is rated against the KPIs they can impact. If they impact the KPI we are working on positively, within the quarter, then they are put on a fast track and prototyped in the quickest way possible to test. Failing often and failing fast has worked the best for me in most cases.

Olga: Is the prioritization based on the business needs? Does it mean that you, product managers, have to have a good solid understanding of business?

Sagar: Within my answer to the previous question I mention the criteria I use to map ideas to which priorities. This mapping is also based on KPIs, which are derived keeping in mind the business goals and needs. Having an understanding of *why?* is very important. As a product manager you need to have an equal or even higher buy-in to the targeted KPI. The success of your product depends on the business it generates (in almost all commercial cases). For this reason, some companies have a business owner to increase the impact of business during product development.

Managing Products of Different Business Areas

Olga: How does it differ to be a product manager of products in different business areas?

Sagar: I can speak from my experience of coming from the gaming business into fintech. The core of your day-to-day and techniques can remain the same across industries, but you need to adapt to the business requirements for a successful product. Learning this is easier if you're open to change and ready to make mistakes.

The Biggest Screw-Up

Olga: Tell me about the biggest screw up in your career as a product manager.

Sagar: While I was working on a free-to-play game, our goal was to increase daily retention KPI. For increasing retention, we introduced a mini-game, which had rewards (including premium ones), which you earn more if you would come back daily. After introducing this, I noticed that it worked really well; therefore to gain more out of the mini game (which our players enjoyed), I introduced a monetization feature on top. Now you could pay in game currency to get through the mini games faster without having to wait. I A/B tested[1] this for a short time and decided to be aggressive and turned it live for all the players. Three to four months after release we started to notice a steady decline in the revenues without knowing what caused it. After much digging into data for a month and a few A/B tests, I realized it was caused due to the release of the monetization feature I introduced on top. This feature allowed users to pay to get premium items faster, creating a drop-in purchase of the premium items using the in-game store over time.

---

[1]A/B testing, in very simple words, is a testing of two versions of the same variable (e.g., web page) to check which one sells more or converts better. Usually it is a slight change so it's easy to manipulate and revert it if needed.

The Biggest Success

Olga: Tell me about the biggest success in your career as a product manager.

Sagar: Along with a very talented small team, I was able to take a game which I was working on, from making early 4-digits figure value of revenue in a day to a decent 5-digit value revenue. I was able to grow the revenues 8-fold in 2 years while I worked on that game. This game was going to be shut down due to early stats, which did not look promising, but thanks to a dedicated team we were able to turn it around.

As you can see, the life of a product manager is a big challenge where the team plays a big role. Let's now have a closer look at this challenge and sort it out!

Preparation

As much as we just want to get our hands dirty and start working on our product, we can't afford doing it without any preparation. We must make sure that all the *stakeholders* are aligned on the initial *requirements*, *deadlines*, *milestones*, and *risks*. We have to make sure that the *responsibilities* and *ownership* are correctly distributed between the team members and that everyone in the team understands their **impact** in the project. If there are external clients, we have to guarantee that we establish a smooth process and correct *communication channels* with them. We might come up with a documented *working agreement* to have everything visible and clear. Your main keywords here are **visibility** and **transparency**. Don't let anyone feel that important decisions are being made without considering their opinion. Don't leave anyone behind. Everyone should feel their impact and their importance in the project. Everyone should feel that they are driving the project to its very success. Then inevitably there will be one.

Requirements and Roadmap

Before gathering the whole team, you should think of *high-level requirements* and build a simple *roadmap*. "Oh my god, alone?" you might exclaim. If it is a small and simple project, then you might consider doing this brain exercise alone and then present it to the team and ask for their opinion. For more complex projects with more stakeholders involved you definitely don't want to be the only one responsible for these important bootstrapping artifacts. Define the key people and brainstorm with them.

Grab someone who has *business understanding*, some *technical person*, and, if applicable, someone responsible from the *client's side*. Go with all these people somewhere where you can have a strategy session without being interrupted.

A place outside the office works better! If it has some nature and outdoor activities, then even better! Have you heard of *focused* and *diffuse* modes of thinking that your brain switches between when you study? Well, turns out, not forgetting about these modes is also useful for any brainstorming sessions. You sit around the table, you present some problem. For some time, you are really focused on this problem and try to work on the solution. After some time, it is a good idea to go for a walk where your thoughts can run freely just like the surrounding nature. This helps to open up the limits around our brains and come to some non-standard and simple solutions.

We had a teacher back when we were studying in Portugal who was also the founder of one of the biggest companies that provides mobile software solutions. This incredibly intelligent sir would have his business meetings on …a golf course! He would explain that the modes of focused and diffuse thinking work pretty nice there. Turns out that the nature around the camp helps thoughts to diffuse, and while you concentrate on your move, you become highly focused. Not only are his successful ideas and solutions produced on golf courses, but all his best contracts and agreements are also signed there! Play golf, sign contracts, generate ideas. Count your revenues. So much profit, don't you think?

It seems we ran away from the main topic of this section. *Requirements and roadmap*, remember? So, you have gathered a small group to define the high-level requirements. What's next? How to do it? What should be discussed in this meeting? Think about the initial version of the product and write down what characteristics it has. Do you remember the picture about the MVP? It starts with a skateboard. If we think about it, we will almost immediately define the needed requirements:

- It must have wheels.

- It must have a board.

- It must have some sort of mechanism that unifies the board and the wheels together.

- It must move using the wheels attached to the board.

- It must have a brake mechanism.

These are indispensable requirements. Without these our skateboard is not a skateboard. Then you can define some nice-to-have features, like beautiful design of the board, ergonomics, jumping capacity, electrical motor, whatever.

That's why you need to have someone with business understanding and someone technical as well. The person with the business understanding will help you to define whether or not this or another feature is indispensable for the business success and business KPIs, whereas the technical person might point out some pitfalls of the implementation on the technical side. All of this is an engineering process. Engineering is about creativity, innovation, technology, and processes. Even Wikipedia knows this:

Engineering is the creative application of science, mathematical methods, and empirical evidence to the innovation, design, construction, and maintenance of structures, machines, materials, devices, systems, processes, and organizations.

Wikipedia: https://en.wikipedia.org/wiki/Engineering

After you define your high-level requirements, you need to define your high-level roadmap. If there is money involved, whoever pays this money would be interested in knowing the project's important delivery milestones. If there is no money involved, the team should be aware of the important days of delivering pieces of their product. Why are dates important? First of all, from our experience, the deadlines are actually powering the process and progress. Without planning some delivery milestones and dates, you can be sure that nothing will ever be delivered. There is no limit to perfectionism. Things can be polished, refined, and improved forever. Delivery dates help to stop this never-ending amelioration process. Second, and it might sound very controversial, the deadlines are pretty motivational. How can something called "deadline," a term that usually collates with stress and pressure, be motivational? Well, this is because each achievement should be celebrated! Achieved milestones must be celebrated with the whole team. The team usually works hard to reach the milestone and becomes happy when the goal is achieved. Make celebrations part of the culture of your team. Work hard, play harder!

That is why it is really important to have a technical person with you. This technical person will help you to run over very rough estimations to create your roadmap. Let's, for example, think of the roadmap for the MVP skateboard.

- Build wheels: 2 weeks

- Build board: 1 week

- Attach wheels to the board: 3 weeks

- Attach the braking mechanism: 2 weeks

- Test: 2 weeks

In total you have a 10-week project. Of course, in real life things will not be as easy as that. You will have to consider the team size, team members' skills, external dependencies (imagine that design is produced by an external agency), the budget, the legal policies, and even the season of the year! Some people, for example, feel a bit depressed and less motivated during winter, which affects productivity. On the other hand, people tend to party more during summer, which might also affect those who suffer from hangovers. :) Don't worry though, your milestones don't need to necessarily be expressed in accurate dates. They can represent the weeks or even the months for long and complex projects. The exact dates can be adjusted as long as the project moves forward. Also, you have your fantastic team that will help you with the roadmap adjustment during the kick-off meeting.

Kick-Off

Now that you already have your roughly described requirements and roadmap, you can gather your team for the *kick-off meeting*. Make it a serious yet a fun event. Serious because we are starting a new project, and everyone should be aligned on the huge responsibility that lies on our shoulders. Fun because new projects must be fun! Because the team is going to participate in a new adventure. Because there will be a celebration. Because great success is waiting for us and we should be ready for it. When people leave the kick-off meeting, they should be totally aligned on the following items:

- What the project is about

- Why this project is important

- What are each person's responsibilities

- What are the deliverables and important milestones

- How we are going to achieve the important results

Every meeting starts with an agenda. Kick-off meeting is not an exception. Prepare your agenda very clearly and send to everyone who is going to participate. Don't hold any tiny detail for yourself. The agenda for the kick-off meeting can be something like this:

- The description of the project (10 minutes)

- Why are we doing this? (5 minutes)

- Discussion of requirements (5 minutes)

- Discussion of dependencies (e.g., technological needs or third-parties dependencies) (10 minutes)

- Timeline and roadmap (15 minutes)

- Roles and responsibilities (10 minutes)

- Questions and answers (10 minutes)

Optionally, you can include the description of the customer (if there is any), the definition of process (if there was not any before), the communication channels, the technical discussions, the budget estimations, etc. Remember, every project is very unique and requires different approaches to be kicked off.

For example, for writing this book (because it is also a project) our kick-off process was pretty simple. We defined our outline and rough deadlines for each chapter, and the publisher created a contract based on that data and sent it back to us. After that we read the contract, signed it, and sent it back. Before each chapter we sat together and had a small brainstorming session of the chapter's content and defining who was writing what for each chapter's section. Thus, our process was smooth and straightforward, but remember, we are a long-running team of two. :)

For our learning platform project, the process was totally different. We sent the first three chapters of the book to our team, so they were aligned on the project and its requirements, and we gathered a meeting with them to brainstorm on the requirements and roadmap. The roadmap timeline was adjusted to the book's chapters deadlines since the product was built during the writing of this book. Also, our team consists not only of those 10 people we presented in the previous chapter. Our team is you. And this fact makes the project even more fantastic. Are you ready? You had better be because you are already on it!

Commitment and Deadline

The word ***commitment*** is drastically important for every project and every second of the project. Let's have a closer look at the definition of this word (just Google it, as it shown in Figure 3-1):

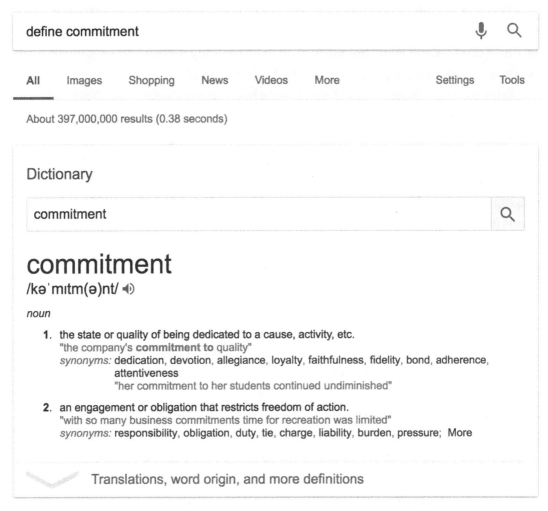

Figure 3-1. *Definition of the word "commitment"*

Check out the synonyms: **dedication**, **devotion**, **loyalty**, **responsibility**, **charge**... Commitment means dedication to the project and to the product, and that is one of the foundations for their success. It means loyalty to the team members.

During the execution of a project you commit to a certain deadline. It is likely that there will be pressure and some amount of stress, which is not necessarily bad if distributed evenly between all the team members.

It is crucial for the project that every team member commits to it and takes full ownership of what they are doing. If at least one team member has the feeling of, "I am just doing this task and going home," instead of, "This is my project and I am totally accountable for," then the project will not be fully successful.

We have been in projects where things were not running as expected. The tough deadlines would come, and there was a lot of work still to be done. Some teams were dealing with it by becoming a unique organism, something big, coherent, strong, and determined. They would try to achieve the committed milestone no matter what. They would help each other not only with project-related tasks but also by making coffee, bringing food, and taking care of some personal issues. These teams would become best friends during the stormy weather and ever after.

In other teams, the members would behave as if they were not a team at all! Each one would continue just doing their job, not being worried about the deadline approaching, and not caring about the other team members.

Needless to say, in the first case the team met the deadline delivering the fully committed feature set, while in the second case some features had to be dropped and some hard conversations had to be held with the client. When we asked the second team why they didn't feel worried about the deadline that was approaching and not delivering the features agreed upon before, they responded that this was not their fault. The fault was on the management. In their opinion, the product manager was responsible for the deadlines and commitment.

Don't let this ever happen on your team. The whole team is responsible. Each and every team member holds the ownership of the project. It is very important to pass on this idea during the very first kick-off meeting. Make everyone accountable, make everyone feel important, and make everyone an indispensable part of the mechanism of success.

A very simple way of making everyone feel their responsibility is to ask about their opinion a lot and using the word "we" or "us" when it comes to success and word "I" or "me" when it comes to a failure.

It is not the product manager, who is building a project; it is the team who is carrying the project through its path to success. It is not the product manager who is dictating the dates of the deliverables; it is a team, estimating those dates and agreeing on them. It is not the product manager who is celebrating the achieved goal; it is the team that is partying hard altogether. All of this doesn't mean that when things go wrong, the product manager can run away from the responsibility by saying, "We as a team failed to deliver the project." In this case, you, as a product manager, must stand up and assume your failures. And, believe us, if your team absorbs the culture of ownership and responsibilities, every single member will do the same.

Requirements for Our MVP

Now it is time to start gathering the requirements for our MVP. As stated earlier in this book, MVP stands for **minimum viable product**, but what does it actually mean? Well for starters, there is no clear answer to that—it just depends... but on what exactly?

When thinking about the MVP, we need to understand the environment and the target. To make it a little clearer, let's do this small exercise:

- A. Are there any other similar products in the market?

- B. What's the target audience? Is it for a specific niche market?

- C. Do I need to have some sort of breakthrough feature to convince people to choose my product?

- D. How long am I allowed to develop the product until it's out?

- E. Do I depend on external parties? For example, do I need some sort of certification or license to start selling my product?

The list can grow infinite, and that can be a problem as it can demotivate you. So, the first rule of thumb when thinking about the MVP is: keep it simple and concise. The important questions that need to be answered will always depend on the kind of product you are about to ship. Some examples follow:

- A. You are building a new social network. If your social network doesn't have a unique selling point (USP) to make people switch from others or join yours from the beginning, you cannot think about shipping it without all the basic features others are offering: liking and sharing posts, searching for content, organizing events, etc.

B. You are building a product X, and it recently went public that company Alpha is shipping a similar product Y. Both of the products will be the next big thing in the market, as there are no others out there. It is extremely important that you are either the first or at least do not wait too long after the other company launches its product. It is acceptable that you reduce the scope of the MVP to be the first in the market and then quickly cover all the features you dropped.

C. There are several applications already in the market that teach you how to cook. They have several features such as liking recipes, commenting on the videos, building shopping lists out of the recipes, you name it. On the other hand, all the content is in English. You want to build the exact same product but for a specific target group: people that speak Portuguese—covering not only Portugal but also Brazil. As you have a USP, it is fine to drop some of the features all others offer. It is not likely that they can compete with you on such short notice as they would have to transform all their content to Portuguese, and that poses a lot of work and resource allocation. As the others might be still thinking or actually converting all their content to Portuguese, you can finish the features you dropped at first and still be the first in the market with a full implementation and in a language that no other competitor has. Not launching all the features and shipping them from time to time can also be a good strategy so you give your customers the feeling that your product is very dynamic, and you are often working to offer them new functionalities.

The exercise that we just did here is pretty simple but also oversimplified. In real life and when there's money involved, a full market research, risk assessment, and report must be made. The decisions will be made taking those into account. Imagine that you have money for 6 months for development and after that you need to start selling your product immediately, so 6 months after launch you are already reaching the goals you and your investors agreed upon. This restriction, whether you like it or not, will influence your MVP.

What you need to retain from all the above is that it is important to think about the MVP before you start and that you cannot always fully control the decisions since you might depend on external factors.

Getting back to our very own specific case, it is quite interesting, and we will tell you why: we are not only competing against other companies but also competing against ourselves. It seems funny, right? But if you think about it, it is true. We already have a platform that is available, exposing a great deal of features and we want to build a new one where the first versions will not offer the same number of features. The good news is that we have a pretty cool USP: our content. This USP will give us leeway not only against our external competitors, but also against ourselves, as the content will not change. This way we can think about our MVP in a different way than we would be thinking if we were just joining the market from scratch.

In EdEra we have three sets of users: students, teachers, and administrators. So here is our first decision: the MVP will only cover the students' applications. This decision was not made out of the blue; we are aware that we do not have much time to come up with a good MVP, so of course we will focus on the most important users of the platform: our actual customers. Besides, we are not launching or administering courses on a daily basis, so we can perfectly live in the early days without a content management system and delegate all that to the development teams, so they do this manually on the database, for example.

Having set the focus, let's build up a list (Table 3-1) of high-level features for our platform. We are splitting the features into logical blocks that will match applications sections such as:

A. Pre-login: login and registration

B. Courses view: the list of courses the user can enroll

C. Dashboard view: the list of courses the user is doing

D. Course view: before enrolling

E. Course view: after enrolling

F. Profile view: edit user information

These are the sections of our initial application. We will now describe them in more detail and what is to be included in which of them. For that we will build a table and assign each feature we want to the sections of the application to which they belong. All the features are described in the user's (student's) perspective.

Table 3-1. *Features for the Education Platform MVP*

Feature	Section	Description
Registration form	A	A simple form with e-mail and password. The user can complete the registration after in the profile section.
Login form	A	A simple form with e-mail and password and a login button.
Recover password	A	A form where the user can type their e-mail address, so a reset link is sent.
Navigation bar	ALL	A navigation bar with the sections of the application. Always visible like a header.
Footer	ALL	A navigation bar with the sections of the application. Always visible like a header.
List all the courses	B	A simple list with all the courses available (might have to be paginated in the future as this list grows); people can click on the course to know more about it.
List all the enrolled courses	C	A simple list (paginated in the future as it can grow) with all the courses the user enrolled and their status. The user can click on the course to continue doing it or check the grading in case it's already finished.
List all the information about the course	D	The user will get the feeling what they will do in the course what they will need and the goals of the course.
Enroll in a course	D	The user can enroll in the course. This can be done only once in a lifetime.
Do the course	E	The user can see the content of the course and interact with it.
Render and play a video	E	The user can play videos that are bound to the course.
Render text	E	An explanation for example for teaching purposes is rendered for the user.
Render and answer a multiple-choice quiz	E	The user can answer a quiz that belongs to the course. The result is saved in persistence storage, so it never gets lost.

(continued)

Table 3-1. (*continued*)

Feature	Section	Description
Provide feedback	E	The user must get feedback if their guess was right or wrong.
Render the correct answer	E	Disclose the answer in case the user wants or guessed it wrong the first time.
Complete a course	E	The user receives a final grading upon the completion of the course. This view is the only view the user can access after the course is finished.
View the user profile	D	The user can check their personal data.
Change the password	D	The user can change their password if the current one is correct.
Change personal data	D	The user is able to change or add their name, gender, and birthday.

When we start laying down the features we want to do for the MVP, it also starts to become clearer how the application will be structured. For example, we can clearly see now that each course has some sort of "modules," like a video or just text and that each of these modules can have quizzes associated with them. This will become even more clear when we start designing, refining, and breaking down each feature into smaller and self-contained user stories, which is exactly what we will do in the next chapter.

Summary

In this chapter we kicked off our project. We wore the hat of a project manager to do it properly. We had an interview with Sagar, a product manager with several years of experience already, so we could get a real feeling about what this role is about.

We became familiar with terms like roadmap, estimations, requirements, kick-off meeting, and prioritization. We discussed how important it is to bootstrap a project correctly and make everyone feel important from the very beginning. We discussed the accountability of the team members, ownership, and responsibility. We also discussed about gathering requirements for the MVP.

We discussed not only how to analyze requirements, but also how to gather the initial requirements for the project we are going to build along this book.

In the next chapter we are going to proceed to the designing stage of our development process. We will wear the hat of a designer and discuss how designers do their work. User stories, mockups, wireframes... Are you ready for these terms? Then let's start, but first let's do a quick check up...

TEST YOURSELF

- What does MVP stand for?

    - Money Value Project

    - Minimum Viable Product

    - Maximum Viable Product

    - Minimum Vulnerable Product

- Your team is following the Scrum framework, you deal a lot with backlogs, prioritizing tasks, and distributing them across the team. You participate in activities such as daily meetings, retrospectives, and planning. Who are you?

    - Project Manager

    - Site reliability engineer

    - Product Manager

    - Product Owner

- You have already defined the initial requirements and agreed on business goals for the MVP with business owners. The team is still unaware of what is going on. What kind of meeting should you gather ASAP?

    - Daily standup

    - Retrospective meeting

    - Offsite event with beers and balloons

    - Project kick-off meeting

- What kind of pronoun should be used in order to create the feeling of everyone's accountability and responsibility?

    - I or me

    - You

    - We or us

    - It

If you answered "Minimum Viable Product—Product Owner—Project kick-off meeting—We or us," then you are good to go to the next chapter!

CHAPTER 4

User-Centered Design

In the previous chapter we analyzed the requirements, committed to a development strategy, and defined a simple roadmap.

In this chapter we are going to talk about one of the most difficult stages of product development: its design. A designer is a person who connects all the dots. Designers link the business needs and the product requirements to the technical challenges and, most important, to the end user. The keyword in this story is user. We are building our products as well as improving and refining them so they can be used. We expect our users to be happy with our product. We expect our products and services to have more and more users.

In this chapter you will wear the hat of a designer and you will see that a good design is not about the ability of drawing. A good design is about the people, their needs and problems, and ways of addressing the needs and solving the problem. The right design puts its user in the center of attention. That is why in this chapter we are going to talk about user-centered design.

This chapter is not about your product's design, this chapter is about your product's user. It does not teach about how to be a designer but rather gives some insights about driving the design process with the user as the center of attention.

© Olga Filipova and Rui Vilão 2018
O. Filipova and R. Vilão, *Software Development From A to Z*, https://doi.org/10.1007/978-1-4842-3945-2_4

Note   If you think that you should skip this chapter because you are not that creative or because you are never gonna be a designer, or because "*all these beautiful things are not my stuff*," please reconsider. Do you remember how you were able to do nearly everything when you were a child? You were able to **sing**, to **draw**, to **dance**… You were able to imagine yourself being an **artist**, a **cosmonaut**, an **actor**… Just at some point of your life, someone told you, *Hey, stop singing, it's awful!* Or maybe something like, *Why are you drawing if you don't know how to do it properly?* Or maybe something like, *You should be a doctor, leave the acting career for those who have talent for that.* During our whole life we develop this fantastic ability of not believing in ourselves. This book is not about giving you some motivational boost or explaining how short your life is and how it is not worth spending not believing in yourself. There are plenty of web resources and TED talks on this topic. We would just like to remind you that *you are creative*. If you don't believe us, check the book called *Creative Confidence* (`https://www.creativeconfidence.com/`). This book written by the creators of d.school (`https://dschool.stanford.edu/`) explains why you are creative and how to be confident in your creativity.

Design Journey—Its Start and End

So, your business requirements are written down, your roadmap is defined, deliverables are specified, and roles are cleared out. Now, finally, it is time for some design, right? No, it's not right. The time for design started at the very moment the idea appeared in your head… or even before. Think about the problem you are trying to solve. Ask a lot of people if they have a similar problem and how would they like it to be solved. Talking to people, identifying their potential problems, and thinking of possible solutions is an intrinsic part of the design process. Your design journey starts at the moment of identifying a problem and becomes intense once you visualize its solution. This journey is a journey without a destination, because ideally it never ends! After the actual implementation you want to keep your users engaged, you want to receive their constant feedback, and you want them to love your product. For that you have to constantly give this love back to them.

Think about your messaging app. Have you ever caught yourself staring at it? Your immediate answer will be "**no,**" but I will assure you that you have stared at your messaging app quite a lot of times. Three dots: does it mean anything to you? Not really? Then look at Figure 4-1.

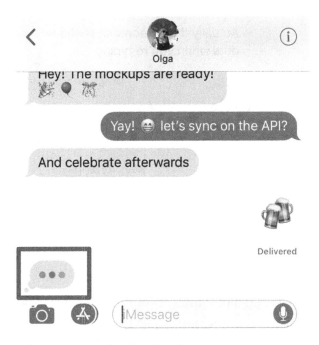

Figure 4-1. *Message's three dots feedback when someone is typing a message to you*

Do you remember these dots? Some applications will explicitly tell you that your respondent is typing (Figure 4-2):

Figure 4-2. *Telegram's three dots feedback when your respondent is typing a message*

Please, don't tell me you are not staring at your messaging app while these three dots magically blink at your face. Look how smart it is! The messaging app would actually be perfectly functioning without this small detail, but this little piece of very simple design makes us, its users, spend more time looking at it than we would if this feedback did not exist. You can find these small things everywhere, in nearly everything. These kinds of things are impossible to think of in the very beginning when you just have a slight idea of your product. These things result out of constant feedback you get from your users, not to mention changing trends. The world is moving around at a total crazy speed. It is impossible that things that were eye-catching yesterday will remain as such tomorrow. If you want your products to be compatible with the world's and users' needs, always keep looking around and always keep listening to your users.

Personas and User Stories

In the previous section we discussed quite a lot about the users and their needs. *User*. Can you establish a special bond, a connection with something that is called "*user*?" When I think of an abstract term "user," the first thing that comes to my mind is robot Sophia. I have no idea why. In order to create a special attachment with users, designers came up with the concept of "**persona**", Persona is a personified user. You have to be able to imagine the person, or a group of people, who will use your product. Your product will always solve **some problem**, but this problem is not common to **everyone in the world**. It will solve **some specific problem** for **some specific group of people**.

For example, if you create a product that helps pregnant women to keep track of their weight, then you can immediately narrow down your user base to females in a very special condition that is being pregnant. You have to keep in mind as well the way your persona uses the devices on which your software product is supposed to run. For example, people of different age ranges use technology in different ways. The same applies to different professions.

We all have our stories; our users are not the exception. What are user stories? **User stories** are stories that help designers to identify their personas and create a special bond with them. You just close your eyes and come up with a story that involves how your product is used. For example, let's imagine a businessman using our learning platform.

Mr. Baggins, a 47-year-old successful businessman, comes home from a conference where he was asked a couple of difficult questions about blockchain. He opens his laptop, opens the website of his favorite learning platform, and types "*blockchain*" in the search box. Two courses appear as a result: one of them is a deep course of 2 months and another is an introductory course that takes 3 hours. Since Mr. Baggins promised to his audience he would give an answer the next day, he enrolls in the second course. He thinks of getting deeper into the subject after the conference, so he adds the first course to his "*ToStudy*" list.

I am pretty sure you can come up with tons of stories like this one. What do we have as an outcome of this story? We actually have a lot of input regarding our learning platform, don't you think? So, our platform should have some sort of *search* mechanism that would allow the user to search for the courses. The resulting list of courses should display the course length for each of them. There should also be the possibility of moving the course to a "*ToStudy*" list. Can you see how many insights you can get just from one user story?

We also got our Mr. Baggins, a serious man, who uses both laptop and phone in his daily life. He is active, and he wants to learn about blockchain technologies. Table 4-1 provides his characteristics.

Table 4-1. *Alex Baggins' Persona*

Name	Alex Baggins
Age	47
Education	Ph.D.
Job/occupation	Businessman in the fintech industry
Income	$125K/year
Lifestyle	Conferences, exhibitions, traveling
Personality	Honest, open, creative
Usage patterns	Proficient PC user
Attitudes and tech usage	Big cloud-based computer systems, online magazines, online education, Amazon, online ticket services

Doesn't it feel good to know your user, even though you just created it? Did you have imaginary friends when you were a child? Being creative is being a child—remove all the boundaries and let your imagination flow. The more stories you tell, the more different users you will come up with and more usage patterns you will identify. Thinking about your users and their stories will help you to establish a special attachment to them. Creating stories feels good and is a common brainstorming practice in the world of software creation, but it's not enough, of course. You have to also go out and meet your users, but that is another story. For now, keep in mind that when we talk about users, we are not talking about some abstract entities, we are talking about our personas, and we already have a special emotional attachment to them.

Types of Design

Since our book is devoted to the software development—particularly to the web applications software development—we will be focused on the design for the web. Talking about design for the web was quite simple some years ago. Any design for the web could be called a **web design**, and everyone who was doing some design for web applications could be called a **web designer**. There has always been a clear distinction between web and graphic design or between print and digital design, but design for the web is simply called web design.

However, things evolve, the web changes, so does the design for web. It gets more complex; it is not only about form, colors, typography, and positioning. It is about the user and about the user's experience. It is about the speed of providing the user the information they need. It is about the amount of data that surrounds us. We live in a big data era and the art of pointing your user in the right direction is the current big design challenge.

The simple term "**web design**" has been split into a large tag cloud of terms and concepts. You might have heard some of them: *UX design, UI design, interaction design (IxD), animation design, information architecture design,* etc.

These are not just some fancy words to introduce more complexity into the already complex enough field, these are the emerged trends dictated by the world we are living in today. Refining and splitting these fields also helps designers and engineers to specialize in a specific field and master it.

There is so much information that your service or product can contain. Of course, you want it to be obvious for your users. You want your users to find whatever they need and find it in a simple and fast way. For that you need to structure your information in the best possible way. So here we are talking about the *information architecture design*.

Depending on the kind of application you are building, there will be different states and transitions between them. For example, when the user logs in, there is a transition between the login page and the actual application page once the user hits the login button. When you search for something on the page, you need a transition between the state when you hit the Search button and the state where the results appear on the page. In these cases, you could use a bit of *animation design* to entertain your users while the application state changes.

The way the user feels about your application is defined by the *user experience design*, and the way the user interacts with your application is defined by the *interaction design*. The way the interface is built is defined by the *user interface design*.

Of course, all these areas intersect, overlap, mix, and combine altogether by offering you a unique flavor of a smooth and nice user journey.

You will rarely find a team that will have people in all the roles we just described. You will find people who are good in several areas. Sometimes one person does all the work. For example, at Feedzai, the company where we've both worked, there was this brilliant guy who would drive the whole design process from initial hand-drawn mockups until the actual implementation in HTML and CSS. During the major redesign stages, an external company specialized in UX design was hired to run through the user research and help to define the perfect interface for the user journey.

Another company Olga worked with had delegated the whole design to an external agency. Do you want our honest opinion about it? Don't do it unless your budget is really limited. The design becomes totally detached from the company's business, mission, and vision, and it's very hard to drive changes. If possible, try to have your own designer on board—someone who lives your product the same way you do.

At OptioPay we have the *creative department* that is led by product managers. This department is composed of an art director—an amazing girl who can easily create simple and great-looking graphics and design whole complex systems. There is also a UI engineer—a guy with a mixed designer-engineer mind. He is able to drive the whole design process, and his real power lies in implementing stuff. He can grab any design and transform it into a production-ready, fully responsive and adaptive interface. What looks like total black magic for us is absolutely obvious for him. There is also a UX designer who connects user experience with the business needs. He drives user research, draws mockups, iterates over them until they are totally obvious to the users, and hands them over to the UI engineers. In the company where Rui works, there are only two designers that do all the jobs—they drive the whole design process, starting from the business brainstorming and low-fidelity wireframes to the high-fidelity mockups and handover to the frontend developers.

Different needs require different approaches, but one thing is true for sure—if your product has a user interface, it automatically becomes user-oriented; therefore, never underestimate the power of design. Your user must be in the center of the whole design and experience concept.

User Interface and User Experience

In the previous section we've discussed different types of design and the major differences between them. The main source of debates, controversial talks, and blog articles is the difference between user interface (*UI*) and user experience (*UX*). These two fields have the blurriest boundary between them. User experience always requires a user interface. An interface can be nearly everything and not necessarily something visible. For example, Alexa does not have a visible user interface, but it has a great user experience!

You can sometimes find products that have terrible interfaces yet very good user experience. For example, Amazon Web Services (AWS) administration console doesn't have an astonishing mind-blowing UI, but it doesn't matter because it has amazing user experience. Whenever we go to the AWS dashboard to monitor some problem or to add some service, we know exactly where to click, where to search, and what to type to find the needed information, as shown in Figure 4-3.

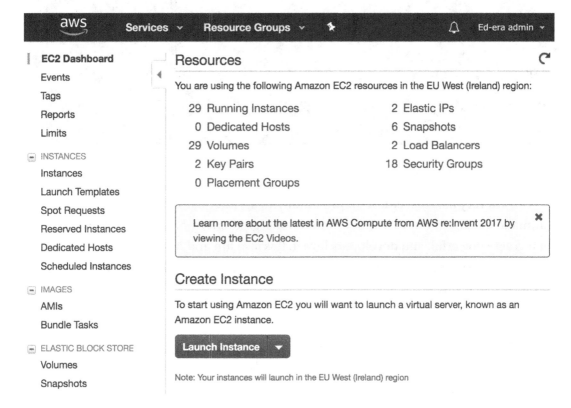

Figure 4-3. *AWS console: just a regular UI, yet a good and powerful UX*

Another example of an ugly UI but great UX is the Linux console. The console allows you to operate your system via commands that you type in the command line interface. No fancy buttons, no beautiful colors. Just text and arrows. But this is what makes consoles so powerful. They do not have distractions; they go straight to the point. That's why developers from all over the world love Linux—Linux' interface is ugly, but it has this powerful console that allows doing everything without ever leaving it! Let's take Vim as an example. Vim is a text editor that you can run on the console. It is easy to find out more about Vim if you are using the console. Just type "`man vim.`" This will give you a complete user manual of the Vim text editor (Figure 4-4).

```
VIM(1)                                                          VIM(1)

NAME
      vim - Vi IMproved, a programmer's text editor

SYNOPSIS
      vim [options] [file ..]
      vim [options] -
      vim [options] -t tag
      vim [options] -q [errorfile]

      ex
      view
      gvim gview evim eview
      rvim rview rgvim rgview

DESCRIPTION
      Vim is a text editor that is upwards compatible to Vi.  It can be used to edit all kinds of plain text.  It
is especially useful for editing programs.

      There  are  a lot of enhancements above Vi: multi level undo, multi windows and buffers, syntax highlighting
, command line editing, filename completion, on-line help, visual
      selection, etc..  See ":help vi_diff.txt" for a summary of the differences between Vim and Vi.

      While running Vim a lot of help can be obtained from the on-line help system, with the ":help" command.  See
the ON-LINE HELP section below.
```

Figure 4-4. *Unix shell:* man vim *command*

Vim is a very nice text editor for programmers. Its interface consists of text commands. It doesn't have buttons, animations, gradients, or any fancy transitions. Yet it is very powerful, and developers love it. It is also fun and has some Easter eggs. For example, try typing ":help 42" in the Vim interface. You will see something like that shown in Figure 4-5.

Figure 4-5. *Vim's Easter egg -* :help 42

There are lots of other examples of the websites with poor UI yet great UX. For example, Hackernews (`https://news.ycombinator.com/`), Reddit (`https://www.reddit.com/`), Craigslist (`https://craigslist.org/`)—these are the examples of ugly yet very popular websites. Hence, you can see that you can have a powerful user experience without having a mind-blowing user interface. Can it be the other way around? Can you have a beautiful user interface yet poor user experience? Oh yes you can! Take Windows 10 as an example. It actually has a pretty nice interface, it looks very modern and fancy, but try, for example, to manage your wireless settings. You will find it a bit complicated and not intuitive at all.

Another example of a service that has some UX problems in the very attractive UI is Invision (`https://www.invisionapp.com/`). Invision is a great product that allows you to create and test your design prototypes. We use it quite a lot. It has a very appealing interface, with smooth transitions, nice colors, and nice fonts... Actually, it also works pretty nice. However, it has some UX issues. For example, imagine you are on the prototypes dashboard where you have a lot of prototypes; hence, you need to scroll. For example, there is a big prototype page, as shown in Figure 4-6.

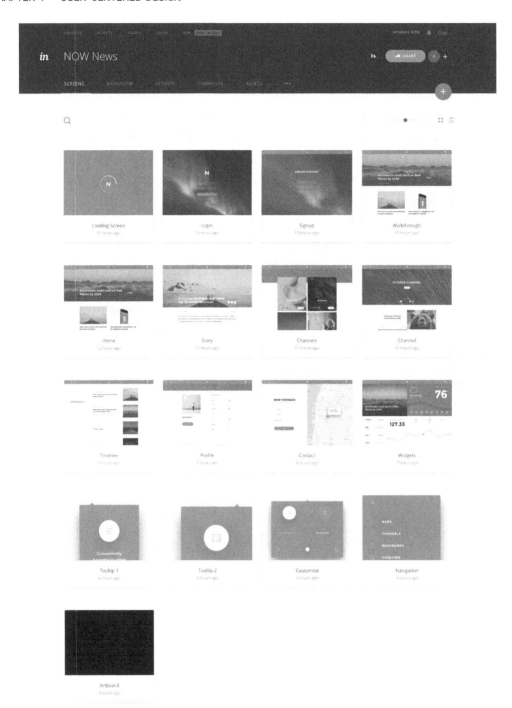

Figure 4-6. *A big scrollable prototype page in the Invision interface*

Imagine that you scroll about half of the page and want to check some particular prototype. So, you click on it (Figure 4-7).

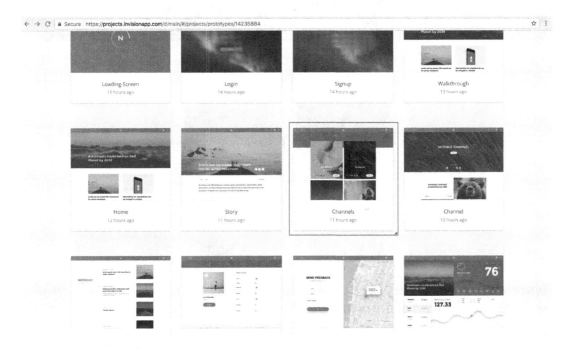

Figure 4-7. *Select one of the prototypes after scrolling*

The prototype is opened on the same page, you do what you need to do in it and then you click back on the browser navigation pane. What do you expect? You expect to come back to the exact same place where you were before you clicked on the prototype—in the middle of the page. What happens instead? The scenario shown in Figure 4-8 happens.

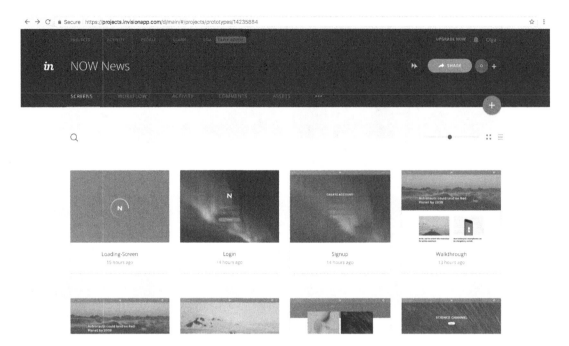

Figure 4-8. *After you click back on the prototype page, you are back to the top of the dashboard instead of the actual place you've been before*

This is a terrible user experience. It is likely that you want to have a closer look at the prototype that is next to the one you've just checked. So, every time you go back you are forced to scroll again and look for the place you have been before.

You can find lots of products out there that have a great UI and great UX all together. Google drive, for example, looks nice, feels nice, and works nice. Twitter is another example that looks nice and is quite intuitive to use. Facebook and Instagram are great examples of something that is not only nice-looking and easy to use, but also so contagious. They made their UX to absorb millions of people and spend their time in useless infinite scroll. That is amazing and scary at the same time.

Of course, you can find examples of bad UI and bad UX in the same product. For example, after Microsoft bought Skype, it became ugly and difficult to use (Figure 4-9).

Figure 4-9. *Skype: example of bad UI and bad UX at the same time*

So, what do UI and UX designers do? Once they start doing their work, they should ask some questions to align with the user and product needs and the business purpose. The questions differ in their nature. So, the UI designer will be concerned with questions like:

- What colors should I use?

- What fonts should I use?

- What is the corporate identity?

As you can see, the user interface designer is worried about the things that you can see. Whereas the user experience designer will ask questions like:

- Who are our users?

- What are the users supposed to achieve while using the product?

- What are the business goals of this product?

Thus, the user experience designer is worried about the things that you can feel. The UX designer is more business-oriented.

Both UI and UX designers are worried about the user. The first is concerned about what the user sees, and the second is worried about how the user feels. Working together, UI and UX designers can deliver great products and make us, users, happy.

Design Process—How Designers Run It

How is the design process structured? Do you just go to your designer and tell them, "Hey, I want to build some online shop!" and then the designer just draws it? Well, it would be great if everything could be that easy. In fact, the design process is quite tedious. We asked a friend of ours, a designer, to describe how she runs her process. Here is her short bio:

Name: Yujia Ma

Description: A UX/UI designer based in Berlin. Likes to solve design problems, create smart user interfaces, and imagine useful interactions, focusing on the user-centered design.

Linkedin: `https://www.linkedin.com/in/mayujia/`

We call her Malu, for short. Here's Malu's story about her design process.

1. *Personas and User stories*

   Malu usually starts with personas and user stories. She recommends creating up to three personas and writing the most important user stories on paper.

2. *Information architecture*

   After writing down user stories and creating personas, Malu proceeds with the information architecture. She defines the information architecture as the structure and order of the product. She recommends thinking about what tasks users can accomplish in your product, and what the flow of users is throughout your product.

   "A good information architecture ensures that your design is logically grouped and interrelated." Take a look at Figure 4-10.

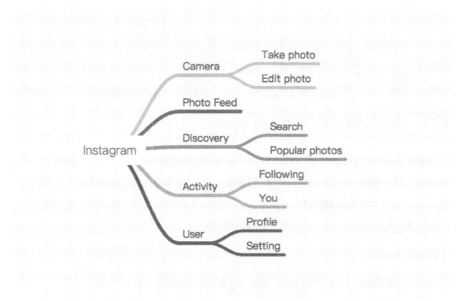

Figure 4-10. *An example of information architecture of the Instagram application by Malu*

3. *Sketching*

    After thinking of the information architecture, Malu draws some
    shapes on paper (as shown in Figure 4-11) to get the feeling about
    how the product looks.

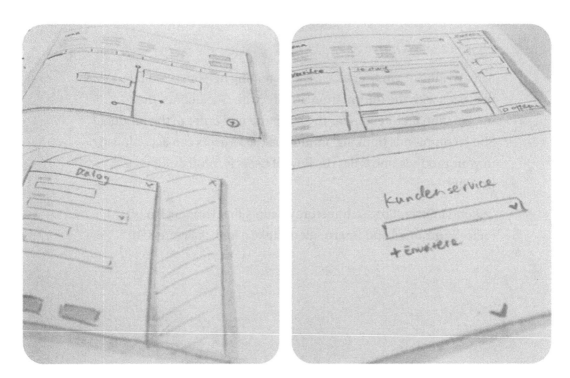

Figure 4-11. *Hand-drawn sketches by Malu*

    Once she feels that her sketches meet and represent the full user
    story, she proceeds to testing. Malu uses the POP application
    (`https://marvelapp.com/pop`), which allows her to test any paper
    mock-up in a variety of device simulators.

4. *Wireframes*

    "Like building a house, you already have a skeleton of your
    application (Information architecture) and you also tried some
    sketch on paper. Now you need to draw the floor plant to make
    sure that the living room and the kitchen are in the correct places.
    To establish the purpose of each page, interactions they have, etc.
    A wireframe gives you sense of the elements' placement on the

page and their relation to each other, but without color, graphics, spacing or typography. Don't forget to make notes to explain the interactions besides your screens."

If you are designing an iOS or an Android app, Malu recommends taking some time to learn more about their graphical user interface (GUI) guidelines first.

- iOs: `https://developer.apple.com/ios/human-interface-guidelines/`

- Android: `https://material.google.com/`

Malu highly recommends considering the following topics while designing a wireframe:

- What needs are the most important?

- What contents and functions should be in the page?

- Do the elements make sense?

- Is anything important missing on the page?

- Does anything make the user confused?

- How can we build connections between pages?

You can design a low-fidelity wireframe using a grey area to replace the real contents, as shown in Figure 4-12.

Figure 4-12. *Low-fidelity wireframe by Malu*

You can also design a higher fidelity wireframe. It's closer to the visual design with the real contents. Designers have many ways to do a wireframe. Malu designs it using Sketch. She has her own wireframe kits for Android, iOS, and web to make the process quick and efficient.

You can find many free resources of wireframe kits as well. In the beginning, you can learn how many basic elements an application should have.

You can also use tools like Omnigraffle (`https://www.omnigroup.com/omnigraffle`), Axure (`http://www.axure.com/`), and Balsamiq (`https://balsamiq.com/`) to create a wireframe.

5. *Prototype*

    After the wireframe, we need to test whether our design works. Malu's process is to upload her sketch file into Invision and make a quick clickable prototype.

    During testing you need to review whether the flow of the product is smooth and consistent. Sometimes Malu prefers to print all screens to make a big board of the workflow. When you connect all screens with a pen, it's very easy to find what is missing and where there exists some logical mistake. Malu also recommends talking with your developer team at this point. The results of the team brainstorming are shown in Figure 4-13.

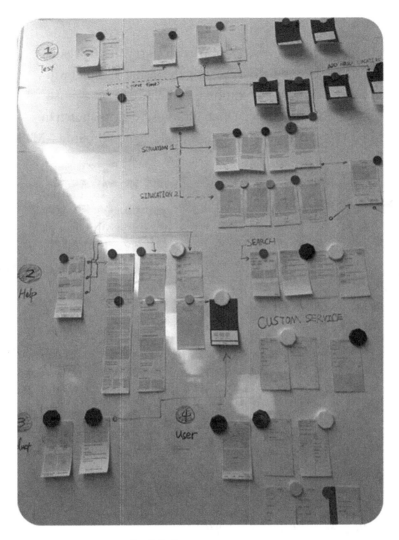

Figure 4-13. *Paper prototype by Malu*

6. *Visual design*

"Wireframes are approved. Yeah! We can start with the visual design! Wait a second before creating the visual design. I will advise you to get more inspirations. It's helpful to get a sense of the style for your product. Open Pinterest (e.g., as shown in Figure 4-14), input some keywords to make a moodboard."—Malu

Figure 4-14. *Pinterest Moodboard by Malu*

Open sketch and do some magic (Figure 4-15):

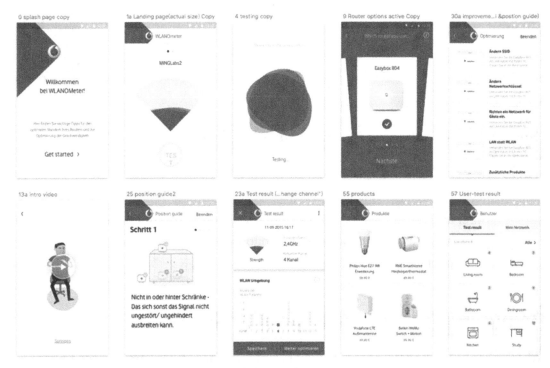

Figure 4-15. *Visual design in Sketch by Malu*

7. *Higher fidelity prototype*

At this point you might be already hungry to start to implement your product. Before doing that, Malu tests her product again. She uses Invision to create a higher fidelity prototype. She finds it as a good way to show the design to others for brainstorming.

"Not enough? I know, everyone likes motion design and animation... OK, you can use Principle, Justinmind, Pixate, After effects, or even just Keynote (the logos of these applications are displayed in Figure 4-16) to do some fancy animations to show the interaction you intend to have."—Malu

Principle   Justinmind   Pixate   After effect

Figure 4-16. *Tools that can be used for designing high fidelity prototype and animations*

8. *Handover*

   After all the testing and brainstorming, Malu organizes her sketch files as well as other design files and hands them over to the developers' team. Let's code!

Designing Our Online Education Platform

Now that we've learned how other designers structure their design process, we can pretend to be designers and start sketching our online education platform. We apply some of the stages and principles of Malu's process. In this section, we will describe what we did to prepare everything for the actual implementation.

Initial Brainstorming

So, we started from the brainstorming. Rui, Safi, and Olga sat together, and Olga told about the expectations from our MVP. We spoke about Personas and came up with some more user stories besides our Mr. Baggins story. Safi asked a lot of questions. She has this special ability of bombarding you with all the questions from several different angles and perspectives. Usually when we run through a brainstorming session with her, we feel like a squeezed lemon, but it does feel good actually! If you will ever build your own product, make sure you have a person like Safi. This person must have a critical and sharp mind, not be shy, and be curious and passionate. So, after the intense brainstorming, we have drawn these sketches (Figure 4-17) on paper.

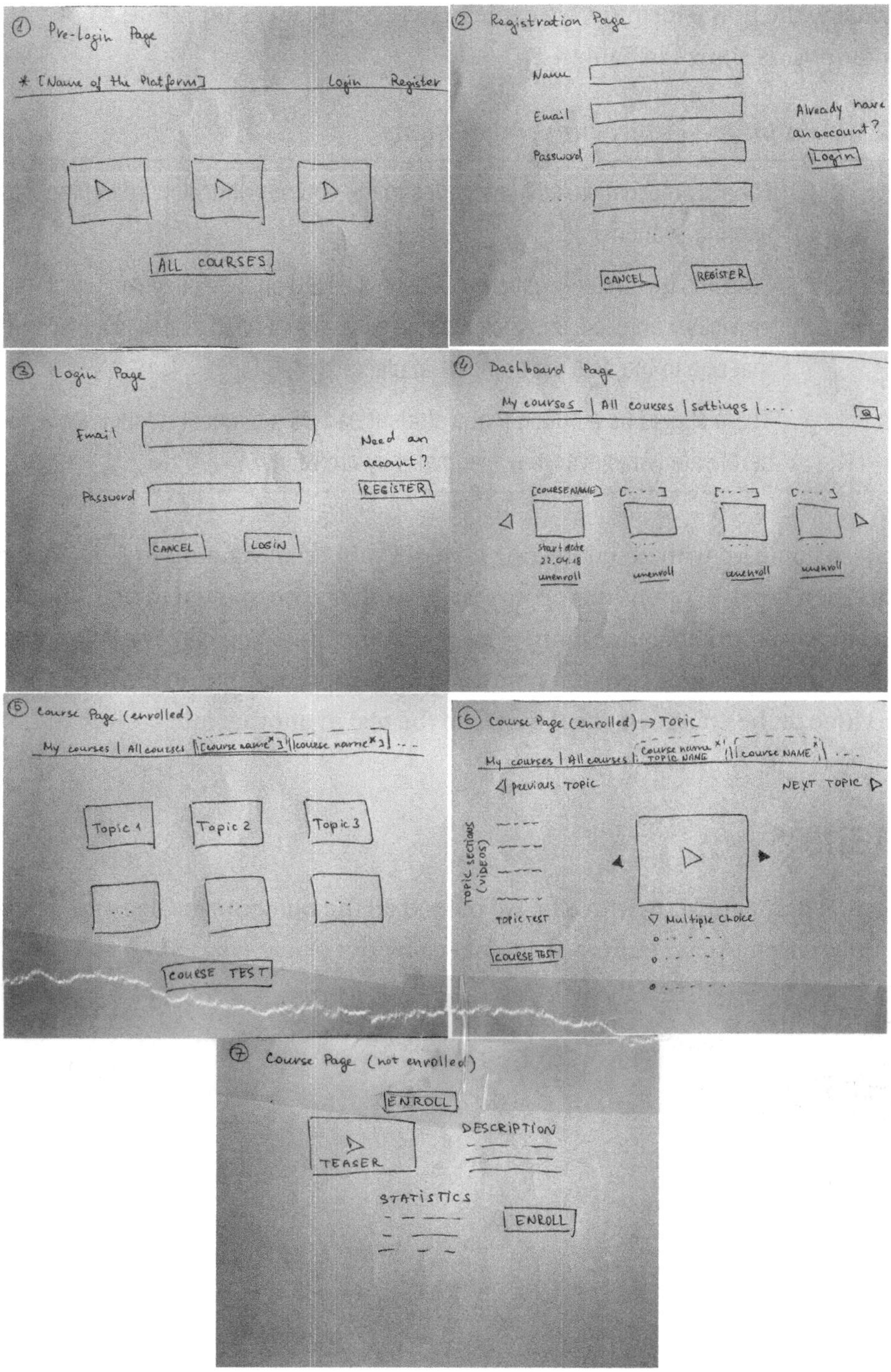

Figure 4-17. *Initial brainstorming mockups for the online educational platform*

Also, during the brainstorming, we came up with some ideas for future implementations, as shown in Table 4-2.

Table 4-2. *Ideas for the Future Implementations*

Categorization of courses	For easy navigation, add categories to the courses and allow searching and filtering by them.
Recommendation engine	Students receive suggestions of courses based on the courses in which they previously enrolled, and their searches (we might need a special consent for that due to the data privacy laws in place).
Certificates generation	There should be a button that a student can click to generate their own certificate (whenever they feel that they are ready).

We've also come up with an interesting idea of a tabbed navigation—check mockup number 6. When the user opens their courses, the courses are opened in tabs, thus allowing us to have more than one course opened at the time. You can even open the same course more than once in different tabs. Imagine, for example, that you can still watch the video of the course in one tab and do the test in another tab.

Wireframes

After the initial brainstorming with Safi, we passed all the outcome to Oleg and he used Sketch to draw wireframes. Figure 4-18 is what came out of it.

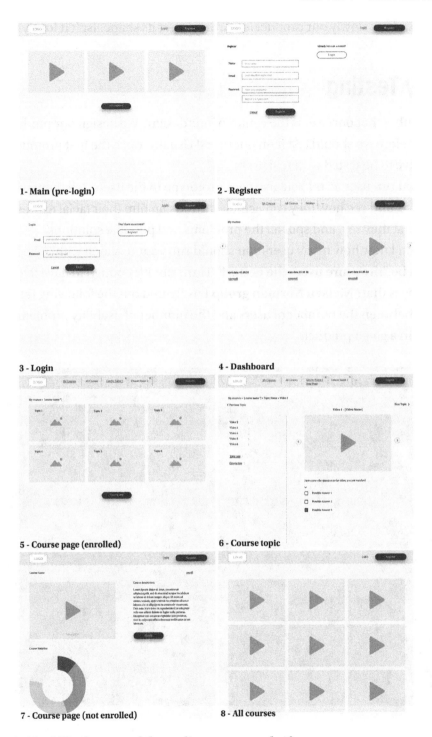

Figure 4-18. *Wireframes of the online courses platform*

You can see how slowly our product is starting to get its shape. Isn't it lovely?

Usability Testing

Do you remember that our user is the center of our design? We design our product for our users, therefore we should test it on our users! Usually, once the first prototypes are ready, they have to be tested with real users.

How do you run user tests? You give your prototype to the users, tell them what they need to achieve, and see how they can achieve it. You can film their facial expressions, write down what they say, and spot all the problems and possible solutions.

How do you know how many users you should run your research with? The logical answer would be "**the more users the better!**" Turns out it's enough to have five user tests! Five! Why is that? **Nielsen Norman group** has figured out the following ratio (Figure 4-19) between the number of users and the number of usability problems that can be found in a given product.

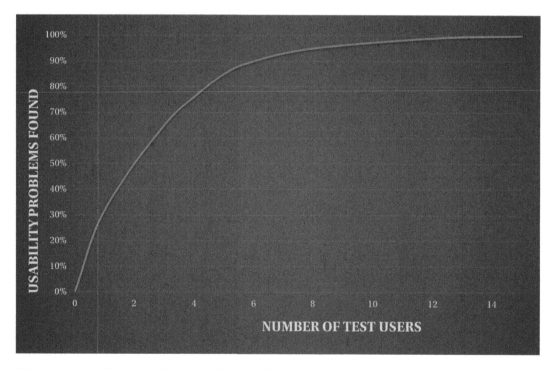

Figure 4-19. *The ratio between the number of test users and usability problems found*

As you can see, starting from five users, the number of problems does not increase as much. Thus, the effort of conducting user testing further is not actually worth it.

Another very important thing that is clear from this chart is that it is better to test with one user than with no users at all. With one test user you can find up to **31% of usability problems**! This is one-third of the problems of your product.

Nielsen Norman group (`https://www.nngroup.com/`) is an American computer user interface and user experience consulting firm. To find out more about the number of test users/usability problems found ration, check this article: `https://www.nngroup.com/articles/why-you-only-need-to-test-with-5-users/`

So, we decided to conduct user testing with one user. We gave the mockups to the user and explained that we are expecting him to interact with the online education platform. Figure 4-20 shows the user's interaction.

Figure 4-20. *Usability testing: better with one user than with no users at all!*

Our user was a 26-year-old male whose occupation is in IT. We could say that the test participant was a heavy online-course user. On one side, that meant he already had an idea how such educational platforms should look and knew his needs and expectations. On the other side, it meant that his expectations were already biased. Due to intense use of similar educational websites, he might have been used to different user interfaces and looked for them, even if they were not optimal. Table 4-3 depicts the results that we recorded during the testing.

Table 4-3. *Usability Testing of Different Pages*

Page	Results
1. Pre-Login page	The page is clearly structured for the user and very intuitive. Two major expectations of the user were: – Classification of videos in different fields – Possible explanations of certifications, or user testimonials. User wants to know exactly WHY this platform could be better than others.
2. Registration page	The user is confused that the registration form is left-justified. He expected it to be placed in the center. – The login button should be placed above the registration form. – The field "name" is redundant. The user wants to have as few fields to fill out as possible. – Additionally, the user expects (from other online educational platforms) that he could register via Facebook or Google API.
3. Login page	The same comment about the field positioning as for 2.
4. Dashboard (My courses) page	The user expects emphasis on his most recent course. – The user wants to see the recommendations for further similar courses. – The logout button is too concise; should not be displayed at all. The user doesn't necessarily want to logout. He would expect the settings section to be in the place of the logout button. – By clicking on that field, he could choose between adjusting his profile, course preferences, and so on to help to improve the recommendation algorithm. And in the very bottom the logout possibility. – The search functionality is missing. The user says in most cases he knows exactly what he is looking for and wants to find it fast.

(continued)

Table 4-3. (*continued*)

Page	Results
5. Course page with topics	The first thing that confuses the user is the button "Course test." The purpose of the button remains unclear. The layout seems to be unusual for the user. For a better course overview, the user would rather expect the topics to be listed on the left side under each other. On the right side, the short topic description and duration, respectively. The search field is missing here as well.
6. Course topic page	The layout looks very intuitive and easily understandable, but the user expected to see more details about the content of the topic (e.g., as a short description below the video), the duration, the teachers, comments from other users, and so on. Multiple-choice questions are rather unexpected at this point.

As you can see, we were able to spot some interesting usability problems that will certainly help us in building our platform. Ideally, we would address all the problems and rerun the testing. However, most of the spotted problems can be addressed during the implementation as future features; thus, we are going to leave the mockups just as they are for now.

Visual Design

After the mockups are ready and the user testing is done, it is time for us to start drawing a visual design. Now we are talking about the UI with its colors, borders, button sizes, and other visual elements. At this point, we are not going to introduce colors, fonts, button sizes, or other elements of design system, because this is part of the corporate identity, and we don't have any corporation; we are just building our MVP. Hence, we will leave it grayscale. The design of the login and registration pageswill look, for example, as shown in Figure 4-21.

Figure 4-21. *Visual design for the Login and Registration page*

These designs were designed by Alexandra Siryk, our designer from EdEra. She is actually the one responsible for designing most of the illustrations of this book. There will not be enough beers to pay her for her hard and amazing work!

Interview With a Product Designer

This chapter is full of evidence stories from real designers. Of course, we couldn't leave you without an interview with one of them, Stan Reimgen, whose Medium profile is shown in Figure 4-22.

Medium

Stan Reimgen
Medium member since Jan 2018

Founder and Designer, working across UX and UI. Built and sold a startup, traveled half of the planet. Now at Fjord Neugelb: http://www.stanreimgen.com/

Figure 4-22. `https://medium.com/@stanbugaev:` *Stan Reimgen, product designer*

This interview was recorded some time ago; it has been unlisted all this time, and now is the time to share it with the world! So here it is: `https://youtu.be/WSEdKyOuat4`. The interview took place in our apartment in Berlin, and the guy from the left is Illia—Olga's brother, the CEO of EdEra.

Summary

In this chapter we spoke about design, its different types, as well as different types of people who work on it. We discussed the main differences between UI and UX, and we explored examples that have good or bad UI and/or UX. We spoke about usability testing, and we've discussed how many users you need to have in order to test your product properly. We ran usability testing with our educational platform. We brainstormed on the features our platform should have and developed hand-drawn mockups and low-fidelity and high-fidelity wireframes for it. Check how well you understand it below.

```
                           TEST YOURSELF
```

- What does UI stand for?

    - Useful Internet

    - User Income

    - User Interface

    - Unique Interface

- You open some website and have a visual orgasm. You see the most beautiful colors, very nice forms, astonishing fonts, and the most beautiful calligraphy. It is so beautiful that you want to immediately use the service even without knowing what the service offers. After some scrolling you find the "join us" button, you click on it, and you are redirected to another beautiful page with some more buttons. In the end you had to click different buttons five times until actually getting to the registration form. This is a clear example of:

    - Good implementation with bad design

    - Very good UI but confusing UX

- • Horrible project management but nice product management

- • Good frontend but bad backend

- According to the Nielsen and Norman group, how many users should be enough to discover most of the usability problems?

  - • As many as possible!

  - • One user is enough—it is better to use it with one person than with no one.

  - • Five users should be enough because testing with five users would uncover about 85% of usability problems.

  - • Usability tests are not needed, product managers can discover all the problems in the product.

- According to this chapter, what or who should be in the center of our design?

  - • Product

  - • User

  - • Business

  - • Experience

If you answered "User Interface—Very good UI but confusing UX—5 users—User," then you are good to go to the next chapter!

Now we are ready for the actual implementation of our MVP! In the next chapter you will become a backend developer and do the invisible yet powerful part—deal with databases, servers, and APIs to prepare our application's data to be created, used, and displayed to our users. Are you ready for hardcore? Let's go!

CHAPTER 5

Backend Development

We've come a long way! We hope you are as excited as we are because this is the first chapter where we'll write code.

In the previous chapter we discussed the design implementation of our product. You saw how everything developed from the concept phase, passing by the flow, mockups, and wireframes until its final visual stage: pixel perfect.

In this chapter we are going to start our project by building our backend application that will support everything needed by the frontend application later. We will start by bootstrapping the project, so it can be built in a way we can later deploy. We will talk about data storage and ways of structuring an application and come up with a good architecture to minimize possible future inconveniences.

Keep in mind that this chapter will introduce a lot of new terms, and we'll provide several definitions and brief explanations, but it won't dive into the details on any of them. The purpose is that in the end you get an idea on what you need in order to build a backend application and how these pieces work together. It will have some practical parts, but as you can imagine the project is considerably big, so we will just guide you through brief examples on how to bootstrap a project and some small implementation details, so you can get a feeling on how backend applications are built.

Note If you are thinking about skipping this chapter because you are more into other topics, such as frontend, we invite you to think twice. We believe that even though you tend to lean more to one side of the development flow, it is important to have some knowledge on how things work together in general. Don't worry, as we won't get into much detail, but just all the steps needed to bootstrap a backend project and also considerations that we need to do when designing a backend application. We hope you are convinced now, and that you'll stay tuned!

© Olga Filipova and Rui Vilão 2018
O. Filipova and R. Vilão, *Software Development From A to Z*, https://doi.org/10.1007/978-1-4842-3945-2_5

About the Stack...

We decided on the following stack because we felt that it is the one we can explain better and be more passionate about. We are not saying that this is the best stack—actually, we don't believe that there's a "best stack"; we believe there are a set of good stacks for what you want to do—some better than others depending on the nature of the project.

There are several things that can help you decide what to choose, either because you are more comfortable with a specific programming language, or because there is one that you feel is better to solve a specific problem you have or just because you are somehow forced to use a specific stack since your company already invested before on it. We usually don't engage in these kind of discussions, as they tend to lead us nowhere.

We decided to write the backend application in Java 8. Why? Basically, because Rui has been working with Java for almost 15 years and he believes that it is a very nice language not only to learn but also for production scenarios. Again, no discussions, this is Rui's personal opinion and not a universal truth!

All examples such as installations, commands, etc., will be done using Ubuntu Linux version 16.04 LTS. If you have another system you'll have to match everything we'll do here to your system, but again we bet it won't be that hard to pull that one off.

The material for this chapter is called "courses-incomplete." It contains the full project, but there are some parts that you will need to complete to make it work. For some exercises, such as the authentication exercise, you will need to use the fully implemented project.

Defining Backend Applications

First of all, let's define what we are actually talking about. When we talk about the frontend and backend, we refer to the client-server model. So, the backend is the part that runs on a server somewhere on the cloud and, among multiple things, is responsible for dealing with data in general terms. This means that it is responsible for receiving requests from the clients to provide data, so they can display.

This seems simple, but there are a lot of topics concerning the backend. Where do we store the data? How do we access it? Who can see what data? All these topics are handled by backend applications. We'll try to break this down for you in a way you can understand all the actors that take a role in what we just described.

Bootstrapping the Project

Now that we decided we are going to do our implementation in Java, we need to come up with a way to build the project. Building a project contains all the necessary steps to make the project executable in the end. In our specific case, it means compiling all the module dependencies and creating a bundle that can run on an application server. For that, we could write scripts or just assume we could do it manually, but believe us, nowadays projects get big really quick, and it's nearly impossible to build them without having a proper Build Automation Tool. In our case we'll use Maven since it's the commonly accepted de facto standard tool to build Java projects.

Maven runs on Java so let's first install the Java Development Kit from Oracle since we'll also need it to compile and run our project. For that we'll use a third-party repository. Just open a terminal and start typing the following:

```
sudo add-apt-repository -y ppa:webupd8team/java
sudo apt-get update
sudo apt-get install oracle-java8-installer
sudo apt-get install oracle-java8-set-default
```

If everything went fine, you should see something similar to that when you run "java -version".

```
java version "1.8.0_102"
Java(TM) SE Runtime Environment (build 1.8.0_102-b14)
Java HotSpot(TM) 64-Bit Server VM (build 25.102-b14, mixed mode)
```

Ignore the "_102" as long as it starts with "1.8" we are set to go. Now let's install Maven. Let's also use a third-party repository:

```
sudo add-apt-repository -y ppa:natecarlson/maven3
sudo apt-get update
sudo apt-get --assume-yes install maven3
sudo ln -sf /usr/bin/mvn3 /usr/bin/mvn
```

All set? Just run "mvn -version" and you should see something like the following:

```
Apache Maven 3.2.1 (ea8b2b07643dbb1b84b6d16e1f08391b666bc1e9; 2014-02-
14T18:37:52+01:00)
Maven home: /usr/share/maven3
Java version: 1.8.0_102, vendor: Oracle Corporation
```

```
Java home: /usr/lib/jvm/java-8-oracle/jre
Default locale: en_US, platform encoding: UTF-8
OS name: "linux", version: "4.12.2-041202-generic", arch: "amd64",
family: "unix"
```

And that's all. We have the environment set for development, but we also need one very important thing: an editor. Again, this discussion could take ages and still lead nowhere, so I'll just drop the one we like to use. It's called IntelliJ IDEA, and you can download the Community version for free at `https://www.jetbrains.com/`.

Build Automation Tool: Maven

What Rui finds cool about Maven is that it's easy to use, easy to read, and has a lot of plugins that can make your life easy. In order to create our project, we need to write down a considerable amount of configuration, since it relies on several dependencies. We'll not do that here. We find it way more interesting for you to just see how things start, because after that it is more of the same.

Maven offers a way to bootstrap projects or create skeletons using archetypes. In our case, we won't use any existing archetypes, we will create the project ourselves by writing it from scratch. To define projects, we use `pom.xml` (Project Object Model) files. Each of these files defines a Maven module. Let's start with the root `pom.xml`, the entry point of our project. First of all, we create a folder to hold the project, let's call it `courses`, for example. Just switch to a folder where you want to keep everything, create the `courses` folder, and the following `pom.xml` inside:

```
mkdir projects
cd projects
mkdir courses
cd courses
cat << EOF > pom.xml
<?xml version="1.0" encoding="UTF-8"?>
<project xmlns="http://maven.apache.org/POM/4.0.0" xmlns:xsi="http://www.
w3.org/2001/XMLSchema-instance"
  xsi:schemaLocation="http://maven.apache.org/POM/4.0.0 http://maven.
  apache.org/xsd/maven-4.0.0.xsd">
  <modelVersion>4.0.0</modelVersion>
  <groupId>com.example</groupId>
```

```
<artifactId>courses</artifactId>
<version>1.0-SNAPSHOT</version>
<packaging>pom</packaging>
</project>
EOF
```

We have used a couple of shell commands (e.g., `mkdir` for creating a folder). If you are not familiar with these commands, please google them (`http://lmgtfy.com/?q=shell+commands`).

This is the root module of the project. You can already build it by calling "`mvn install`". It won't build anything yet, since it's empty. We suggest that at this point you open an Integrated Development Environment (IDE) of your choice (we'll use IntelliJ IDEA, as we stated before). The first thing you define is the project coordinates, meaning the values that uniquely identify your project:

1. **groupId**: Should be unique, usually most projects use the domain name of the company or project if it's the case. In our case we'll use `com.example`.

2. **artifactId**: Matching the folder that holds the module. In our case `courses`.

3. **version**: The current version of our project.

4. **packaging**: The type of module. In this case, we say it's a `pom` module, which means that it's a module that will hold other modules.

Since our project is still under development and there's no release, we use the suffix "`-SNAPSHOT`". Don't worry about this, you can learn more about it if you want by checking the documentation; but just so you roughly know what it means, it just tells Maven that your project is still under development and subject to changes.

As our project is a Java project, we need to compile it somehow, and for that Maven already has a plugin to do this for you. Let's include it in our root `pom.xml`:

```
(...)
<properties>
  <java.version>1.8</java.version>
  <maven.compiler.plugin.version>3.7.0</maven.compiler.plugin.version>
</properties>
```

```
<build>
  <pluginManagement>
    <plugins>
      <plugin>
        <artifactId>maven-compiler-plugin</artifactId>
        <version>${maven.compiler.plugin.version}</version>
        <configuration>
          <source>${java.version}</source>
          <target>${java.version}</target>
        </configuration>
      </plugin>
    </plugins>
  </pluginManagement>
  <plugins>
    <plugin>
      <artifactId>maven-compiler-plugin</artifactId>
    </plugin>
  </plugins>
</build>
(...)
```

It's always a good idea to keep the versions of your dependencies and plugins in the property section of your root POM so it's shared among all the sub-modules you create. This makes it easier in the future to upgrade and make sure all modules are using the same version. Yes... you might at some point need to use a different version for a specific module, but you can always override that definition later, so don't worry about that.

What we just specified is that we will write our project in Java 1.8 and that we want to produce Java 1.8 packages. The plugin management section is where you specify the plugins, version, and configuration to be used. The build section means that you want this project to use the plugin configuration you just defined in the management section. By doing it like this, every module in the project will use this configuration, meaning that you don't need to write it for every module.

It is likely that you will use *common* functionalities across the whole project, so it's a good practice to create a module that holds your common functions. Usually this module is a simple module with as few dependencies as possible, so try not to include heavy frameworks. In our case, we are going to create a module called commons:

```
mkdir commons
cd commons
cat << EOF > pom.xml
<?xml version="1.0" encoding="UTF-8"?>
<project xmlns="http://maven.apache.org/POM/4.0.0" xmlns:xsi="http://www.
w3.org/2001/XMLSchema-instance"
  xsi:schemaLocation="http://maven.apache.org/POM/4.0.0 http://maven.
  apache.org/xsd/maven-4.0.0.xsd">
  <modelVersion>4.0.0</modelVersion>
  <artifactId>commons</artifactId>
  <version>1.0-SNAPSHOT</version>
  <packaging>jar</packaging>
  <parent>
    <groupId>com.example</groupId>
    <artifactId>courses</artifactId>
    <version>1.0-SNAPSHOT</version>
    <relativePath>../pom.xml</relativePath>
  </parent>
</project>
EOF
```

So, we just created a module called commons that inherits all the configuration from the main root module, as we stated in the parent section. As you might have noticed, this new module is different from the other one, as it's not a module that holds other modules but produces an actual JAR artifact. A JAR is nothing but a zip file with code that can be run. We just need to do another thing to complete the linkage between the parent and the newborn "commons" child. We need to tell the parent that this module belongs to it. For that we create a section called modules and include the commons module in the parent pom:

```
(...)
<modules>
  <module>commons</module>
  </modules>
  (...)
```

As previously said, the configuration for the project gets quite big, so we invite you to take a look at the final version and explore it, get acquainted with the structure, but again don't worry much about it. The purpose of this small exercise is just for you to learn the terms and how to create a project from scratch using Maven. If you now run "maven install" in the root of your project, you will see that the "commons" model is also built:

```
(...)
[INFO] Reactor Summary:
[INFO]
[INFO] course ................................ SUCCESS [  0.479 s]
[INFO] commons ............................... SUCCESS [  1.314 s]
[INFO] ------------------------------------------------------------------
[INFO] BUILD SUCCESS
[INFO] ------------------------------------------------------------------
[INFO] Total time: 1.947 s
[INFO] Finished at: 2018-04-23T22:22:46+02:00
[INFO] Final Memory: 10M/193M
[INFO] ------------------------------------------------------------------
```

What we just did was to create a project structure using Maven. Even though there is no code or nothing to build, this is how you build a project from scratch. This structure we have just created is ready to grow, so we could just start adding more dependencies, plugins or even create our new modules! You can take a look at the full project if you are interested in how it looks like when it's complete.

Database

As previously stated, the backend is responsible to handle data. This means that it is responsible for fetching and storing these data, and for that it makes use of databases.

In software engineering, most of the time when we refer to databases, we are referring to relational databases (RDBMS), but any form of organized data can be called a database. There are several types of databases: persistent, in-memory, relational, column store, document store, or even plain text files. The list can get bigger as time goes by and new ones come into play, but in our case, we will talk about relational databases.

Even though non-relational databases have been gaining a lot of popularity in recent years, relational databases are still widely used. Let's just lay down some pros and cons of relational databases so you understand exactly what we are talking about.

Pros

1. Structured data leading to no duplications

2. Constraints on the data, leading to less faulty data from the applications

3. Relations between the data can have constraints, making it safe to build relations by making sure they actually exist.

4. Transactional support, meaning that we can create a session, do a set of operations, and if something goes wrong all of them are reverted, and we end up in the previous state.

5. Isolation from other sessions; no changes are seen by them until the session that introduces the changes is closed by a commit (this actually depends on the isolation level, which is out of the scope of this explanation).

Cons

1. Not easy to scale horizontally (by adding more instances and not just upgrading the hardware). Just a side note, in general most of the vendors do not even provide such feature. That's why NoSQL databases were developed—to address that problem. The Aurora RDBMS from Amazon AWS provides an in-between solution, where it is possible to build a cluster where the read workload is distributed. I must say, better than nothing!

2. Data is normalized, which means that sometimes in order to collect some simple information, we need to create complex queries or joins that pose drawbacks in performance

3. No complex objects, as they mostly work with simple types such as numbers, strings, dates, etc.

Does it mean we should always use RDBMS? Of course not! We should use whatever fits our needs better. In general, Rui always likes to think about a hybrid approach, use a RDBMS to structure data and use a document store with searching capabilities when we need complex objects, for example.

In our case and for development purposes, we will use a database that we won't need to install and configure. It's called H2 and we can use it as embedded, meaning that it will run inside our application. Of course, for production scenarios, this is not an option, but it's quite a good solution for developing, so we don't care about all the rest. If we later decide to change the database, there is no problem since we will be using an *Object Relational Mapping (ORM)* library that abstracts and translates all the instructions to the database vendor that we want. This is possible, mainly due to *SQL* (Structured Query Language, special language that is used to "talk" to databases in order to store, modify, and retrieve data) being a standard and that most of the vendors follow that standard.

When designing a database schema, we often use *Entity Relation (ER)* diagrams where we state the entities (tables) and their relations. For the purpose of the example we are building right now, we will work with only two entities: user and course, as shown in Figure 5-1.

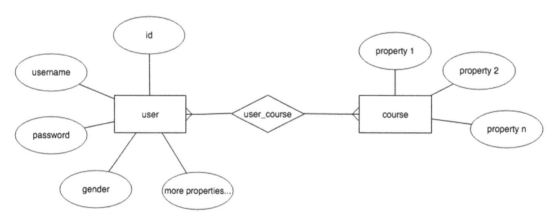

Figure 5-1. *Entity Relation diagram of the user and course tables*

In the diagram we are establishing the relation between the user and course entities. This relation is an N-to-N relation, meaning that a user can enroll in several courses and a course can be enrolled by several users; as a result, a new entity called user_course comes into play. This new entity will contain both primary keys from the user and course entities. These keys are known in this new entity as foreign keys.

Before we continue let's define some of the terms we just mentioned. We invite you to learn more about them; Wikipedia and Google can help you with that.

1. **Table columns and rows**: Table is a structure that holds data in a column and row fashion. Data gets into the table using the rows, while the columns dictate what data is there (very similar to an excel sheet).

2. **Primary key**: A key that uniquely identifies a single row in the table. In modern schemas the primary key is often a number that is assigned to the row when it gets created.

3. **Foreign key**: A key that identifies a row on another table. In this case if you combine the user key with the course key, you can say that user X is doing the course Y.

4. **Relation**: Defines how the tables relate to each other. N-to-N relations result in another table with the primary keys of both tables as foreign keys; 1-to-N relations do not result in more tables but will result in a foreign key on the N side of the relation, referring to the primary key of the "1" side.

These are the very basic things you need to know about relational databases. If you feel adventurous, you can still google for "first, second, and third normal forms," but these concepts are not really easy to digest the way they are usually described.

So, at this stage we have three tables to care about: user, course, and their relation user_course. There are two main types of SQL statements: *Data Definition Language (DDL)* and *Data Modification Language (DML)*. They are quite explanatory; the former is used to create or define (schema) how our data gets stored and organized. The latter is used to interact with the schema we define—insert, update, and delete data. We will not get into detail about them, as we have a nice tool that will do this for us. It is called **liquibase,** and it is an open source library that helps us define database schemas and keep track of their changes. We invite you to check the liquibase project—specifically the changelog.xml file—for the whole database structure. Too complicated? Let's try to match only the ones we defined earlier in this chapter:

```
<changeSet
  id="20180225-1700"
  author="Rui Vilao">
```

```
  <createTable
    tableName="user">
    <column
      name="id"
      type="BIGINT(19)"
      autoIncrement="true">
      <constraints
        primaryKey="true" />
    </column>
    <column
      name="create_time"
      type="datetime"
      defaultValueComputed="CURRENT_TIMESTAMP" />
    <column
      name="update_time"
      type="datetime" />
    <column
      name="username"
      type="VARCHAR(256)">
      <constraints
        nullable="false" />
    </column>
    <column
      name="password"
      type="VARCHAR(128)" />
    <column
      name="salt"
      type="VARCHAR(128)" />
    <column
      name="name"
      type="VARCHAR(256)" />
  </createTable>
</changeSet>
<changeSet
  id="20180424-2230"
  author="Rui Vilao">
```

```
<createTable
  tableName="course">
  <column
    name="id"
    type="BIGINT(19)"
    autoIncrement="true">
    <constraints
      primaryKey="true" />
  </column>
  <column
    name="create_time"
    type="datetime"
    defaultValueComputed="CURRENT_TIMESTAMP" />
  <column
    name="update_time"
    type="datetime" />
</createTable>
</changeSet>
<changeSet
  id="20180424-2231"
  author="Rui Vilao">
  <createTable
    tableName="user_course">
    <column
      name="id"
      type="BIGINT(19)"
      autoIncrement="true">
      <constraints
        primaryKey="true" />
    </column>
    <column
      name="create_time"
      type="datetime"
      defaultValueComputed="CURRENT_TIMESTAMP" />
```

```xml
      <column
        name="update_time"
        type="datetime" />
      <column
        name="user_id"
        type="BIGINT(19)">
        <constraints
          nullable="false" />
      </column>
      <column
        name="course_id"
        type="BIGINT(19)">
        <constraints
          nullable="false" />
      </column>
    </createTable>
    <addForeignKeyConstraint
      baseTableName="user_course"
      baseColumnNames="user_id"
      constraintName="fk__user_course__user_id"
      referencedTableName="user"
      referencedColumnNames="id" />
    <addForeignKeyConstraint
      baseTableName="user_course"
      baseColumnNames="course_id"
      constraintName="fk__user_course__course_id"
      referencedTableName="course"
      referencedColumnNames="id" />
  </changeSet>
```

We start by defining a table named users with an id, username, password, etc. Then we define a table, courses, that for now only holds the id and some other metadata such as creation time and update time (especially useful to keep track of changes). We then define a relation table called user_course, where we say that it relates to the user table and the course table. Pay attention to the primary key—here, we could perfectly say that the primary key could be user_id and course_id together, but we want for people to be able to enroll more than one time in the same course, but not at the same time. It seems perfectly valid that you enroll in one course, finish it, and later you want to start it again—a complete new instance of the course with everything empty (quizzes, answers, etc.).

Now that you are curious how all this works, open our project and compile it as a whole (project's root folder):

```
mvn clean install -DskipTests
```

Once you are done with that, run the following to create the database:

```
cd liquibase
mvn liquibase:update
```

This will create some database files in your /tmp directory. If you are using Windows you might have to change the temporary folder in the url parameter of the pom.xml of the liquibase project and also in the persistence-layer.properties file (inside the persistence-layer module). At this stage you have a simple database created in your system. If you run this command again, you will notice that nothing happens, since there are no new changelogs to be applied. Now if you would want to add a column, for example, you could create the new change set, compile the project, and run the command again, and only that new change would run. Pretty cool, isn't it?

If for some reason you end up with issues on your database while trying it out or you want to delete it, just remove all files, starting with courses, in your tmp folder:

```
rm /tmp/courses.*
```

And we're done with databases. If you are interested in this topic and you want to deep dive a bit more into it, there are plenty of materials on the Internet. We invite you to check it out!

Authentication

Authentication is the way of proving to some entity that you are, in fact, who you say you are. For this to be possible, an authority comes into play. A good example is the following: when going to another country, you take your passport with you. Once you arrive at your destination, you will have to hand your passport to the officer in charge. In this example, you are the entity trying to authenticate, the passport is your token of authentication, and the officer is the authenticator, meaning the one that will or will not give you access based on the fact that he trusts the authority that issued your passport.

In software engineering it's no different. There are several ways to implement authentication, several methods and techniques, and guess what: yes, there is no such thing as the best way that works for everything; every case is a case. Even for the *HTTP Basic Auth*, which is one of the most discouraged ways of authentication because the user and password travel both side-by-side together in the same request and must be included for every single request, there's a place. The *OAuth2* protocol, the one we'll be using for our project, also uses HTTP Basic Auth when asking to authenticate users, and payment service providers (*PSPs*) also use Basic Auth to push notifications to the merchant's servers, among other examples that are outside the scope of this section.

OAuth2 is one of the most popular authentication protocols used nowadays. We believe the reason it became so popular is because of the feature that you can delegate the authentication to a trusted authority. Imagine that you want to build your own website, but you don't want to implement your authentication mechanism. You could simply delegate this part to Google or Facebook, for example. But this is just one of the modes OAuth2 provides for authentication. It's called the `Authorization Code Grant`. In our example, we will use the `Resource Owner Password Credentials Grant`, which means that the user will provide a username and a password to authenticate with our authority. Ready? Let's start! For this exercise use the complete project "`courses`".

Switch inside our project and compile it:

```
mvn clean install -DskipTests
```

Then switch inside the module called `rest-api` and run it (if you don't have the database set up, just run "`mvn liquibase:update`" inside the `liquibase` module).

```
mvn tomcat7:run
```

We configured a `tomcat7` Maven plugin with our module, so we can run a server with our application. Tomcat is one of the *de facto* servers to run Java applications, but of course there are plenty of them. This will open up a port listening on 8080. Let's now try to authenticate a user:

```
curl -u webapp:test -X POST localhost:8080/oauth/token -H "Content-type: application/x-www-form-urlencoded" -d "grant_type=password&username=test@example.com&password=123456a$"
```

You will see that the response is

```
{"error":"invalid_grant","error_description":"Bad credentials"}
```

In fact, that's ok... that user doesn't exist yet on our database! Let's register it:

```
curl -v -X POST localhost:8080/api/v1/public/users -H "Content-type:
application/json" -d '{"username":"test@example.com","password":
"123456a$"}'
```

```
curl -u webapp:test -X POST localhost:8080/oauth/token -H "Content-type:
application/x-www-form-urlencoded" -d "grant_type=password&username=test
@example.com&password=123456a$"
```

Now the response consists of two tokens:

```
{"access_token":"7977c2f9-6664-4bdf-9bab-8d8ce6f0bc44",
"token_type":"bearer","refresh_token":"587d6ee2-5cb2-479d-b64f-
9bd8724f56e1","expires_in":86399,"scope":"read write"}
```

Let's describe what we just did here. In order to authenticate a user on the authentication server, we need to authenticate the call to our authentication server using the HTTP Basic Auth; hence we use the credentials "webapp" (user) and "test" (password). Then we pass to the body of the request our user credentials (the one we just created). As a result, we receive two tokens:

1. **Access token**: The token we will use to make subsequent requests. This token is used to access the server's resources and it is usually a short-lived token. This increases the security, because if for some reason someone grabs a hold on this token, it won't have access for long.

2. **Refresh token**: The token we will use to get a new access token once the one we are using expires.

If the access token we just received expires, we can renew it by not sending the user credentials again (this is what happens when, for example, you open an app on your phone after 1 or 2 days—you don't need to type in again your credentials). To renew the token, we would have to do the following:

```
curl -u webapp:test -X POST localhost:8080/oauth/token -H "Content-type:
application/x-www-form-urlencoded" -d "grant_type=refresh_token&refresh_
token=587d6ee2-5cb2-479d-b64f-9bd8724f56e1"
```

and you receive a new pair of access and refresh tokens. For the simplicity of our setup, we are storing all these tokens in-memory. This means that when we restart the server or if we later in production decide to add new servers to our server farm, these tokens will be no longer valid. This can be easily fixed by storing it in a persistent storage (like a database) or use *JSON Web Tokens (JWT)*, which are auto-contained tokens where the token itself describes the user and their security aspects. Now you can start using the token to make requests like the following (remember that for you, the tokens are different!)

```
curl -v -X GET localhost:8080/api/v1/secured/users/me -H "Content-type:
application/json" -H "Authorization: bearer 7977c2f9-6664-4bdf-9bab-
8d8ce6f0bc44"
```

Where you would get something similar to

```
{"id":1,"password":null,"name":null,"age":null,"gender":null,"username":
"test@example.com"}
```

Just to wrap up, we would like to introduce you to a new term that goes hand-in-hand with Authentication. This term is **Authorization**. People often misuse them, but they are actually very clear. We already defined authentication as being the mechanism that verifies someone is actually who or what they say they are, while authorization means basically what they are authorized to access. For example, right now our online education platform will only provide access to students, but in the future, it will provide access to administrators and teachers. The authorization is often done by assigning roles when the user authenticates. In our case, we assign the STUDENT role. In the future, we might need to have some metadata in the database, so we can inject the proper roles when the users login.

Development

Let's start doing some coding! For this section you will use the "courses-incomplete" project. Before we start let us describe how our application is structured. We split our application into logical modules where some of them also translate to physical modules. The stack is as follows (Figure 5-2).

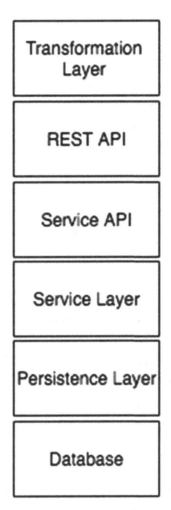

Figure 5-2. *Application stack*

The hierarchy works with self-contained blocks where the modules on top can see all of the modules below them, but not the other way around. It is a good practice to do so, because if in the future you come up with a new project, it's easier and cleaner to reuse these modules. Let's come up with a real-life example; it is very likely that at some point we need a Customer Management System (CMS). Since it will operate in the same database, we could easily share the persistence layer where we already have all the objects that map to database entities and relations. Let's now do a brief introduction of each module and their role in the project.

119

Database

The database module is the database engine we chose for the project. In our case, we chose to use H2. The bridge between our realm and this module is done with the help of Spring Data, Hibernate, and the H2 driver. These layers of abstractions help us to be able in the future to change the database engine without worrying much about the interaction with the database itself. In general, we should be able to live with these abstractions for most of our projects, but sometimes we need to bypass them in order to use some features that are not supported by the framework. This is somehow ok, but you need to know that once you do that, you might be introducing some dependency that in the future might become complicated to handle. So, if possible, we should avoid it.

Persistence Layer

The persistence layer is the set of features we create to interact with our database. In it we define, via Java objects, how our database looks for our applications. We also define a set of repositories, which are no less than a set of queries that our upper layers will use to fetch and store data. These repositories use entities that we define to map our tables, their columns and the relations between those tables.

Service Layer

Here is where most of the logic resides. This module is responsible for interacting with the persistence layer to store, change, and retrieve data. In this module we also validate our data before being stored, and we also define how faulty operations should be handled. For example, if the upper modules try to fetch something that doesn't exist, we throw an error. If they try to store something that already exists, we throw another error. Those errors are then handled by the upper modules in the way they think is best. Those can be suppressed or propagated with proper error codes to, for example, the clients making the call.

Service API

The Service API is a set of interfaces that the service layer implements so the upper modules do not have to deal with the specifics of the actual implementation of the service layer. This is not that obvious, but it is more kind of a way to prevent a possible growth on the project complexity. Imagine that in the future we want to come up with a payment module. It is very likely that this payment module needs to use features from the service layer as well, but we want to make it separate. This way we can put this module aside and still be able to communicate with the service layer since the API is known to us.

REST API and Transformation Layer

The REST API exposes our application to the outside world via REST endpoints. It is responsible for translating the way we talk to our clients to the way we talk to our backend application. For example, the user object we work with on the frontend application might not have the same structure or data as the one we use internally. The REST API knows this and can also ask to transform data back and forth with the help of the translation layer so that this communication is properly done. Moreover, and you might have already noticed this, we introduced versioning in our API. This is one of the most important things to do nowadays since every known product now is available also in several platforms, mainly mobile applications. If you only think of a frontend application that is maintained by you and people fetch its code every time they want to use it, we wouldn't need versioning, right? We control everything, so we can make changes and release everything altogether, but… what about mobile applications? People do not update their mobile applications immediately after release—sometimes they even keep using old versions for months! If, for some reason, you need to introduce a breaking change in your API, you can continue to support the version before and make this change only for the version 2 (the new one you will fork just to keep the others compatible). Versioning is something that you must always keep in mind when designing APIs. You don't need to know immediately what to do and how to do it, but you should be prepared; in our case our preparation is to have a dedicated URL for version one and dedicated formats for that version.

Implementing the Registration

For this exercise use the "courses-incomplete" project.

Do you remember the feature "Registration form" from Chapter 3? Let's implement the backend part of it from scratch now so you have a feeling on how it is to implement an end-to-end feature in the backend.

So, we are requested to enable users to register themselves on the platform. You might have noticed already that we have two different realms on the API: secured and public. They are quite self-explanatory; the public doesn't require authentication and the secured does. Because of course users cannot authenticate before being registered, this endpoint must be public. Open the `PublicUserController.java` file. Now we need to introduce you again to some new information. When designing a REST API, we rely on HTTP methods for specific kinds of operations:

1. **GET**: Used to retrieve data. In any case you should not modify data when calling such request, unless you want to do some sort of tracking, but never related to data itself. Clients making a GET request will NEVER expect that data can change. GET endpoints are nullipotent, meaning that calling them will never have any side effect.

2. **POST**: We use this one to create new entities. This means that if you try to create another entity that is the same—for example, two users with the same username—it must fail. More on that later in the example.

3. **PUT**: Used to update the full entity. This means that when a user makes such call, it is expected that the whole object is replaced with the new one being sent.

4. **PATCH**: Replaces the non-null elements in the entity. It should be used, for example, if we just want to update the name of the user, but not the entire user. This is the most preferable way of updating data. In general, we discourage people to use PUT and use PATCH in its favor.

5. **DELETE**: Use this method to delete entities. Sometimes deleting is not really a physical delete, but just an invalidation making it not visible anymore for listing or retrieving (GET); might work as some sort of flag for dirty.

Ok, back to our example! We want to implement the create new user method, so we need to expose a POST method.

```
@RequestMapping(method = RequestMethod.POST)
@ResponseStatus(HttpStatus.CREATED)
public UserV1Dto create(@RequestBody UserV1Dto userV1Dto) {
    return transformationsV1.user2Dto(userService.create(userV1Dto.toUser()));
}
```

What we are doing here is the following: we are transforming the `UserV1Dto` to a user object our service layer (and the ones below) understand—`userV1Dto.toUser()`. Then we send this user object to our service layer via our service api. We will get into that in a minute; let's focus on what's happening here right now. Then this service responds with the same object enriched with more information, such as the user id (since the user id is created only when we store the user in the database). We grab this result and transform it again into a `UserV1Dto` and send it back to the user with a default response status of `CREATED` (201). When possible use and abuse of proper HTTP codes; the frontend clients will thank you for that. You might have noticed that we are not specifying the endpoint, but don't worry—in fact, we are specifying it on the class level "`/api/v1/public/users`". What happens in this case is that the endpoint for creating an entity is the same as the root of the endpoint, but of course with the method `POST`.

Let's now take a look at the service layer implementation. What we need to do here is the following: check that the user doesn't exist already and fail if it does; validate the input—mainly the username and password; and store the information on the database getting back with an id so the user can be referenced later. In order to validate the user's e-mail address, let's use regular expressions (regex). Luckily, we don't have to come up with this, as a lot of people already did it, and to be honest this kind of thing is where you usually introduce bugs... so let's use something that has been already built (from `http://emailregex.com/`).

```
(?:[a-z0-9!#$%&'*+/=?^_`{|}~-]+(?:\.[a-z0-9!#$%&'*+/=?^_`{|}~-]+)*|"(?:[\
x01-\x08\x0b\x0c\x0e-\x1f\x21\x23-\x5b\x5d-\x7f]|\\[\x01-\x09\x0b\x0c\
x0e-\x7f])*")@(?:(?:[a-z0-9](?:[a-z0-9-]*[a-z0-9])?\.)+[a-z0-9](?:[a-z0-9-
]*[a-z0-9])?|\[(?:(?:25[0-5]|2[0-4][0-9]|[01]?[0-9][0-9]?)\.){3}(?:25[0-
5]|2[0-4][0-9]|[01]?[0-9][0-9]?|[a-z0-9-]*[a-z0-9]:(?:[\x01-\x08\x0b\x0c\
x0e-\x1f\x21-\x5a\x53-\x7f]|\\[\x01-\x09\x0b\x0c\x0e-\x7f])+)\])
```

Quite big don't you think? Maybe it's not a good idea in general to embrace the adventure of coming up with these regexes on our own. Both regexes are already there in the code so you don't need to do anything. Let's just code the logic of creating a user.

```
@Transactional
@Override
public User create(User user) throws AlreadyExistsServiceException {
    validateUserCreation(user);
```

```
if (userRepository.findByUsernameIgnoreCase(user.getUsername()) != null) {
    throw new AlreadyExistsServiceException("Username already exists.");
}

final String salt = UUID.randomUUID().toString();
user.setPassword(passwordEncoder.encode(user.getPassword() + salt));
user.setSalt(salt);
return userRepository.save(user);
}
```

Salt? What the hell is that? First things first! We call the validation—we'll get into more detail after—and then the first thing we need to know once the validation is done is whether we already have a user with the same username, in our case e-mail address. If it's the case, we throw an exception. The kind of exception we throw here is important because we've set up an exception translation controller on the rest-api layer that will translate this exception to the right HTTP error code (you can check that in DefaultExceptionHandler.java). Once we are good with that check, we will work on the user password. The salt technique is a good technique to scramble a bit more the passwords on our database. This is handy because when we hash passwords on the database, the input will always generate the same output, that's why this can be done like that. So, imagine that someone somehow steals our database data. The first thing they would try would be to group all the hash passwords that are the same. Then they would try to figure out the most popular, which is the candidate to be the most vulnerable since it's a common one. Once our nice hacker figures out that popular password, it means that all the other users with the same hash will have that password! Bummer... the salt solves this exact problem. By adding some random information to the password, the hashed passwords will always be different, so if for some reason this hacker out of the blue gets one password, even if other users have the same password, it will make their life way more difficult. Cool, isn't it? And yet so simple. This of course means that when we authenticate a user, we need to take this into consideration and do the exact same thing: add the salt to the user input and compare with the hashed password we have on the database.

Once we are done with that we set all the data we generated, the hashed password, and the salt together and save the user. As for the validation, if you are still interested, it is as simple as that:

```
protected void validateUserCreation(User user) {
    Preconditions.checkNotNull(user, "User cannot be null.");
    Preconditions.checkNotNull(user.getUsername(), "Username cannot be
    null.");
    Preconditions.checkNotNull(user.getPassword(), "Password cannot be
    null.");

    if (!EMAIL_REGEX.matcher(user.getUsername()).matches()) {
        throw new PreconditionFailedServiceException("Username is not
        valid.");
    }
    if (!PASSWORD_REGEX.matcher(user.getPassword()).matches()) {
        throw new PreconditionFailedServiceException("Password is not
        valid.");
    }
}
```

Let's try it out! Compile everything (mvn install -DskipTests on the root of the project). Then let's do some tryouts:

```
curl -v -X POST localhost:8080/api/v1/public/users -H "Content-type:
application/json" -d '{"username":"test@example.","password":"secret"}'
```

The response:

```
{"reason":"Precondition failed: Username is not valid."}
```

Another one:

```
curl -v -X POST localhost:8080/api/v1/public/users -H "Content-type:
application/json" -d '{"username":"test@example.com","password":"secret"}'
```

{"reason":"Precondition failed: Password is not valid."}

```
curl -v -X POST localhost:8080/api/v1/public/users -H "Content-type:
application/json" -d '{"username":"test@example.com","password":"w1secret$"}'
```

**{"id":1,"password":null,"name":null,"age":null,"gender":null,"username":
"test1@example.com"}**

And now if you try again with the same user:

```
curl -v -X POST localhost:8080/api/v1/public/users -H "Content-type:
application/json" -d '{"username":"test@example.com","password":"w1secret$"}'
```

{"reason":"That resource already exists: Username already exists."}

Before we continue with more examples, let us tell you how the URL structure works when you use REST. We already discussed the methods. This is important because the methods together with the URL define sets of operations. In general, it's a good practice that your URLs are nouns in the plural form when they point to actual resources, such as users, courses, programs, etc. There is no consensus when it comes to actions; some use verbs, others use underscore and the verb (e.g., _search, _start, _stop). In general, we like the approach with the underscore, since it clearly states that you are doing some operation and not dealing with resources in general. Let's define a table with the operations and URL structure and their outcome. The example is with the users' resources, as shown in Table 5-1.

Table 5-1. *REST Methods on* users *Resource*

URL	GET	POST	PUT	PATCH	DELETE
../users	Retrieves the list of users (forbidden)	Creates a new user	Replaces the list of users with a new one (not used and kind of dangerous)	Not used	Deletes a collection of users
../users/1	Gets the user with the id 1	Not used	Replaces the user (with the id 1) data with a new one	Changes specific data for the user with the id 1	Deletes the user with the id 1

Don't stress it too much now! You will learn them as your needs progress.

Let's include the PATCH functionality. Do you remember about it? It's the one that is used to update the information of an entity, but only the elements we want (the non-null ones). So, this call must be made with the user already authenticated so we need to do it on the "secured" branch of our URL tree. Open the SecuredUserController.java file and start coding the PATCH.

```
@RequestMapping(value= "/{id}", method = RequestMethod.PATCH)
public UserV1Dto patch(@AuthenticationPrincipal UserDetailsImpl user,
                       @PathVariable("id") Long id,
                       @RequestBody UserV1Dto userV1Dto) {
```

```
if (!id.equals(user.getId())) {
    throw new ForbiddenServiceException("Not your user.");
}

return transformationsV1.user2Dto(userService.patch(id, userV1Dto.
toUser()));
}
```

Maybe you didn't see that coming, but there are two things that need some consideration in this implementation. The first one is that if the user is in the session, why do we need to pass the id? Well, we actually don't need to pass it, but in this way, you are complying to the REST standard. So, we strongly encourage you to do it like that even if it's not needed. Nevertheless, if you actually do it, be careful. In our case, we added the validation to check if the user trying to be edited is the actual owner of the resource and if it's not the case, we just throw a forbidden exception that will be mapped to the 403 (Forbidden) error code. This way you make your API prepared for the future. Remember that for now we will only allow students, but in the future, we might want to enable for customer service to edit some of the user's information, and in this way it's already semi-prepared! As for the rest of the code, it seems self-explanatory; we'll just say that you specify a variable (id in this case) inside brackets and you use the @PathVariable to inject its value into the Long id variable.

So, what about the service layer? For now, we only implemented the PATCH for the name of the user, but we could extend it to all of the attributes that can be edited (id of course not included!). Pay special attention to the password, which needs some additional processing and not just a mere replacement.

```
@Override
@Transactional
public User patch(Long id, User user) {
    // Remember that if the user doesn't exist, this throws not found!
    final User storedUser = get(id);

    if (user.getName() != null) {
        storedUser.setName(user.getName());
    }
    // Add more in the future!

    return userRepository.save(storedUser);
}
```

That is easy, isn't it? Let's try it out!

```
curl -v -X PATCH localhost:8080/api/v1/secured/users/2 -H "Content-type:
application/json" -H "Authorization: bearer 35d8cda1-0f54-411e-a2a1-
b57c8cf42b75" -d '{"name": "test"}'
```

We just tried to modify a user that is not ours, so we get:

```
{"reason":"Forbidden: Not your user."}
```

Let's now try it with our user:

```
curl -v -X PATCH localhost:8080/api/v1/secured/users/1 -H "Content-type:
application/json" -H "Authorization: bearer 35d8cda1-0f54-411e-a2a1-
b57c8cf42b75" -d '{"name": "test"}'
```

We get an update!

```
{"id":1,"password":null,"name":"test","age":null,"gender":null,"username":"
test@example.com"}
```

As you see, the name is now "test". Let's verify whether it really got persisted.

```
curl -v -X GET localhost:8080/api/v1/secured/users/me -H "Content-type:
application/json" -H "Authorization: bearer 35d8cda1-0f54-411e-a2a1-
b57c8cf42b75"
```

And indeed it is!

```
{"id":1,"password":null,"name":"test","age":null,"gender":null,"username":"
test@example.com"}
```

We hope you got an understanding on how things work. Most of the cases are pretty much the same. We are not a big fan of PUT; we prefer to code everything with PATCH, but there might be some use cases. Anyway, the PUT method might lead to bugs if you forget to implement something; everything gets overwritten.

As for the DELETE, it's basically the same—we receive the id as a path variable and we perform the operation, which usually doesn't mean an actual deletion but just a deactivation.

We already prepared a test suite for you to start coding some tests. Let's move on to that topic now!

Testing

We will have a dedicated chapter related to testing where we will describe the most common types of testing and when they must be applied. Nevertheless, it makes sense that we cover some testing on the code we just wrote. We'll do some unit or better integration tests, since we will be using other systems such as the database or the authentication system.

These kinds of tests are usually done by calling a set of operations and asserting the result with what we expect. Let's just look at the /me example. What we do is authenticate the user and call the /me endpoint, and we expect that the user returned is the same user in the session (the one we authenticated). So, we write the following:

```
@Test
public void getUserInTheSessionTest() throws Exception {
    final MockHttpServletResponse result = mockMvc.perform(get("/api/v1/
    secured/users/me")
            .header("Authorization", "bearer " + getAccessToken())
            .contentType(MediaType.APPLICATION_JSON))
            .andReturn()
            .getResponse();

    assertThat(result.getStatus()).isEqualTo(HttpStatus.OK.value());
    final UserV1Dto user = readJson(result.getContentAsString(), UserV1Dto.
    class);
    assertThat(user.getUsername()).isEqualTo(testUser.getUsername());
}
```

The test user is set for every test by the class AbstractRestApiTest.java. What we are checking is that the HTTP result code is of the OK type, and the user returned is the actual user we use in the authentication.

How could we test the creation of a user? We need to cover several things, such as creating a user with all valid data, invalid data such as invalid username or password, and even the case where we try to register a user that already exists. The following is the latter case.

```
@Test
public void createAUserTwiceTest() throws Exception {
    final MockHttpServletResponse result = mockMvc.perform(post("/api/v1/
    public/users")
            .contentType(MediaType.APPLICATION_JSON)
            .content(writeJson(UserV1Dto.builder().withUsername(
            "ex1@example.com")
                    .withPassword("123456a$").build())))
            .andReturn()
            .getResponse();

    assertThat(result.getStatus()).isEqualTo(HttpStatus.CREATED.value());

    final MockHttpServletResponse result2 = mockMvc.perform(post("/api/v1/
    public/users")
            .contentType(MediaType.APPLICATION_JSON)
            .content(writeJson(UserV1Dto.builder().withUsername(
            "ex1@example.com")
                    .withPassword("123456a$").build())))
            .andReturn()
            .getResponse();
    assertThat(result2.getStatus()).isEqualTo(HttpStatus.CONFLICT.value());
}
```

For the first call, we expect the CREATED HTTP status, but for the second one we expect the CONFLICT error code. Feel free to add more tests—get acquainted with the testing framework! Writing tests is fun and it will secure your code for future changes. This is the first line of defense for your code, so make use of it! In order to run tests, you need a test database, but don't worry, we already prepared that for you! Switch inside the liquibase module and run

```
mvn liquibase:update -Ptest
```

This will create a test database in your /tmp folder (again, Windows users, you might need to change that). Now switch back to the rest-api module. If you run mvn test, this will run all the tests that are in the module, but you can also run tests from one class only by specifying the class name like the following:

```
mvn test -Dtest=RestApiUserTest
```

And you can even specify a single test by adding the test name to the test variable

```
mvn test -Dtest=RestApiUserTest#getUserInTheSessionTest
```

Summary

In this chapter we discussed how a backend application can be structured and some of the technologies typically involved. We started by defining our database layer, then our service layer, until we reached the top, which is the entry point to our application, the rest-api.

We provided some implementation examples, so you could get in touch with backend development using the Spring framework for Java. In the end, we created some integration tests to cover some of our code base.

In the next chapter, we will start implementing the frontend of our application. We will connect it to what we just did on the backend, authentication and resource manipulation. Stay tuned!

CHAPTER 6

Frontend Development

In this chapter we are going to wear the hat of a frontend developer and connect whatever the designer did to the backend that was developed in the previous chapter.

Have you realized that every role we talk about is actually connecting something to something? The product manager connects business needs and development, the designer connects product and business goals to the user needs, the backend developer connects data to the product, and, finally (actually, not yet), our frontend developer will connect the backend and the design. Yes, software development is all about connecting several blocks.

We, software engineers, aim at connecting people and technology. Some people see technology and its progress as a problem, and we want to show that it is, in fact, a problem-solver. Let's do it together, step by step. In the previous chapter, we prepared the behind the scenes for our data. In this chapter, we will use the prepared endpoints to bring the data to the user and display it in the user interface.

There will be programming here as well, so embrace the fact that there is no software creation without coding and be prepared to write some code. "But I wrote some code in the previous chapter," some might say. Yes, that's true. It is a bit different, however. The main difference between the backend and the frontend code relies in the fact that you can immediately see the results of the frontend code directly in your browser.

Note   If you are totally sure that frontend is not for you, you might want to skip this chapter and move on to the testing and DevOps. Or, maybe you are already an experienced frontend developer and this chapter might seem a bit basic for you, but if you think that coding is hard, and you are not made for this and that the previous chapter had already enough coding for you, please take a minute, take a deep breath, and reconsider.

© Olga Filipova and Rui Vilão 2018

O. Filipova and R. Vilão, *Software Development From A to Z*, https://doi.org/10.1007/978-1-4842-3945-2_6

In this chapter we are going through the fun process of showing how easy it is to program interfaces and make them look however you want them to look.

Disclaimer   All the code samples that appear in this chapter were tested in Chrome, Safari, and Firefox browsers. We don't guarantee these samples work in Internet Explorer.

Let's Code!

Open your favorite text editor and type, "Hello my dear friend! ♥" Exactly like this. Now save this file as hello.html.

If you use TextEditor on macOS, choose Format -> make plain text

---

After saving your file open it with double click. You will see how your browser window opens, as shown in Figure 6-1.

Hello my dear friend! ♥

Figure 6-1. *Your first HTML file rendered in a browser*

Do you want to discover more? Or wasn't it convincing enough yet? Open the file in the editor again and just add a couple of things:

```
<div style='text-align:center'>
  <h1>Hello my dear friend!
    <span style='color:red'>&hearts;</span>
  </h1>
  <img src=http://thecatapi.com/api/images/get?format=src&type=gif />
</div>
```

Save the file, open it in your browser, and you will see something like this Figure 6-2.

file:///Users/olga/Desktop/hello.html

Hello my dear friend! ♥

Figure 6-2. *Adding the color to the text, playing with images, and centering the content*

Every time you refresh the page, the cat picture will change. This is, actually, how the internet works—it is just full of cats, all the rest is just noise.

It's a bit frustrating to have to refresh the page every time you want to change the cat picture. Let's just add a last line of code. Open the file in your text editor, and add the following section:

```
<div style='text-align:center'>
  <h1>Hello my dear friend! <span style='color:red'>&hearts;</span></h1>
  <img src='http://thecatapi.com/api/images/get?format=src&type=gif' />
</div>
```

```
<script>
  const src = 'http://thecatapi.com/api/images/get?format=src&type=gif'
  setInterval(() => {
    document.getElementsByTagName('img')[0].src = src + '&ts=' + Date.now()
  }, 3000)
</script>
```

You can copy this code from the `beforeyouskip.html` file.

Refresh the page in the browser and have a look. You will see that every 3 seconds the cat picture changes.

Are you still with us? We know cats are amazing, but we have some work to do.

With just a couple of lines of code you were able to center things on the page, add a picture and some colors to the text, and make the things change on the page without having to refresh it. How amazing is that? And even if the process of coding is not convincing enough to make you to continue to read this chapter, I am sure the cat is. So, let's try to understand what frontend is and where it starts.

Where Does Frontend Start?

We have discussed design, we have also implemented some deep behind-the-scenes backend parts. Where does frontend start? Actually, it has already started. While thinking about design, we were concerned with how the frontend developers would implement it. While working on our backend, we were already thinking how we will pass the data to the frontend.

So, what is frontend? Frontend is a visible part of our application and a connection between it and the backend. Thus, besides being a face of the application, frontend has some invisible parts that connect this face to the brain, which is located on the backend.

Also, frontend applications must get data and display it in an attractive and dynamic way. Do you remember the picture that we drew to explain the parts of the frontend, as shown in Figure 6-3?

HTML   CSS   JS

Figure 6-3. *HTML, CSS, and JS: Three pillars of frontend development*

You see that it consists essentially of three parts: HTML (hypertext markup language), CSS (cascading style sheets), and JS (JavaScript). What are all these? The HTML code defines the structure of our interface; the CSS defines its style; and the JS defines how it changes overtime, and it is responsible for communicating with the backend while guaranteeing that all the changes that happen to data are propagated to our interface. These are the three pillars of frontend development. Of course, you might have heard a lot of stuff around web development—a lot of buzzwords like less, sass, react, redux, vue.js, bootstrap, material design, serverless (uhh) —but remember, in the end browsers really understand and can interpret these three things: HTML, CSS, and JavaScript. Basically, the browser parses our HTML code, styles it with our CSS code, and interprets our JavaScript code to apply whatever we tell it to do.

Actually, you have already used all three of them in the previous section! Check it out—the structure of our document is defined by HTML:

```
<div>
  <h1>Hello my dear friend! <span>&hearts;</span><h1>
  <img src="...">
</div>
```

The styling (colors, alignment, etc.) is defined by CSS:

```
<div style='text-align:center'>
  <h1>Hello my dear friend! <span style='color:red'>&hearts;</span><h1>
  <img src="...">
</div>
```

And, finally, the dynamic part of the page (changing the cat picture) is defined by JavaScript:

```
<script>
  const src = 'http://thecatapi.com/api/images/get?format=src&type=gif'
  setInterval(() => {
    document.getElementsByTagName('img')[0].src=src + '&ts=' + Date.now()
  }, 3000)
</script>
```

So, you've already tried all of them. Also, we figured out that the frontend starts in the early stages of the development process. You probably ask yourself now: where and when does frontend end? Well, it actually never ends. Once your application is shipped to production, you will find yourself in a constant process of changes and improvements. You will have to guarantee that your product is compliant with the modern web standards, new users' needs, and new business goals. Your main wish is to always be on top. That's why the process of developing frontend for your application, as well as any process related to it, will never stop unless you decide to step out of your product and leave it alone in the big wild world of the web.

Let's discuss in more detail each of three pillars.

Markup and DOM

Markup is the skeleton of our application. Markup defines the structure of your page and the placeholders for its content. For more than a couple of decades (developed in 1993), HTML has been used for creating web pages and web applications.

In a nutshell, the HTML document is composed of a set of tags, their attributes, and the content for these tags.

- HTML tag: can be seen as a container that defines a semantic of an enclosed content. Each tag is written in the angle brackets (e.g., <p> - paragraph tag). Tags can open and close—for example, <p> defines a start of a paragraph while </p> defines its end.

- HTML attribute: some tags can have some attributes that tell and define a little bit more about the tag container besides its semantics. Attributes can have different values. The attributes are written inside the opening tag, and their values are written inside quotes after the equal sign. For example, the `title` attribute can be applied to any tag and will create an effect of appearing text while you hover the mouse over the element that contains this title (e.g., `<p title="my nice paragraph"></p>`).

- Content of the HTML tags: whatever text appears inside the tags is the content of your page. It will be rendered and displayed by browser as a text with applied semantics and basic styling of wrapping tags and their attributes. For example, Figure 6-4 will be rendered as a simple paragraph with the title appearing once you hover the mouse over it: `<p title="my nice paragraph">Hello reader! </p>`

Hello reader!

my nice paragraph

Figure 6-4. *How browser renders paragraph with the applied title attribute*

There are a lot of different tags that can be used to structure your document. We have already spoken about the paragraph tag <p>, you have seen the tag for the image <img>, but before we proceed to some other tags, let's talk about DOM.

Document Object Model

DOM (document object model) is basically a structure created by the browser once it opens any web page. It is represented as a tree since the browser render engine reads the markup code from top to bottom (Figure 6-5).

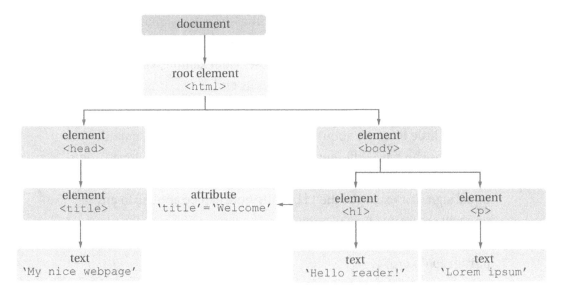

Figure 6-5. *DOM tree representation*

In this diagram you can already see that there is some root element called html and that there are elements called head and body. Let's talk about them before we proceed to any other HTML tags.

So, the <html> element encloses your whole web page. It tells the browser that this document is an html document, so the browser knows exactly how to read and interpret it. Inside the html tags there are two main containers: <head> and <body>. <head> tag contains all the meta data about your web page—its title, description, language, any search engine optimization (SEO) related data, favicon path, etc.

All the content that will appear on your page should be contained inside the body tags. It makes sense, actually, head is for short descriptive information, and body is for all the rest. Thus, the basic structure for the html file without a content will look as follows:

```
<html>
  <head></head>
  <body></body>
</html>
```

Note that the tags are like boxes with the content inside of them. Boxes can contain other boxes, and those can contain other boxes as well. Hence, the html tag contains head and body tag, and, in turn, the body tag will contain lots of other tags defining structure and content of the webpage.

Headings

Let's talk about some of the tags. We've already spoken about the paragraph tag: <p>. A content inside the p tag will appear as a new paragraph.

If you want to highlight titles of your page, you can use heading tags. The heading tags start from the biggest heading, <h1>, and go until the smallest heading, <h6>. Thus, in between you have <h2>, <h3>, <h4>, and <h5>. Try to create a content in different heading tags in your html file, and check how it looks in your browser:

```
<h1>Hello reader!</h1>
<h2>Hello reader!</h2>
<h3>Hello reader!</h3>
<h4>Hello reader!</h4>
<h5>Hello reader!</h5>
<h6>Hello reader!</h6>
```

It will look as shown in Figure 6-6.

Hello reader!
Hello reader!
Hello reader!
Hello reader!
Hello reader!
Hello reader!

Figure 6-6. *HTML headings tags from h1 to h6*

Hyperlinks

Of course, there is no internet without hyperlinks. Do you use Wikipedia? Have you ever caught yourself in the situation where you were looking for, let's say, Siamese cats and ended up after 5.5 hours knowing everything about blockchain technologies and the impact of marijuana legalization? Wikipedia hyperlinks are evil. Let's see what HTML tags are used to produce this evil. The tag is called anchor and is written as <a>. Do you remember about attributes? This tag only works if you provide an attribute called href to it (href means **h**ypertext **ref**erence). Makes sense, right? If we want to send the person somewhere, we should provide them a reference of where to go. The actual content of the tag will be the text you would like to appear on the page as a link. Let's say we want to send the person to the Google website and we want the word "google" to appear as a hyperlink on the page. Then the markup code will look as the following:

```
<a href="https://www.google.com">Google</a>
```

You can also reference the pages of your own website, providing the relative path to them.

The path can be rather relative or absolute. Absolute path means that you provide the whole path starting from the root of your (or any other) server, and relative path means that you provide the path relatively to the current document.

So, for example, if we have a page called hyperlink1.html and want to reference a person to another page called hyperlink2.html that lies in the same path, we would do the following:

```
<a href="hyperlink2.html">Go to the second page</a>
```

Check the html pages hyperlink1.html and hyperlink2.html inside the code folder for this chapter.

By default, the links are opened in the same tab as where you are. If you want the links to open in the new tab, you can provide another attribute called target with the value _blank:

```
<a href="https://www.google.com" target="_blank">Google in new tab</a>
```

Images

Just as the internet cannot exist without hyperlinks, it cannot exist without the images. You have already used the image tag; it is written as <img>. It must have an attribute called src (source of the image), but it doesn't contain any content, because its content is actually defined by the image source. Since all the html tags must be opened and closed, it closes itself. Such tags are called "self-closing" tags. So, it is written as:

```
<img src="http://via.placeholder.com/350x150" />
```

Like the href attribute of the anchor tag, the src attribute can also have both absolute or relative values. So, you can put images near your html file and provide a relative path to them in your src attribute. For example, if we put an image called cat.png inside the img folder we can display this image using the img tag like this:

```
<img src="img/cat.png" />
```

By default, the image will appear in its original size. Sometimes it's not really appropriate because the size of the image might not fit the layout of our page. To solve this problem, the html specification allows you using width and height attributes applied to the img tag. If you only specify one of those, the other one will scale accordingly. The size can be specified in absolute values (e.g., pixels):

```
<img src="img/cat.png" width="500px" />
```

or in relative values, in percentage (this will be the percentage relative to the parent element). If our image is a direct child of the body tag then the relative width will be relative to the body and occupy the exact portion of the screen that we indicate:

```
<img src="img/cat.png" width="40%" />
```

Check the code in the file called image.html. Try to resize the browser page. You will notice that while the image for which width is specified in pixels always remains the same, the other one, for which size is specified in percentages will adjust accordingly to the browser size.

When the web page elements easily adjust to the size of the device in which they are opened, it means that they are responsive and adaptive.

Responsive and adaptive are very important concepts of the web nowadays. There are so many devices, and you want your product to run in all of them. Or... maybe not? That is why it is crucially important to understand your user. You have to know pretty well what devices are being used the most and make sure that your product is perfect on those devices. Nowadays, software is being built based on the paradigm of "mobile-first," which means that number one priority is to make sure that the product will appear nicely on mobile devices. It is quite understandable—people these days use mobile devices a lot more than desktop devices.

Forms

Since we started talking about users, let's think about the interaction and communication with them. A lot of times besides displaying some content to your user, you want to receive some data from user or some confirmation.

While I am writing these words, it is May 25th, 2018, which means that the EU-GDPR (European Union General Data Protection Regulation) has started today. Don't underestimate the power of this law while asking for data from your user! But before you think about laws, you would like to know how do you use HTML to ask data from your users, right? The HTML specification has a way of doing it using the <form> tag. Inside the form tag you can have lots of inputs asking for user data. Let's talk about these input fields.

Input tags (<input>) are also self-closing tags that can have several attributes specifying the exact input field type. By default, and you don't even need to provide any attribute for this, the input will be of type text. It is a generic input where you can write any text:

```
<input />
```

It will render on the webpage as shown in Figure 6-7.

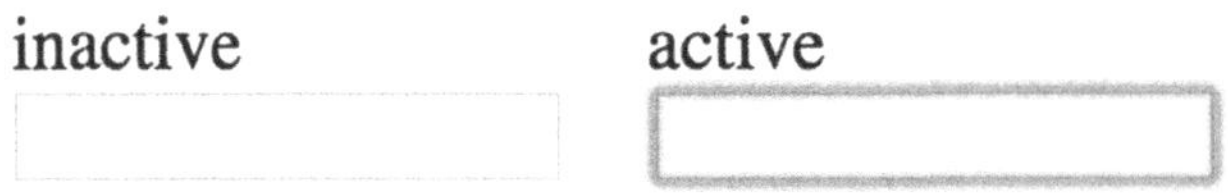

inactive   active

Figure 6-7. *Active and inactive input tags*

It is possible to have different types of inputs by providing the attribute called type to the input tag. The values can be very different, for example:

- password

- number

- date

- e-mail

- checkbox

- range

- search

For example, this form:

```
<form action="">
  Name: <input type="text" placeholder="Type your name" />
  Password: <input type="password" />
  Age: <input type="number" />
  Email: <input type="email" placeholder="example@gmail.com" />
  Your favorite color: <input type="color" placeholder="#eee" />
  Date of birth: <input type="date" />
</form>
```

will render as shown in Figure 6-8.

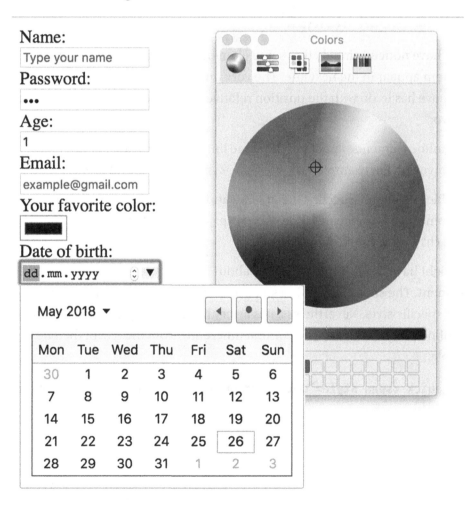

Figure 6-8. *The form with input fields of different types*

Check the code with different types of input fields in the file `form.html`.

Of course, now you ask yourself, "Ok, and what should I do with all this data?" That is a fair question, and at this point the plain HTML is not enough. Somehow, we need to collect this data and give it to our backend for processing, storing, or taking some actions. Let's come back to this later.

Besides providing some semantics to the elements of your page, you want to give your page some structure and define some important divisions. That is why HTML specification offers you a very important element called `<div>`. The `div` tag means division. This tag doesn't have any style attached to it, but it is very useful to separate chunks of content from each other and style them differently.

Inline and Block Elements

You might have noticed already that some elements appear in the same line, while some of them appear in the next line. The very important characteristics that all the elements have has to do with the position relative to the previous element. It can be any of these two:

- Inline elements: appear in the same line where they are being invoked. For example, `<a>`, `<img />`, `<span>` are inline elements.

- Block elements: occupy the full line and the next element will be rendered from the new line. `<div>`, `<p>`, heading elements (`<h1>`-`<h6>`) are block elements.

You might have noticed that we talked about the `span` element as an example of an inline element. The span element is a small and invisible tag that doesn't provide any context or specific style. Nevertheless, it is a very important tag, as is `div`, because it can be used inline to style the wrapped content differently from the rest of the line. For example,

```
<div>The quick <span style="color: brown">brown</span> fox jumps over the
lazy dog</div>
```

This piece of code will render as shown in Figure 6-9.

The quick brown fox jumps over the lazy dog

Figure 6-9. *Span element used to style one word inside the full phrase*

We can talk a lot about HTML, its specification, different tags (we haven't covered, for example, list tags `<ul>` and `<ol>` or media tags such as `<video>` or `<audio>`), their attributes, and different kinds of magic that are possible to achieve using this simple, yet powerful markup language, but we believe that we provided enough information for you to be able to search for the information you are interested in regarding this topic. Let's check it with this simple exercise.

EXERCISE ABOUT HTML

Create a simple html page that contains the following:

- Header saying your name

- Your picture

- Couple of paragraphs about yourself

- Links to your social profiles (e.g., linkedin, github) or just a link to `https://www.apress.com/` if you don't have any social account

- Add a simple form asking for the name and e-mail of the person who is reading your profile and a submit button

In the end, your page should look similar to this Figure 6-10.

I am Olga

I am a software engineer. I solve problems and love challenges.

New technologies and development processes drive me and make me happy.

I believe that learning and knowledge sharing are the power for everything.

Github Facebook Twitter

Who are you?

What is your name?

What is your email?

Contact me!

Figure 6-10. *Create a markup to produce similar rendered result*

You can find the code for this page inside the `exercise.html` file.

Now that you are an expert in creating HTML structure for your web pages, let's start styling them!

Style

Of course, we cannot enjoy our web pages if it's just plain black text, even if it's nicely structured into paragraphs, divisions, anchors, and other nice components. We need to adjust colors, fonts, size, alignment, positioning, background, and many other things to make our page appealing for an eye and capable to run in any browser of any device. This is where CSS comes in handy, and this is what we are going to talk about in this section in addition to different kinds of layouts and ready-to-go design systems.

CSS is a language that is used to describe styling rules for the HTML markup. The term *cascading* simply defines a priority scheme when more than one styling rules match the same element.

The styling rule is written in a simple format—the name of the rule followed by the colon and its value. So, for example, the rule for the red text color will look as the following:

```
color: red;
```

Of course, the rules must be applied to something; they cannot just fly in the air. The rules can be applied to some specific element or to the group of elements. This depends on the way you decide to specify those rules. There are essentially three ways of specifying CSS rules:

- Inline: the CSS rule is attached to a given element inside the tag attribute called style: `<p style="color: red;">Hello! Here's the red paragraph</p>`

- Internal stylesheets: CSS rules are written inside the `style` tag inside the head element of your html file. The rules must be written inside the blocks defined by the selectors. For example, to apply `color: red` rule to all the paragraphs, you would write the following:

```
<style>
  p {
    color: red;
  }
</style>
```

- External stylesheets: the CSS rules are written the same way they would be written inside the style tags, just in the external file that has a `.css` extension and imported to the html file using the special tag `<link>` contining the path to the CSS file inside the `href` attribute: `<link rel="stylesheet" href="style.css">`

What are the advantages of each of them? If you just need to tweak one specific element, you can go for the inline style. If you need to specify similar styles to different groups of elements, but it's not too many styles, you can create them internally in the same file inside the `<style>` tags, but if you have a big complex stylesheet describing different styles, or animations for different groups of elements, you should choose the external stylesheet. Check the files `inline-style.html`, `internal-style.html`, and `external-style.html` for each of three types of the stylesheets usage.

You might have noticed that when we specify style rules inside the `<style>` tags or in the external files, we wrap the rules in the block of the corresponding element to which the style should apply:

```
p {
  color: red;
  font-size: larger;
}
```

Does it mean that we can only specify styles for tags? What if we don't want all the paragraphs to look the same? Actually, the block to which we can specify the style rules can be pretty complex. This block is called selector, and this is one of the most important concepts of the web development.

Selector defines the group of elements to which we want to apply some specific style. It can be described by tag, class, id, or a mix of them.

Turns out the html elements can have ids and classes attached, and these can be used as well as CSS selectors. Let's talk about them.

- Id of the element is an attribute (id), whose value must uniquely identify the element. For example, `<p id="first">This is my first paragraph</p>`

- Class of the element is an attribute that can identify more than one element, usually used when you need to style or select more than one element in the same way. For example, `<p class="important">This paragraph contains some important information</p>`

The way we write selectors for class and id are different from the way we write selectors for tag. So:

- Selector for tag is just a tag name:

  - `p`—selects paragraph tags

  - `img`—selects img tags

  - `div img`—selects img tags inside div blocks

- Selector for an id of element is the value of the id preceded by #:

  - `#first`—selects element with id "first"

- Selector for class is written as name of class preceded by a dot:

  - `.important`—selects all the elements that have class "important"

  - `p.important`—selects all the paragraphs that have class "important"

  - `div img.important`—selects all the images that are inside divs and have class important

  - `#first .important`—selects all the elements inside the element with id "first" that have class "important"

Check more about selectors on the w3c page: `https://www.w3schools.com/cssref/css_selectors.asp`.

Also check the code in the file `selectors.html`.

Now that you know how to select elements and write blocks that will contain the CSS rules, let's talk about the rules themselves. What rules can we apply? What can we do with CSS? I think nowadays you can only ask, "What can't we do with CSS?" because CSS is really powerful nowadays! If you google by "projects built with only CSS," you will be totally amazed. Of course, in this book we will not draw any Mona Lisa portrait with CSS. We are just going to talk about the generic rules. You will do all the rest, ok?

Let's start from the basics. Colors. To change the color of the text, you apply "`color`" rule with any value you need for it. The values for colors can be specified in different formats:

- The name of color itself (e.g., `black`, `red`, `yellow`, etc.)

- The hexadecimal color code (e.g., `#000000`, `#ff0000`, etc.)

- The rgb specification (e.g., `rgb(0, 0, 0)`, `rgb(255, 0, 0)`)

In the same way, you can change the background color. You can rather use the "`background-color`" css rule or "`background`" rule. The difference between both is that while `background-color` rule is used for explicitly defining the background color, the `background` rule can contain more properties—for example, background image. Each of the parts that can be specified within the background rule can also be specified in the individual property, like "`background-image`", "`background-position`", etc. Check more about the `background` CSS rule in the w3schools page: `https://www.w3schools.com/cssref/css3_pr_background.asp`.

It is also possible to specify some gradient for your background. For example,

```
#gradient {
    background: linear-gradient(blue, yellow);
}
```

Let's talk about sizes. You can specify sizes for your elements using CSS and their width and height properties. The values for these properties can be absolute or relative. For example,

```
div {
  height: 200px;
  width: 20%;
}
```

Let's talk about fonts. Fonts are a special part of web development where it is possible to talk hours after hours because typography is actually something pretty much correlated with the whole concept of design and even architecture. Different types of typography are used to deliver different types of messages, and there are some specific fonts that we associate to some specific things. For example, you would not use the same font to create a punk poster as you would to write a scientific paper. Different spacing between paragraphs and letters transmits different messages. Different line width is used for different needs—for example, important articles in the newspaper will use different width for the line than, let's say, an online CV document. CSS provides lots of properties to play with fonts, their types, and characteristics. Font-related properties are the following:

- `font-family`: specify the font family, provide several of them for the fallback. For example,

```
p {
  font-family: "Times New Roman", Times, serif;
}
```

- `font-size`: specify font size. Again, you can specify font size in absolute units (e.g., pixels) or in relative units (e.g., in em). 1em is equivalent to the current font size which is usually 16px.

```
p {
  font-size: 1.5em;
}
```

- `font-style`: can be rather `italic`, `oblique`, or `normal`:

```
p {
  font-style: italic;
}
```

- `font-weight`: specify the weight of your font:

```
p {
  font-weight: bold;
}
```

Besides the font formatting to change the way the text looks, CSS allows applying innumerous rules to the text itself. Properties such as `letter-spacing`, `vertical-align`, `direction`, `line-height`, `text-ident`, and `text-transform` are just some of the properties that can be applied to the text. Check in more detail about them in the w3schools page: `https://www.w3schools.com/css/css_text.asp`.

Another very important thing to explain about CSS is its box model, which is shown in Figure 6-11. Each element is like a box, and its size is composed of the size of its content, margin, padding, and border.

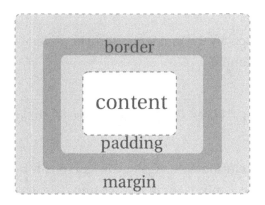

Figure 6-11. *CSS box model*

So, if you define the width of your `div` as 200px and add margin, padding, or border properties, you should sum them up to get the final width of the element. Let's talk about these three properties:

- Margin: defines a space outside the element. This property is composed of top, right, bottom, and left margin values:

  ```
  margin: 20px 10px 10px 20px;
  ```

  If you specify only one value, the element will have the same margin for all 4 sides:

  ```
  margin: 10px;
  ```

  You can also specify each of the sides separately, using `margin-top`, `margin-right`, `margin-bottom`, and `margin-left` properties.

- Border: defines a border around the element. It can be dotted, dashed, solid, rounded. The line of the border can have different thickness. You can also specify different borders for different sides of the element, and, of course, you can define the color for the border.

  ```
  border: dashed gray 2px;
  ```

- Padding: defines the interior space between the borders of the element and its content. The way how you define paddings is very similar to the margins:

```
padding: 20px 10px 10px 20px;
```

Or:

```
padding: 10px;
```

Check the file `box-model.html` to play with paddings, margins, and borders.

In this section, we have covered basics of CSS, like its box model and styling text and colors. There is so much more that you can do with CSS—for example, animations. Oh yes, you can do crazy stuff using just CSS rules. We will leave it for your individual learning; you will find the whole internet of resources on CSS animations. Let's just talk about a very important topic when it comes to implementing user interfaces: layout.

Layout

One of the most important challenges of CSS is to provide an easy way for developers and designers to distribute their content on the page in a way that looks nice and doesn't break in different screen sizes.

It is quite obvious that you don't want your content to be sequentially distributed over the page from top to bottom. You want to have some grid, some boxes, some interesting structure. Before the good and fancy CSS of present day, people would structure their content using tables (programmers' hell!).

After that, people would create absolutely positioned layouts and layouts based on the float property of CSS; "`float: left`" would tell the element to stick to the left side of the parent element, while "`float: right`" would tell the element to stick to the right side. Combined with the relative width, it would allow building more or less flexible layouts.

Now that we are talking about flexible layouts, it's time to talk about flexbox—a popular CSS tool that allows composing flexible responsive layouts using easy-to-understand properties.

Flexbox (flexible box) is a way of positioning elements inside the container in a row or in a column in a specific order and in a suitable way. Flexbox guarantees that even if the sizes of the elements are dynamic, the layout remains flexible for any device. To use flexbox, apply `display: flexbox` property to the container: `.container {display: flex;}`

Inside the flexbox container, elements can be displayed in the columns or in a row. You can specify it by applying the "`flex-direction`" property with the value `column` or `row`. You can align items in any way that you like (using `align-items` property), and you can tell the elements to wrap when needed; this is useful for the responsive layouts. There is a lot more about flexbox, try to play with it a bit using this guide: `https://css-tricks.com/snippets/css/a-guide-to-flexbox/`.

Not so long ago, another value for `display` property came to help flexbox: grid.

Grid layout is a powerful tool for laying out content of the web page that operates in a 2-dimensional space. You specify the rules for both columns and rows for your layout. In order to tell the container that it will become a grid, use the same as you would use for flexbox, just replacing `flex` value for display property with `grid:.container {display: grid;}`

Note that we said that the `grid` came to help `flexbox`, not to replace it. These two tools can complement each other in order to achieve powerful flexible responsive layouts. The main difference between them is that *grid* operates in a 2-dimensional space, while flexbox is great for the unidimensional spaces where we need columns or rows to have a needed behavior. Grid is something that operates more on a layout level, whereas flexbox operates more on the content level. Flexbox listens to the content and adjusts to it, while grid basically dictates the structure. Therefore, grid should be used for defining a large-scale layout, while flexbox can be used on a smaller-scale level for flexible elements. Play with both. The guide for the grid can be found here: `https://css-tricks.com/snippets/css/complete-guide-grid/`.

Now you know a lot about using CSS for not only defining colors, sizes, and fonts but also for positioning elements on the page. I guess it's time to consolidate your knowledge and check yourself with this simple exercise.

EXERCISE ABOUT CSS

Do you remember the mockups of our learning platform? Do you remember pages for login and register? Use what we've just learned to transform the html inside the `exercise2.html` into that shown in Figure 6-12.

Figure 6-12. *Login screen with applied style*

- Apply your knowledge of both `flexbox` and `grid` system to build two-column layout for the main content and to display label and input elements the way they are displayed on the mockup.

- Apply your knowledge of margins, paddings, and borders to make the login container, input elements, and buttons look like they look on the mockup.

- Apply your knowledge of styling colors and background to color all the texts and background exactly how it appears on the mockup.

Check yourself in the `exercise2-solution.html`.

I hope you enjoyed being a UI engineer and creating a user interface according to the mockup built by our designers. Let's now see how current technologies can help us in outperforming in these tasks.

Design Systems

In a nutshell, a design system is a set of pre-defined HTML components with already applied CSS rules that define all your design, starting from the color schema of your product and defining the classes for laying out its content. Having the design system defined, you just enjoy the process of composing your software without being worried about defining styling, positioning elements, writing complex CSS rules, and creating animations for transitions. If you want to build your own design system for your product, kudos to you and good luck. If you, like us, don't have enough resources and patience for that, then you can use one of those that already exist.

I will give you a couple of examples of those.

Bootstrap is a great framework that comes with everything you need to build interfaces. Check it out at `https://getbootstrap.com/`. It is open-source and totally free. Check the file `bootstrsap.html`, where we show how to implement our login form using Bootstrap's grid system and classes to style the components.

Another popular framework is Foundation (`https://foundation.zurb.com/`).

Another one developed by the folks from Google is called Material design and can be found at `https://material.io/design/`.

The idea behind all these systems is very simple: the developers should focus on developing products, and these tools should help them in achieving the needed visual effects in a fast and friendly way. However, if you find yourself fighting with the tool for quite a long time to make things work the way you want them to, and you know that you could achieve this effect by writing a couple of lines of CSS code, then just drop the tool and write your own CSS code. Remember: tools are here to reduce your development time and not to increase it!

Pre-Processors and Template Engines

As you can see, writing HTML and even CSS code is not rocket science. It requires some discipline, though, because you can easily end up with a huge codebase that is hard to maintain, but it's not difficult at all. However, developers are the laziest people in the world, so they critically assess every symbol that they have to write and can easily say, "This is too verbose!" or, "There is a lot of repeated code, let's do something about it!" So, for example, when it comes to the HTML code, they decided that the symbols of opening and closing tags (< and >) do not contribute to the overall purpose so they came up with the new languages where they removed it. Or, for example, why should we repeat the code for things like footer in every page of our website? The developers like the DRY and KISS principles very much—that's why they constantly come up with new languages to make their life easier.

DRY principle means "Don't Repeat Yourself" and KISS means "Keep It Simple Stupid!"

These languages are called pre-processors or templating engines for HTML and are basically programming languages that decrease developing time by providing a means of code reusability and reducing the amount of code itself. After writing in these languages, you have to apply special tools called transpilers that will transform this code into the HTML and CSS again, so browsers are able to process them. There are plenty of them. So, for HTML you have, for example, the following:

- HAML: HTML abstraction markup language

- Jade: template engine

- Mustache

- HandlebarsJS

Let's, for example, compare the code written in HTML and in Jade. Consider this piece of HTML code:

```
<div class="container">
  <div id="main" class="row">
    <h2>Log in</h2>
    <form>
      <div class="form-group">
        <label for="email">Email</label>
        <input type="email" class="form-control" id="email"
        aria-describedby="emailHelp" placeholder="youremail@example.com">
      </div>
    </form>
  </div>
</div>
```

In Jade, you would do something like this:

```
.container
  #main.row
    h2 Log in
    form
      .form-group
        label(for='email') Email
        input#email.form-control(type='email',
        placeholder='youremail@example.com')
```

It will be very similar in HAML:

```
.container
  #main.row
    %h2 Log in
    %form
      .form-group
        %label{:for => "email"} Email
        %input#email.form-control{:placeholder => "youremail@example.com",
        :type => "email"}/
```

As you can see, template engines for HTML remove unnecessary code and even provide means to reuse templates inside the templates; so, for example, you can have a template for footer and just include it in other templates, so you don't have to repeat the code. That is pretty useful.

There is something similar for CSS as well. The two most popular tools for CSS are Sass (https://sass-lang.com/) and LESS (http://lesscss.org/).

Sass is a CSS extension language that means "Syntactically Awesome Style Sheets". Less is another pre-preprocessor for CSS, which is inspired by Sass, written in JavaScript, and whose tagline is, "It's CSS, with just a little more."

One very useful thing offered by both Sass and Less is variables. Imagine you have some specific color that you use all over the page in different elements. Let's say, pink, #f28fe9. You will have to repeat this color code in all the places where you want to use it. Imagine that for some reason you have to change this code to slightly lighter pink,

#ffb6c1. Of course, there is a nice feature called find and replace, but still, it is tedious. What you could have done in Sass or Less is to simply declare a variable called pink and use and reuse it all over the code:

```
/ Variables
@pink:        #f28fe9;
@light-pink:  lighten(@pink, 10%);

// Usage
a,
.link {
  color: @pink;
}
a:hover {
  color: @light-pink;
}
```

Now if you need to change your pink color to something darker or lighter, you change it in one place only! How awesome is that?

Besides offering the language support to make your code reusable and friendly, both Sass and Less offer some ready-to-use component libraries, support for Grid system, different themes, etc. If you are into this subject of making the web prettier using CSS, we strongly advise you to take a look and play with all these tools.

Dynamic Content

Now that we know how to implement our user interfaces using HTML and CSS, it is time to make them live! In this section, as you might have already guessed, we are going to talk about JavaScript! JavaScript is a high-level interpreted programming language.

Being high-level programming language means that the code is closer to human than to the machine, so it's easy for humans to read. Being interpreted means that it doesn't need to be compiled before being executed (like, for example, Java). It is interpreted by browsers during the runtime.

Being an interpreted and not compiled language on one hand reduces the development time, since you don't need to compile code every time you change it; on the other hand, it's more error-prone since you might discover errors only during the runtime.

Please note, although half of the name of the JavaScript language is Java, it doesn't have anything to do with the Java programming language! Some people even say, "JavaScript to Java is like Car to Carpet."

Since JavaScript runs on the client side, it has access to the properties of the browser of the client; again, be careful about the information you access and use—the data protection laws don't sleep!

Development Tools Console

The easiest way to try JavaScript is using the development tools console. It exists in most of the browsers. We will show the Chrome developer tools here. Figure 6-13 shows how you open it.

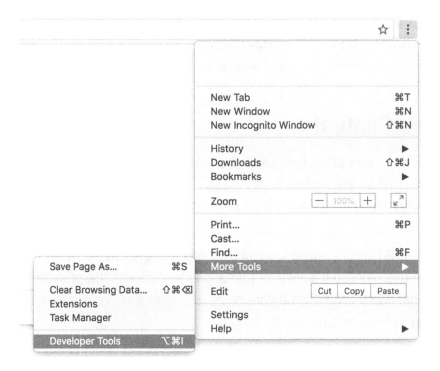

Figure 6-13. *Opening developer tools console in Chrome*

In some systems, you can simply press F12. In macOS, you have to press command-option-I (it has to be different, right?). With developer tools opened, click on the *Console* tab. Now you can type some JavaScript code, and it will immediately execute it. Type, for example, 2 + 2 followed by Enter. You will see something like what is shown in Figure 6-14.

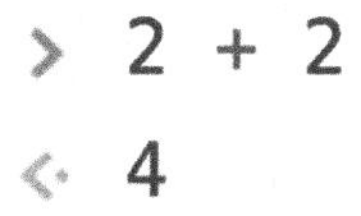

> 2 + 2
< 4

Figure 6-14. *JavaScript executed in chrome devtools console*

Now type new Date() and click Enter. Date() is a built-in JavaScript function that allows operations with date and time.

Type alert(new Date()), and you will see a popup with a new Date. Alert is another built-in JavaScript function that displays these ugly popups. Please don't use it.

Variables

JavaScript also has variables. To declare a variable in JavaScript, use the keyword var followed by the name of variable. For example, type var myVar = 10; Click enter and now type myVar. The number 10 will be displayed. Type var a = 10; var b = 20;. Now type a + b. Play a bit with variables using console.

Including JavaScript

Of course, writing JavaScript in the browser's console is a fun process, but you might already be wondering, "Ok, and how do I use it in the applications? I'm not going to the user's browser console typing some things there." Of course, you aren't! You include your JavaScript code in your pages the same way you include your CSS. You can, for example, make it internal for each html file using <script> tag and writing some JavaScript there:

```
<!DOCTYPE html>
<html lang="en">
<head>
  <meta charset="UTF-8">
  <title>JavaScript Alert</title>
</head>
```

```
<body>
  <script>
      alert(new Date())
   </script>
</body>
</html>
```

If you open this page (alert.html) in the browser, the popup with the current date will appear.

It can also be external and be imported into your html page using empty `script` tag with `src` attribute:

```
<script src="script.js"></script>
```

Let's see how we can display date on the webpage using JavaScript. JavaScript allow replacing content of the HTML elements. You can obtain the reference to the element using one of the "`document.getElementBy...`" functions.

For example:

```
document.getElementById(container)
```

Now you can access this element's different attributes, including '`innerHTML`', which defines whatever is written inside this element. If you change this value, it will automatically change on the page. For example, if we create a `div` with id '`date`', obtain its reference, and assign the value of the `new Date()` to its `innerHTML`, we will end up with the date showing up inside the `div`:

File 'date.html'

```
<body>
  <div id="date"></div>
  <script>
    document.getElementById('date').innerHTML = new Date()
  </script>
</body>
```

It looks a bit ugly though, don't you think? What if we wanted to display a date like: "today is May, 28". How would we do that? The date object created by the `new Date()` function has a lot of methods we can use on it to access different date properties. For example, `getMonth()` gives you the current month, `getDate()` will give you the day of the month, and so on. If you want to use the name of the month, you could use the internationalization API: new Date().toLocaleString('en-us', {month: 'long'})

EXERCISE ABOUT THE DATE OBJECT IN JAVASCRIPT

Use the knowledge about Date() function to display the date in the form "Today is May 28" in the browser. Use file exercise3.html as a base.

- Apply your knowledge about variables.

- Use getElementById() function and it's innerHTML property.

- Apply your knowledge of accessing different properties of the Date object.

Check yourself in the exercise3-solution.html.

What if we wanted to display the current time instead of the current date? We could do something like:

File time.html

```
<body>
  <div id="time"></div>
  <script>
    var date = new Date()
    document.getElementById('time').innerHTML = `Now it is ${date.
    getHours()}:${date.getMinutes()}`
  </script>
</body>
```

Note that instead of appending strings with the plus sign like we did in the previous exercise, I used JavaScript template literal.

Template literals in JavaScript are wrapped in the back-tick (` `) character instead of double or single quotes. These literals can contain JavaScript expressions inside them that are indicated by the dollar sign and the curly braces: ${expression}.

If you open this file in the browser, you would see the current time. What if you wanted to update it each time you click some button? JavaScript DOM objects (the ones you obtain using `document.getElementBy...` functions) have some properties related to the events that can be applied to them—for example, `onclick`, `onblur`, `onchange`, `ondblclick`, etc. Then you can call any action on this event. For example:

```
button.onclick = function () {
  alert('Button clicked!')
}
```

Let's do it for our time update. We have to create a button element on the page, obtain its reference, and tell that it should fill the `innerHTML` of the time `div` with the new time:

File time-with-button.html

```
<body>
  <div id="time"></div>
  <button id="update">Update time!</button>
  <script>
    var button = document.getElementById('update')
    button.onclick = function () {
      var date = new Date()
      document.getElementById('time').innerHTML = `Now it is ${date.
      getHours()}:${date.getMinutes()}:${date.getSeconds()}`
    }
  </script>
</body>
```

Open this file in your browser and click the button.

Functions

Do you remember that developers strive for code reusability? That is why JavaScript has functions. We can wrap some JavaScript statements into them, rather than typing those statements just using functions.

To declare a function in JavaScript, invoke the function statement followed by the name of the function, parenthesis, and curly braces for the function body:

```
function myFunction () {
  // JavaScript statements
}
myFunction()
```

For example, we could put the code that creates a time string and writes it in the time div into the function and call this function inside the onclick callback:

```
function updateTime () {
  var date = new Date()
  document.getElementById('time').innerHTML = `Now it is ${date.
  getHours()}:${date.getMinutes()}:${date.getSeconds()}`
}
var button = document.getElementById('update')
button.onclick = updateTime
```

Isn't it a bit boring to have to click a button every time we want to see the updated time? Wouldn't it be nice if it would just update itself periodically? Actually, JavaScript provides this function called "setInterval". This function receives two arguments: a callback function, to be called periodically, and a time interval, from which the callback should be invoked. For example, if we would like to append "hello" to some div every second, we could do something like:

```
setInterval(() => {
  textDiv.innerHTML += 'hello'
}, 1000)
```

Note that the units of the time of the interval are provided in milliseconds—thus, 1000 equals 1 second. We could also print some counter and update it inside the setInterval function:

File set-interval.html

```
var counter = 1
var textDiv = document.getElementById('text')
setInterval(() => {
```

```
textDiv.innerHTML = `Hello for already ${counter} times!`
counter++
}, 1000)
```

The notation `counter++` just means that we are increasing the value of the counter by one. This is a shortcut for the statement `counter = counter + 1`

The possibilities of JavaScript are endless, and we could spend another ${counter} pages just talking about it. If you feel enthusiastic about this topic, take some online courses, go to a codecamp, go to meetups, and start building stuff. There is nothing more efficient for learning than getting your hands dirty.

EXERCISE ABOUT SETINTERVAL IN JAVASCRIPT

Use both `setInterval` function and `updateTime` function that we've implemented before to automatically update time on the page.

Check yourself in the `exercise4-solution.html`.

You have already realized, haven't you, that the developers are lazy and creative creatures, and they are never satisfied with the way things work. They always keep trying to improve the things so they have to type less code and can be more efficient and productive. That is why they came up with hundreds of different frameworks to make their lives easier and work less. Let's talk about frameworks.

Frameworks

Of course, you can write the whole software using just plain JavaScript, but all these years developers were not sleeping and developed a bunch of frameworks to help you to structure, create, and maintain all kinds of JavaScript applications—from small to a huge scale, starting from famous jQuery, Backbone, Ampersand, React, Angular, Meteor, Ember, Vuejs... The list is endless. Some of them come with already pre-built themes, Sass and Less support, reusable components, utility functions, plugins, add-ons, etc.

How does one choose what to use? My suggestion would be: don't use frameworks just for the sake of using frameworks. If you have a simple web page that you can create and maintain on your own using plain HTML+CSS+JS stack, do it! In the end, all the code built with frameworks will be transpiled into this trio. Of course, if you have a big-scale architecture, a lot of data to deal with, different transitions, conditions, and huge complexity, then totally yes, check frameworks. Keep in mind that frameworks require some learning curve. Check comparison tables and decide what and how you need.

Sometimes when you work in a team and you start a new project, there might be a discussion on what to use. What Olga usually does in these cases is distribute different frameworks within the team members, establish some deadlines (let's say, end of the week), and schedule 20-minute presentations. Each person has to prepare a POC (proof of concept) using the chosen framework and present it to the group. Then the group decides which of the frameworks answers the project's need most.

Olga personally likes Vue.js because it can be used for very basic needs without having to install the huge bunch of tools and can also be scaled for big projects with complex architecture. If you are interested in learning Vue.js while building interesting projects with it, check out these books that Olga wrote:

- *Learning Vue.js 2* `https://www.packtpub.com/web-development/learning-vuejs-2`

- *Vue.js and Bootstrap 4 Web Development* `https://www.packtpub.com/web-development/vuejs-2-and-bootstrap-4-web-development`.

Not so long ago, a lot of web developers were using jQuery (`https://jquery.com/`) to modify the DOM structure and communicate with server (among thousands of other things offered by this framework). jQuery, in fact, is easy to understand and to use. Its beauty lies in how nicely it simplifies all the DOM-related operations. For example, this line of code:

```
document.getElementById('container').innerHTML = 'hello'
```

can simply be replaced by

```
$('#container').html('hello')
```

if you use jQuery.

jQuery provides tons of handy functions to deal with your web elements. `.hide()`, `.show()`, `.toggle()`, `.fadeOut()`, `.animate()`—these are only few of operations you can run on your elements using jQuery.

jQuery also provides an easy way for communicating with the server. Do you remember in the previous chapter we talked about REST methods (GET, POST, PUT, DELETE, PATCH)—methods that are used to operate and retrieve from the server? jQuery provides an easy way of calling these methods on given endpoint and retrieving data or passing it to server. jQuery's method is called `ajax()`, and it receives a URL as an argument and, when needed, data to pass to server.

Ajax means asynchronous JavaScript and XML. This is actually one of the most misleading abbreviations in web development. First, using ajax, you can run both synchronous and asynchronous calls. Second, no one uses XML anymore for transporting data through the network.

To use the `ajax()` method, you simple call `$.ajax(URL, [data])`. Check the full documentation on the official jQuery page: `http://api.jquery.com/jquery.ajax/`.

Besides the ajax method, jQuery provides shortcuts like `.get()` and `.post()`. This way you don't need to pass the configuration object as a parameter specifying which HTTP method you want to use in some specific case.

Let's use jQuery to login on our application. We know that the endpoint for the login is `oauth/token`, we have to use method POST, and we have to pass username and password to it.

First, let's run our server application. Go inside the `server-integration` folder, ensure that you have Java 8 installed, and run:

```
mvn clean install -DskipTests
cd liquibase
mvn liquibase:update
cd ..
mvn tomcat7:run
```

Now if you open your page on `http://localhost:8080/oauth/token`, it will throw an error. Of course, this should be called as a POST method and pass the username and password to the server. Do you remember our login page that you had to style? For this example, we have put it into the `rest-api/src/main/webapp` folder so it runs on our server. To check that it actually runs, open `localhost:8080/login.html`.

If you fill the form with some data and click on the login button, nothing will happen. What we want to happen is that by clicking on the button, the jQuery post method is called on the oauth/token endpoint with username and password. We have to also pass grant_type property to it to indicate that it is password. So, our call will look like the following:

```
$.post('http://localhost:8080/oauth/token', {
    grant_type: 'password',
    username: <EMAIL>,
    password: <PASSWORD>
})
```

How do we get values for e-mail and password? Do you remember how easy it is with jQuery to manipulate the DOM and retrieve things from it? In order to retrieve value from some input with jQuery, you can use .val() method. So, for example, to retrieve value from the e-mail input you should call $('#email').val().

Another important thing to understand about jQuery *ajax* methods is that they are promises.

Promises are very special asynchronous functions in JavaScript that return values in the future. We don't wait for them to finish their execution; instead we call method .then() on them with the provided callback, and this callback will be executed once promise method finishes its execution, or, speaking scientifically, resolves. Of course, promises can fail as well, the callbacks for failures are executed inside the .catch() method of promise.

Thus, our post should have both the .then and .catch methods attached so we can execute some code when the login is successful or when it fails. This will look like the following:

```
$.post('http://localhost:8080/oauth/token', {
    <...>
})
.then(result => {
  // Do something
})
.catch( error => {
  // do something
})
```

What should we do if the login is successful? Well, we could redirect the user to the courses page. You can simply do it assigning the `window.location` property to the one you need:

```
window.location = 'http://localhost:8080/courses.html'
```

INTEGRATING LOGIN PAGE WITH THE BACKEND

Use `server-integration` folder's code as a base. Run the server as described in the `README.md` file. Create a new user using the `createuser.sh` script. In this exercise, you have to be able to login with the user with `test@example.com`/`w1secret$` credentials.

You only need to modify things inside the `rest-api/src/main/webapp` folder. There you can see three html files, `css`, and `js` folders. We've extracted the needed CSS to the `style.css` file inside the css folder, and we added jQuery code to the `js` folder and imported it into the `login.html` file.

- Use `$.post` method inside the login function with 'oauth/token' url.

- Redirect user to the `courses.html` page if login is successful.

You need to modify the code inside the `<script>` tag inside the `login.html` file to finish the implementation of the login functionality.

Check yourself in the `server-integration-solution` folder.

In this example, somehow we knew that the endpoint for the login was "oauth/token" (ha! "somehow" means I read the previous chapter where Rui implemented those endpoints).

On the other hand, it's not the usual case that the frontend and the backend folks write a book together, therefore knowing in advance what everyone would do next. So, the frontend people need to understand how to use the API provided by the backend. For this, we should talk about contract. Yes, when we (developers) work together, sometimes we have to sign some kind of agreement in order to make our work nice and smooth.

Contract Between Frontend and Backend

We already stated that JavaScript is responsible for retrieving data from the backend and displaying it on the frontend; it is also responsible for collecting data on the client side and passing it to the backend. Of course, all of this data should follow some format; we can't just pass anything to the backend because it will not know how to interpret it. Also, we can't get data from the backend and display it on the frontend without knowing which format the data comes in. That is why developers communicate a lot in order to establish some kind of contract. You will never find frontend and backend departments that just work separately. You already saw that at any stage of the process, there's a lot of communication back and forth between people of different roles: product owner talks a lot to business people and then to developers and designers; designers are constantly involved in the brainstorming with developers; and backend developers should be involved in the early stages in the discussions to understand what kind of data is there and when and how it should be stored, retrieved, and displayed. Frontend developers communicate a lot with designers to know how to display the data and with backend developers to know which data will be provided and in which format.

There are different ways of establishing this kind of agreement. What we usually do is to design a JSON file with the API description—this way frontend doesn't need to wait for the implementation to be ready, we can just mock some server responses and work with fake data until the server-side is ready. It happens a lot.

So, since we (Rui and Olga) are working on the backend and the frontend of our online courses platform, we had to establish a kind of contract. Rui created a JSON file for Olga describing the API. Note, it is still very basic API—it's not complete, but it shows pretty much what we mean by the contract.

JSON (JavaScript Object Notation) is a common format used in web development. This format is easy for humans to read, easy for the browser to interpret, can easily be iterated by JavaScript, and is easily generated by any backend language.

So, the part of this JSON related to the course list looks like following (we need the information regarding the path itself and the definition about the course object):

```
"paths" : {
  "/api/v1/public/courses" : {
    "get" : {
      "summary" : "Lists the available courses.",
      "operationId" : "list",
```

```
      "responses" : {
        "200" : {
          "description" : "The paginated list of available courses.",
          "schema" : {
            "$ref" : "#/definitions/PageCourseV1Dto"
          }
        }
      }
    }
  }
},
"definitions" : {
  "CourseV1Dto" : {
    "type" : "object",
    "properties" : {
      "id" : {
        "type" : "integer",
        "format" : "int64"
      },
      "name" : {
        "type" : "string"
      },
      "description" : {
        "type" : "string"
      },
      "durationHours" : {
        "type" : "integer",
        "format" : "int32"
      },
      "active" : {
        "type" : "boolean"
      }
    }
  }
}
```

This is just a small example of what the JSON object might look like. Of course, it is far from being complete, but it's important that it exists and is up to date, so everyone is on the same page of how API can look.

At some point, this "contract" becomes enormous and hard for humans to follow. There are a lot of tools out there that not only allow nice visualizations of your API files but even their testing. One of these tools is called Swagger (`https://swagger.io/`). It has an online editor where you can paste your JSON or YAML (yaml is yet another format widely used—particularly for describing APIs) and get a nice visualization of your API. Just open the swagger editor (`https://editor.swagger.io/`) and paste `swagger.json`, which you can find inside the `rest-api/target` directory. You will see something that shown in Figure 6-15.

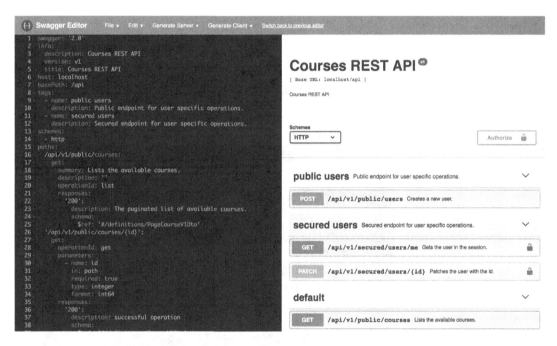

Figure 6-15. *Visualization of the API by Swagger*

If you click on the methods, you will see the description of the underlying objects as well as the description of the error and success codes (Figure 6-16).

Figure 6-16. *Detailed description of the underlying user object*

Now that you know how the frontend communicates with backend, how the API works, how to implement the design, and how to make it work, you are ready to choose your favorite framework and start implementing frontend for our application.

Creating the Frontend Application for Our Platform

We have already implemented the HTML page for the login page for our platform and styled it using CSS. We have even established the communication with server using jQuery. Let's get some flavor for the development with frameworks and use Vue.js and Material design system to develop our frontend.

First, make sure you have npm installed on your system (`https://docs.npmjs.com/cli/install`). For the compatibility of versions, I use version 8.11.1. As a personal advice, install nvm (node version manager), as it will allow you to install different versions and switch them as needed. Now let's install vue command line interface:

```
npm install vue-cli -g a
```

Now we want to create a Vue project. There are different ways of doing that; we want to use the template that uses material design. It's called vuetifyjs (`https://vuetifyjs.com/`), and to bootstrap a new project using this template, use vuetifyjs/nuxt template. Vuetify, as we already pointed out, is a material design framework, and nuxt (`https://nuxtjs.org/`) is a tool designed for vue that makes already easy-to-use Vue framework even easier. It basically abstracts all the client-server communication and routing while we focus on the UI part.

So, let's create a project and call it frontend:

```
vue init vuetifyjs/nuxt frontend
```

Now switch inside the frontend folder and run yarn install and yarn run dev:

```
yarn install
yarn run dev
```

If you don't have yarn installed, install it globally: `npm install yarn -g`. If you open your browser on `localhost:3000`, you will see the default vuetify index page. The beauty of the underlying `nuxt.js` is that it provides you with the out-of-the-box implementation of routing and transition between pages. Everything located inside the `pages` folder becomes a route. Go on and create pages `login.vue`, `register.vue`, `dashboard.vue`, and `courses.vue` inside the `pages` folder. We are going to use single file components.

Single file components in Vue are the files that have template, style, and script all in the same file. Ideally these are small reusable components.

Create the template section in each of the created pages and just write down the section name. For example,

```
// pages/login.vue
<template>
  <div>Login</div>
</template>

// pages/register.vue
<template>
  <div>Register</div>
</template>
```

Change the default layout so its navigation bar contains the links to these pages:

```
// layouts/default.vue
<template>
<...>
<v-toolbar fixed app :clipped-left="clipped">
  <v-spacer></v-spacer>
  <v-btn flat router :to="'login'" exact>
    Login
  </v-btn>
  <v-btn flat router :to="'register'" exact>
    Register
  </v-btn>
  <v-btn flat router :to="'courses'" exact>
    Courses
  </v-btn>
</v-toolbar>
<...>
</template>
```

Click on these buttons and check how beautiful it is to transition between pages (Figure 6-17).

Figure 6-17. *The transition between pages*

Note how we didn't do anything for this to happen!

We have implemented the login and register pages. There is also a basic code for the courses page. Check the code in the `frontend` folder. You have to run `yarn install` and `yarn run dev` in order to run the frontend code in the developer mode. Note that you have to have the server up and running in order to make it work.

Some explanations:

- We've used `@nuxtjs/proxy` plugin to redirect the requests to our server that is located under `localhost:8080.` You can find it in the `nuxt.config.js` file

- We've used `vue-resource` plugin for the communication with the server. You can find the corresponding code inside the `api/index.js` file

- We use Vuex for centralized store management. You can find the corresponding state, actions, mutations, and getters inside the `store` folder.

- Note that we use the courses endpoint to get the list of courses and display them on the courses page. However, the displaying itself is not fully implemented—we just print out the names of the courses. Use what you've learned so far to render them nicely!

Play with this code, change it, add components, use them, reuse them, abuse them. It is a fun and crazy process!

IDEs

Of course, you can write your code using a simple notepad or even the vim editor, but for sure you have already asked yourself what is the most suitable coding environment for the web development. Again, there are plenty of them. Olga is using Webstorm—this is an IntelliJ family IDE, the same that Rui is using for the backend development. But there are plenty of others: sublime, atom, vim (yes, vim), brackets... Visual Studio code IDE developed by Microsoft has gained a lot of popularity lately. Yes, those guys finally started doing something for the open source community, and they have achieved some great results. I suggest that you try some of these editors before choosing your favorite one.

Summary

In this chapter we wore the hat of a frontend developer to implement the interface that we designed earlier and connected it to the backend implemented in the previous chapter. We have actually completed our acquaintance with the implementation for our MVP. It's time to test it! Let's move to the next chapter, where we will try the hat of a quality assurance engineer and implement some tests that will not only assess some functionalities of our system but also ensure its quality from end to end. If, until now, we were enjoying the process of building software, in the next chapter we will have to do something quite opposite—enjoy the process of destroying it. When you test your software, you have to forget the part of how it was hard to build it. It's better that you break something now and fix it than if your users find bugs and become disappointed.

Now let's move to the next chapter and break stuff!

CHAPTER 7

Testing Our Product

In the previous chapter, we finished the frontend development. Does it mean we are done with the development? No! Writing tests is also part of development. In this chapter we will discuss what types of testing there are out there, how to do them, and when to use them. In this chapter we will explain the difference between manual testers and automation testers and discuss several testing platforms and frameworks. We hope you enjoy and that by the end of this chapter you know how extremely important that topic is.

Different Types of Testing

Different types of testing serve different needs. It doesn't mean that one can be used in favor of the other or that some types are better than others, all of them have their purpose, and, depending on the nature of the project, some might be more important than others. This section discusses some types of testing, the ones we believe are most important for our use case, but there are more, and we invite you to take a look if you are interested.

Unit Testing

As the name states, **unit testing** means testing a small part (units) of code. This kind of testing is done as individually as possible, meaning that it is advisable that the code being tested runs isolated from other pieces of code. In most of the cases, what's being tested is a method, a class, or even a module, and the test cases should be independent from each other (e.g., *test B must not be expecting that something is created by test A in order to pass*). Depending on the nature of the application, the setup can be more or less complex. In our case, for example, we need to handle database calls; this means that we had to set up everything in a way that all the database changes are only valid during the test and then discarded.

© Olga Filipova and Rui Vilão 2018
O. Filipova and R. Vilão, *Software Development From A to Z*, https://doi.org/10.1007/978-1-4842-3945-2_7

This kind of testing is the first line of defense for your code. You might ask, "Why do I need to write this test if I can just verify if manually?" It is a good and valid point, but only if you assume that your code will never change, and we all know that is not true in most (if not all) of the cases. Writing unit tests will prevent further changes to break your code base in the future, since you are asserting the expectations of several actions. If tomorrow your new colleague is performing the task of changing something and deletes some parameter you were using before, the test will fail.

Sometimes it is common to use **Parameterized Unit Testing,** meaning that the input is generated by the testing framework and not by the one writing the tests. In most cases, it is hard to set up these kind of tests since the modules being tested are too complex. Imagine that we were to use parameterized tests to test the user creation. Our restrictions with passwords and e-mail would make it complicated to provide a good seed to generate data. On the other hand, if you just created a memory structure, such as a list or a map, that is generic, parameterized testing would fit perfectly. Again, the right tools for the right job!

Unit tests are often written during development since they provide a way to test code immediately without having to have all other parts attached. It is also a good practice to provide several tests that run different parts of the code, such as *"if"* *branches* or *"loops."* In our case, this would reflect on, for example, testing the user creation. If you only provide test cases where the user is new, you are never testing the case where we need to throw an exception because you are registering the same user, and that branch of code would be left without any test.

The advantages of unit testing are enormous, and we advise that all projects have them. First of all, it helps us to find inconsistencies or errors at an early stage of development. Second, as mentioned before, it protects possible future changes or huge refactors from breaking your code, especially if it's written in a language with compile time such as Java.

The downsides of unit testing are that usually the person writing the test is the same that wrote the code, which leaves the test biased. It's also nearly impossible to provide tests for all possible combinations, which might lead you to think that just because the tests are passing, your module is bullet proof. People often argue about how close to reality those tests are, because it's not easy sometimes to come up with real-life examples for most of the tests. This is a valid point, but we believe anyway that it brings benefits.

An example of a unit test for our project is the user registration. Registering a user is an isolated event that uses mostly one module where there's no interaction with other code besides the framework code and the database. What we mainly verify with this test is that the user is registered successfully, that the username is the same as we provided, and that the id is not null (returning the id when creating entities is of special importance, as we might need to immediately reference the newly created entity). Several other tests also apply as unit tests regarding registering users. Such tests will verify other branches of the code, such as invalid passwords or usernames that already exist.

```
@Test
public void createAUserTest() throws Exception {
      final MockHttpServletResponse result = mockMvc.perform(post
      ("/api/v1/public/users").contentType(MediaType.APPLICATION_JSON).
      content(writeJson(UserV1Dto.builder().withUsername("ex1@example.
      com").withPassword("123456a$").build())))).andReturn().getResponse();

      assertThat(result.getStatus()).isEqualTo(HttpStatus.CREATED.value());
      final UserV1Dto user = readJson(result.getContentAsString(),
      UserV1Dto.class);
      assertThat(user.getUsername()).isEqualTo("ex1@example.com");
      assertThat(user.getId()).isNotNull();
}
```

Integration Testing

Integration testing in software development is used to assert that different modules can work together. During this testing phase the interface contracts are checked, meaning that it will be verified that *module A and module B can work together given the previously agreed interfaces*. Let's define that in our case we would consider integration testing as a set of tests between modules of the same application or project, meaning modules within the backend application and modules within the frontend application, but never between both of them. A good example of a possible integration test would be to log in a user and try to make a secured call. The previous example asserts the integration of the login module and an endpoint, where the latter would only work if the former works as well.

Since there are many modules involved, several techniques can be used for this kind of testing. Again, this depends on complexity and how fast the modules can be finished from development.

The **big bang testing**, as the name suggests, waits for the *"perfect storm"*—that is, for all the modules to be ready in order to start writing or performing tests. In big bang testing, all the modules are integrated in one go, hence eliminating the need of stubbing or mocking other modules in order to start building tests. The downside is that one needs to wait for all the modules to be ready in order to test them altogether. This might seem acceptable, but if some modules take months to be completed, then it doesn't seem appropriate. The incremental testing addresses this exact problem by creating mocks or stubs for the modules that are not ready yet.

This kind of testing will not 100% assert the integration of the two modules of course, but it will verify that the data transfer between the two modules is working properly and that the contract is being met. For the incremental approach and depending on the nature of the project, you might use a *bottom-up* approach where the low-level modules and typically the ones with less dependencies are tested first. For this you will need some sort of driver or traffic/content generator to make that module run. For the *top-down* approach, it's mostly the other way around, so we start by testing the high-level modules—typically the ones with several dependencies—and for that we will need to create stubs or mocks.

In agile environments, where the release cycles are typically around 2 weeks, big bang is mostly used. It is also not common that you will come up with two or three modules from scratch in one iteration, meaning that you will build your application in blocks and add new modules on an iterative basis. This leads to the fact that when we actually need to do the integration testing, most of the modules already exist, and we can write the integration testing without having to wait for other modules or creating stubs/ mocks or drivers to fake data.

We could give you several examples of tests that we can do, but we will leave you one that we believe is important since involves several modules even some provided by the framework we are using in our backend. We will test if the refresh tokens are working properly in this case. For a refresh token to work properly we not only try to get new access and refresh tokens using a previous refresh token, but we also verify that this new access token is valid and that we can use it to access protected endpoints and resources.

```
    @Test
public void refreshTest() throws Exception {
 final String accessTokenAfterRefresh = readJson(mockMvc.perform(post
 ("/oauth/token")    .contentType(MediaType.APPLICATION_FORM_URLENCODED)
```

```
.header("Authorization", "Basic d2ViYXBwOnRlc3Q=")
.content(String.format("grant_type=refresh_token&refresh_token=%s",
getTokens().get("refresh_token"))))
.andReturn()
.getResponse().getContentAsString(), new TypeReference < Map < String,
String >> () {}).get("access_token");
```
```
final MockHttpServletResponse result = mockMvc.perform(get("/api/v1/
secured/users/me")
    .header("Authorization", "bearer " + accessTokenAfterRefresh)
    .contentType(MediaType.APPLICATION_JSON))
  .andReturn()
  .getResponse();
assertThat(result.getStatus()).isEqualTo(HttpStatus.OK.value());
  final UserV1Dto user = readJson(result.getContentAsString(), UserV1Dto.
  class);
  assertThat(user.getUsername()).isEqualTo(testUser.getUsername());
}
```

You can find the whole example and dependencies in the RestApiUserTest.java and AbstractRestApiTest.java. The acceptance of this test is not only that we can make calls with the new access token, but also that the token we generated was actually for the same user.

System Testing

System testing is a term that combines several types of testing. Usually this testing phase occurs after the integration testing and aims at verifying that the system can work properly as a whole. In our case, for example, this would be testing that the frontend and the backend are working properly together. For this kind of testing, no knowledge about the internals of the product is required, code- and logic-wise making it a black-box testing phase.

The *black-box testing* can be either *functional* or *non-functional*. Functional testing focuses on checking if the system is meeting the requirements specified early, whereas non-functional testing focuses on checking how the system performs under heavy load and stress situations. Some examples of functional testing include interface errors or improper handling; errors in database structures or behaviors; and incorrect implementations or functionalities that are missing. The advantages of this testing technique are that because the testers do not have any information about the internals of the application, they can help point out discrepancies between the specifications and the actual implementation better than someone who has knowledge because they are not biased. Also, these testers do not need to possess programming skills to perform this task. Being nearly impossible to test all the cases, thus leaving some paths left untested, is one of the main disadvantages of this kind of testing technique.

We will not dive into all the possible tests that are performed during this phase, as there are many of them, and depending on the nature of the project, some might be applicable while others are not, but if you are interested in this topic and wish to know more, feel free to dive in a bit further—Google will be your friend!

Acceptance Testing

Acceptance testing is one of the last levels of testing, especially when shipping a new product. During this testing phase, the software application will be tested for compliance between the specification and the implementation, taking into account that the business requirements or contracts are also being met. Like in the previous testing phase, this one is also carried out using black-box testing. These tests are done on a high level of abstraction from the implementation, with the focus on how the final clients will use the product.

Depending on the nature of the product, two stages might apply during the testing. The first stage is the one where the acceptance is performed internally by a team belonging to the same company that implemented the product, but usually not someone that was involved in the development per se. Such teams include Product Management, Customer Service, Business Development, or even the Sales department. The other one is performed externally by people or companies that were not involved with the development. In this case there can be a Customer Acceptance Testing, where the company that asked for the service is responsible for verifying that everything conforms to the established contracts; or, in the other case, it might be a User Acceptance Testing where a set of end-users are responsible for testing and providing feedback. Sometimes that is referred also as *Beta testing*.

Regression Testing

Regression testing is one of the most important test phases when maintaining and evolving a product. Its purpose is to ensure that new code changes do not affect the previously tested and stable version of the software.

Even though you feel that minor and isolated changes are unlikely to have an impact on the system as a whole, the probability is always there. Believe us when we say that because sometimes you just don't see it coming and even if you know the whole code base from point A to point B, at some point you will break something. Sometimes it is not even your code, but some framework you are using. Just to give you an example, just by accepting empty lists on a function that is using Hibernate queries with the IN clause can cause a bug in your code. Does it mean they are wrong? Well it's complicated. If you try to write a query in SQL using "`... WHERE column IN ()..:`" it will fail, so who should take care of that? The mapping library or the programmer? This might result in an endless discussion, so let's leave it here; what's important is that you get the point that even a tiny thing that seems harmless can break your code, and you might realize it only when it's already in production. In this case, if you previously had a test that was checking for empty lists and gracefully accepting the failure, by changing the code to allow empty lists, that test would fail—not only from the acceptance point of view, but it would also result in an error. So as you can figure out, during regression you don't write new tests; you just run the previous ones against your new version. This is the reason why it is extremely important that you cover your code with as many meaningful tests as possible. Regression tests can be performed on any of the previous phases discussed in this section (Unit, Integration, System, or Acceptance); but in general, in our opinion they are mostly useful for Unit, Integration, and System Testing. Sometimes this kind of testing can be time- and resource-consuming, so make sure you are aiming at the right target—a bit contradictory from what we have said before, since every minor change might break your code, but nevertheless sometimes you will have to take some risks if you want to ship changes fast. One way to get past this problem is to invest in automation.

Automate everything! On every branch push, make the unit and integration tests run, have nightly builds running the system tests, and leave only what is not suitable for automation to human manual testing—for example, acceptance testing.

Who Is Testing What?

As much as there are different types of testing, there are different types of people who test. At this point we should answer the question: when does the testing start? As you might have guessed, considering that you have read the previous chapters, the testing of a product starts from the very early stages, sometimes even before the product exists. When we start defining our requirements and thinking about business goals and needs, we already know what we expect from the product's functionalities; therefore, we can imagine and define how it can be tested. Ideally the testing scenarios are defined before the implementation.

When product owners define the features and pass them to the developers, they can and should already define the acceptance criteria for each feature and the test case scenarios. So in the end of the implementation it is easy to test what has been done.

During and shortly after the implementation, the first line of defense is built by developers. Developers should guarantee that the code is covered by unit tests and that the feature is functioning as described by its acceptance criteria. Ideally, they should also implement some automated tools that check that none of the previous functionality is broken; unit tests already do the job, but it is important to check at least that the happy path is not broken.

Happy path is a full journey of the user through your product, imagining that no problem has occurred. So, for example, if it is an e-commerce platform, the happy path starts on the registration page and ends on the successful checkout page.

Some companies rely heavily on developers to do their testing and truly believe that they can guarantee the quality of the product because they can develop any automated solution for testing it. Thus, these companies don't have anyone besides developers testing their code. The developers write unit tests (probably some automated tests), product managers test the product for some happy path (maybe even in different browsers), and the testing is done.

However, we believe that the testing also should be done by people other than developers. Even if the developers are brilliant engineers, the mindset for testing a product relies on the will of breaking it. Remember those car tests—they are being exposed to real crashes. This is because when the car is out there, anything might happen to it; therefore it is important to test how it reacts to crashes and any other unexpected conditions. There is no difference between cars and the software we build. Once we ship it, it will run on a totally unknown road full of unexpected actions coming from our users. That is why to properly test it, we need to try hard to break it. It is better that we find breaches ourselves and fix them right away rather than our users running broken software. Well, with that being said, let me ask you a question. When you build something, how likely would you be willing to break it? Imagine IKEA furniture and imagine yourself spending the full weekend assembling it piece by piece, part by part. Would you be willing to break it? Would you be willing to hit it with hammer to see how reliable it is? Of course, you will not! Even if you are asked to do something harmful to your furniture to explore its reliability, you will do it with lots of care and love. Developers are doing the same with their code. It is very hard for a developer to apply any harmful actions to the code that they've been building with so much care and love. That is why we believe it is wrong to rely on developers to test their own work. That is why we belong to those old-school guys that believe that every team should have a dedicated Quality Assurance Engineer, or tester.

There are different kinds of testers. One of the simplest forms of testing the product is checking it manually. That is why we have manual testers.

Manual QA Tester

Manual testers are those who would spend time manually interacting with the product, trying to come up to scenarios where features can be broken. For example, consider the login form. A developer would probably test it by introducing the correct e-mail and password and clicking on the *"Login"* button, whereas a good tester would type any nonsense in the input field. Do you know this famous joke about a QA engineer?

A QA engineer walks into a bar. Orders a beer. Orders 0 beers. Orders 9999999 beers. Orders -1 beers. Orders asdqweqads beers.

Oh yes, good testers are amazingly creative. There is this guy we were lucky to work with that would come up with totally crazy scenarios. Sometimes he would come to us and say something like: So, I've typed this in the input field "*QWADASDasodjaioqwehyq2o239190q283qasdasd*", refreshed the page, clicked on the "back" button, and stopped the server at the same time, and then this error happened.

And you would just look at him with your eyes wide open and think: man, what have you just smoked? Can I also have it?

This guy, by the way, is managing a team of 10 QA engineers in one of the biggest startups in Berlin right now.

It feels good to have manual testers on your team, and that contributes to the overall quality not only because they are testing your software but also because developers start to write better code. Why is that? We will tell you a story. Once, Olga worked as a frontend developer on a team that had a manual QA engineer. Every time the engineer would go to Olga, saying: "**Olga, I have a question...**" Olga would start trembling because usually the statement that followed the question would contain a bug introduced by Olga's code. Olga wanted so hard to deliver the best quality possible just to not to hear this question again and again, so she not only would improve her coding techniques but also the overall processes within the team, such as code reviews and pair programming.

Automation QA Tester

Of course, manual checking is important; however, sometimes the tasks for the manual tester become very repetitive. This becomes pretty obvious and worrying when it comes to regression testing.

Just a reminder, **regression testing** relates to checking the essential functionalities that have to run every time a new feature is introduced to ensure that this feature hasn't broken anything. The tests for this feature are added to the suite of regression tests.

Imagine that you have a set of 10 regression tests, each of which takes 5 minutes to check. Imagine that you have to support two browsers: IE and Chrome. Let's not even discuss the versions of these browsers, focusing only on the latest versions. Thus, to fully test the application's functionality, you would need a bit more than 2.5 hours of manual testing. If it's a one-time only job, that's acceptable, but your product is not frozen in time—it's being developed and improved, and new features are being introduced. Therefore, regression would have to be run quite often, and with time it will become a big waste of resources. There are lots of things that can be automated in this process. For example, if we are dealing with web applications, we can write automated tests using frameworks that simulate the browser interaction and instruct them to check that as a result of some specific interaction, certain results must appear on the page.

Automation testers are those who define the scenarios and write these tests. Automation testers know how to write code, use frameworks, and leverage infrastructure to simulate live environments.

For example, the automation test for testing the login functionality could be written like the following:

```
open("/login");
$("input#login")).setValue("test@test.com");
$("button#login").click();
$("#username").shouldHave(text("Hello, test!")); // Waits until element
                                                    gets text
```

Depending on the framework that is being used for the automation tests, they can be written in several programming languages. It is common to use *Selenium* (https://www.seleniumhq.org/) as a framework for automated tests which is primarily written in Java. Therefore, there are a lot of automation testers that specialize in writing automated Selenium tests in Java. However, there are wrappers for selenium in different programming languages, including JavaScript. Sometimes they are even easier to use. It is quite easy to choose what to use—if you have a dedicated automation tester, give them the freedom to choose the language and the framework they are comfortable with. If your automation tests must be written by developers, then they will write them in a language of their choice. We've worked at companies that had dedicated QA engineers that were writing entire test suites in Java, whereas we have also worked at companies where frontend developers were responsible for writing automated, or the so called end-to-end, tests in JavaScript. Flexibility for the win!

From Manual to Automation Tester

How does a manual QA tester become an automation tester? Well, learn a lot. It is essential that you know how to write code. It is essential that you understand the basics on how web protocols (e.g., HTTP) work. It is important also to have basic understanding of infrastructure tools, scripts, servers, and databases. Ideally you first dive deeply into the testing mentality and then step by step you learn the basics of computer science and specialize yourself into automation.

There is another career path for manual testers though, and we've seen it happen quite often (Figure 7-1). Note that testers work closely with product managers to understand the requirements, define acceptance criteria, define different ways the product has to be tested to guarantee that all the supported browsers are covered, etc. Thus, with time, they develop a very sharp and good understanding of product, its caveats, growth strategy, goals, and needs. At some point in time, these people find themselves in product manager or product owner positions. So, if you are a manual tester, at some point in your career you might be presented with two possible directions: automation testing or product management. The decision will happen quite naturally, and you will not even notice it—if you are into tools, infrastructure, scripts, and tech, you will mostly choose automation tester path; if you enjoy processes, product development and improvement, definition of features, and product strategy, then you should definitely follow the product manager's path.

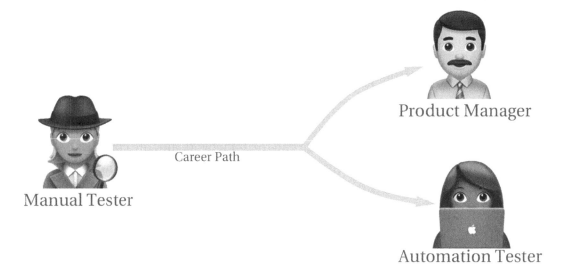

Figure 7-1. *Career path of a manual tester*

If you decide to follow the automation tester path, start digging into programming languages with focus on testing frameworks. Study the basic concepts of client-server architecture, communication protocols, and web and mobile tools that allow debugging and monitoring applications.

At some point you might decide to get some certifications. The most famous one for testers is called *ISTQB* (*International Software Testing Qualifications Board*; https://www.istqb.org/). This certification has different levels and sublevels. ISTQB certification centers exist worldwide and the exam should be paid. You might find plenty of online preparation resources. If you find this topic is interesting for you, we suggest that you use those preparation tools. Even if you decide not to go for a certification, it is a very good chance for learning, not only from the perspective of testing itself but also for understanding processes and standards used in the software development world.

Tools, Platforms, and Frameworks

There are many tools that can make the life of a QA tester easier. These range from tools that allow writing manual test specifications to complex frameworks to be used for writing code for automated tests.

Before we start discussing the tools for test management, let's discuss tools for task management because tests are associated to some development tasks.

One of the most famous task management platforms for agile software teams is JIRA (`https://www.atlassian.com/software/jira`). It is developed by Atlassian, and it is so powerful that we cannot even imagine what it cannot do. Figure 7-2 shows what a JIRA board looks like.

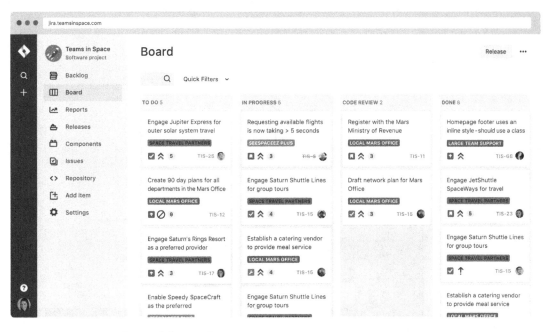

Figure 7-2. *JIRA board for task management*

Developers from all over the world love and hate JIRA. It is a big love because, as we already mentioned, it is very powerful and there is nothing that can't be done. At the same time, it is monstrous and quite complex to configure it properly given the needs. Sometimes you think that you introduce a small change that will affect a very specific part of the project configuration, and all of a sudden, every user becomes affected by your change! Or, you change a filter for the board, forget to change the privacy of the filter (it is not obvious that it should be changed), and the team is not able to see the board anymore. We had lots of interesting and funny stories related to managing JIRA. Some companies even invite external agencies to run workshops for the employees on how to use JIRA. However, it integrates with nearly everything, and lots of tools integrate with it, making it an obvious candidate. Sometimes using JIRA for small projects might seem that we are trying to kill a fly with a cannon, and for that we can use other simpler solutions. *Wunderlist* and *Trello*, for example, are very lightweight and easy-to-use tools. You can use them as web-based tools as well as standalone applications.

Figure 7-3 shows what Wunderlist looks like.

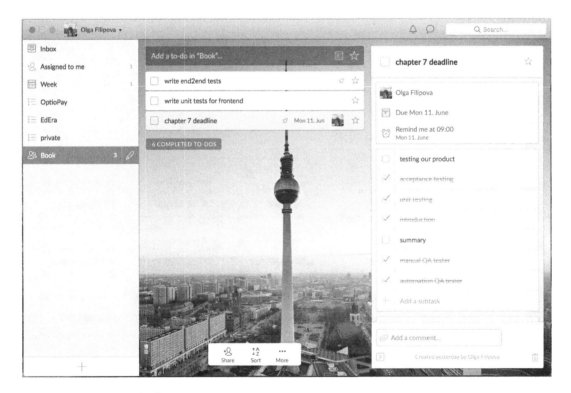

Figure 7-3. *Wunderlist*

Yes, this is the famous TV tower in Berlin in the background. The thing is, the application was developed by the Berlin-based startup called 6Wunderkinder. It was acquired by Microsoft, but it still continues to be a great and easy-to-use product.

What software to use to manage your tasks is up to you. What we can tell you is that tools like Wunderlist and Trello can be used for simple and not just software-related tasks, like "*buy bread*." Trello allows having multiple boards and teams; therefore, it can be used for more complex projects but still can be used for personal use. We don't know anyone who uses JIRA for small personal tasks. JIRA comes into the stage when you deal with big software projects developed within agile teams.

Now that we have a rough idea of what tools can be used for defining the tasks and features, let's talk about tools that can be used to define test cases.

Of course, you can write your test cases in a simple text file. You can also use some more structured editors like Excel. Or you can use some software specifically designed and built for the task. These tools help us to structure test cases, steps, and results. You can specify the release cycles and bind those tools to the continuous integration and continuous delivery pipeline. When you work on the test cases specification, you work closely with product managers and the development teams because the test case must reflect the business value and risks of the tested feature. The developers must be involved too, because they can provide valuable input on the amount of effort needed to implement some expected results or the impact on development if the feature doesn't behave as expected. Remember though, it is quite important that whatever you use for the test specification, you somehow integrate it with your task management tool; otherwise, it will be quite difficult to manage and to associate your tasks to the corresponding test cases. There is the possibility to specify a test case as a part of task, but then, when the task is DONE, the test will be also considered done, and you have to repeatedly run it as a part of the regression tests suite.

For JIRA there is a plugin called **Zephyr** (`https://bit.ly/2mpiThF`). This tool allows specifying tests, attaching them to the corresponding tasks, and running them whenever needed. Another similar tool is called testrail (`http://www.gurock.com/testrail/`). It's a web-based solution that seamlessly integrates with JIRA and provides all sorts of methods for dealing with your test scenarios, including all possible visuals like reporting and charts (Figure 7–4).

Modern test management for your team

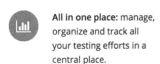

Manage all your testing efforts in a central place

Web-based on your own server or hosted by us

Modern user interface for a fast and productive team

All in one place: manage, organize and track all your testing efforts in a central place.

Web-based: easily access TestRail with your entire team – either hosted on your or our servers.

Modern interface: testing with a beautiful and highly productive user interface.

Figure 7-4. *Testrail (`https://bit.ly/1TrocHO`)*

Specifying test cases is not enough—someone needs to run those tests and tell the system when tests fail or pass. These tests can be defined and run manually rather than by manual QA testers or product owners. Some of the tests can be automated.

Of course, there are a lot of tools and frameworks to automate those, starting from those that require coding skills to those that can be implemented by product managers.

One of the most popular frameworks for UI testing and probably the first one you will hear if you step into this field is *Selenium*. Selenium is a set of tools developed in Java that allows executing all kind of web interaction using the Java programming language. One of these tools is a standalone Java server that allows connecting to any browser through a simple API. Another tool is the framework itself—a Java library that contains a vast range of commands to execute whatever you can imagine on the browser, starting from opening a browser on a specific URL and going further with clicking, hovering, typing, dragging elements, etc. As just a simple interaction with a browser is not enough, Selenium also provides several ways for us to check certain conditions to assert the tests. You can use any assertions library along with Selenium to assert whatever you need to assert. Let's consider, for example the **login** functionality. Consider that we want to assert that after a successful login, the user name appears in some specific box in the website header. For this test, we need to input the username and password, click on the button, and check for the text. Java code for this test using Selenium library will look like the following:

```
webDriver.findElement(By.cssSelector(("input[name=username]"))).
sendKeys(username);
webDriver.findElement(By.cssSelector(("input[name=password]"))).
sendKeys(password);
webDriver.findElement(By.cssSelector(".loginBtn")).click();
assertTrue(webDriver.findElement(By.cssSelector(".userbox")).getText().
contains(username));
```

A little bit cumbersome, but still readable. There are plenty of frameworks and wrappers that make your life easier. For example, there is a wrapper for Selenium called Selenide (http://selenide.org/). It wraps ugly huge chains of Selenium statements into both elegant and short human-friendly ones. The same test using Selenide could be written as follows:

```
$("input[name=username]").setValue(username);
$("input[name=password]").setValue(password);
$(".loginBtn").click();
$(".userbox").shouldHave(text(username));
```

Isn't it awesome?

You might prefer any other language for coding UI tests. There are selenium wrappers for lots of them. For example, for JavaScript there is a very nice and elegant solution called Nightwatch (http://nightwatchjs.org/). If you are a JavaScript developer, you don't need to step out of your comfort zone and use other programming languages for testing your UI. You can, and you should, use the same language to write both your code and your tests. The syntax of Nightwatch is very similar to Selenide.

To write the test for the login functionality using Nightwatch, you would do something like the following:

```
browser
  .setValue('input[type=email]', username)
  .setValue('input[type=password]', password)
  .click('.loginBtn')
  .assert('.userbox').toHaveText(username)
```

Who writes automated tests? As we already pointed out, sometimes there are dedicated automated QA engineers who implement automation, sometimes it has to be done by developers. Some companies invest in QA departments, other companies foster a culture of "developers being responsible for quality." We have seen QA departments composed of one member who would do everything—from manual testing to defining a complex infrastructure for running automated tests written by them every time a new release occurred. We have also seen quite big QA departments composed of manual testers, automated testers, release managers, and experienced infrastructure personnel. We have also seen no QA department at all—developers would write all the tests, and the infrastructure personnel would help set up the correct tools to run them every time they needed to run.

If there is no QA department and the team does not possess enough resources to write automated tests, product managers can use some visual tools that use Selenium (or any other frameworks) behind-the-scenes for UI testing. For example, **Katalon studio** (`https://www.katalon.com/`) is a powerful framework that allows recording browser interactions that can be replayed every time you need, asserting that the result of the run is the same as it was at the time of the recording. Another example is **Pingdom** (`https://www.pingdom.com/`). This tool is designed for website monitoring, and one of its features is called transactions monitoring (`https://www.pingdom.com/product/transaction-monitoring/`). This tool is not free, but it's simple to use. The downside, however, is that it only run tests in Chrome, and if you really need to run checks of your applications in other browsers, you will have to do that on your own.

Since we mentioned cross-browser testing, we have to talk about **Browserstack** (`https://www.browserstack.com/`). This is a powerful web-based tool for cross-browser and cross-device testing. It is not free, but it offers a vast range of possibilities, from manual testing using remote browsers to automated tests. Basically, you can write your automated UI tests using any Selenium framework and connect them to your

Browserstack account, specifying the platforms and browsers in which to run your tests. Another tool similar to Browserstack resource that is very popular nowadays is **Sauce Labs** (`https://saucelabs.com/`).

If you don't want to spend money and invest in Browserstack or similar tools for cross-browser testing, but you still need your tests to run in multiple browsers, you can set up **Selenium grid** by yourself. You will have to set up machines (physical or virtual) with operating systems and browsers you need to test your application. Then you will have to set up your Selenium server instance to serve as a hub that connects to these different machines. Ideally you have to configure some infrastructure that allows you to run all the tests on demand. This configuration requires some programming and DevOps experience. Usually it's done by experienced QA engineers or developers/DevOps personnel.

Figure 7-5 is a screenshot of a comparison of a couple of tools from a presentation that Olga did once for her frontend team so they could decide on what tool they could use for UI testing.

	Can be done by anyone	Easy to install and configure	Can be integrated in the CI/CD pipeline	Flexible	Easy to use	x-browser, x-device
Nightwatch + Selenium Grid	✗	✗	✓	✓	✓	✓
Nightwatch + browserstack	✗	✓	✓	✓	✓	✓
Pingdom	✓	✓	✗	✗	✓	✗
Katalon	✓	✗	✓	✓	✓	✓

Figure 7-5. *Comparison of different tools for run automated tests*

If you are not into hiring QA testers or allocating resources for testing, you can always decide to go for a "crowd-testing" platform, which is very popular nowadays. Basically, these platforms connect your applications to thousands of testers all over the world. You can register as a tester and spend your day clicking on buttons of different projects and filling out bug reports, or you can register as a business proprietary and tell what, how, and when you need the testing to be performed. Some examples of such platforms include test.io (`https://test.io/`) and rainforest QA (`https://www.rainforestqa.com/`).

As you can see, there are plenty of options out there. It doesn't really matter what you choose—what really matters is that you find a right balance between spending time and spending money on testing what is really important to test. It is important that you find bottlenecks and define exactly what needs to be automated and what can be tested manually. It is important that you assess all the risks and impact of different testing approaches. It is also really important that at least the happy path of your product never fails. This is what makes your users loyal to your product.

Testing Our Product

We have been discussing a lot about different types of testing and different people who participate in different types of testing. Enough discussing, we have some work to do. We have to test our platform. In the previous sections you have already checked how to create unit and integration tests for the backend module. Now let's cover some frontend code with unit tests, run some manual tests, and write some automated tests for our user interface. Remember, now you will be wearing the hat of a destroyer. Don't be gentle to your product—your main purpose is to break it!

Manual Testing

Manual testing of software happens quite often for frontend developers. While they are developing a new feature, they always check the page in the browser to see the result of their work. However, this is not a fair testing—as we have already mentioned, we developers test for the positive outcome and don't try to actually break what we have just done. So, if we are implementing, let's say a login page, we will for sure test if we can authenticate with the correct credentials, but it's unlikely that we start testing negative scenarios like "introducing invalid e-mail" or "clicking on the login button with the password field empty." That is why it is useful to delegate our manual testing to someone else, like product owners or a dedicated QA tester.

In our case, we were pretty lucky because a friend of ours is currently learning how to become a tester, and she happily agreed to test our platform. She is a real person whose name is Natalia, and she is currently working as a bank clerk and wants to switch to IT. She decided to embrace this journey by becoming a manual tester. She spent a couple of weeks reading some articles, talking to people who currently work as QA engineers, and learning the dynamics of this work, and now she is ready to get her hands dirty. So, we gave her a link that was pointing to the implementation we had at this stage and asked her to test the registration and login functionalities. The outcome of her testing was a test case specification sheet and a bug report. Let's have a look at them.

Test Cases

For the **login** and **registration** functionalities, Natalia decided to test a happy scenario—the case when all the fields were set correctly—and some negative scenarios—the cases where some fields were invalid (e.g., invalid e-mail format) or even empty. She wrote down the test title, test steps, and expected behavior. Also, and very important, she wrote down the operating system and the browser she used for tests. Specifying these things makes it easier for developers to later reproduce the bugs, as they might occur only under certain conditions. In a nutshell, Figure 7-6 shows how her test table looked.

Test Case # and Title	Test Steps	Expected Behaviour	Browser	Operating System
TC01 - Successful Register	Click on the "Register" button at the header of the page Fill in all mandatory fields Click on "Join us" button	The user is redirected to the dashboard page	- Google Chrome 66.0.3359.139 - Internet Explorer version 11 11.431.16299.0	Windows 10
TC02 - Preview password	Fill in the password field Click "Show" button	The user is able to see the introduced string	- Google Chrome 66.0.3359.139 - Internet Explorer version 11 11.431.16299.0	Windows 10
TC03 - Invalid email	Fill in invalid email Click on the "Login" button	Error message is displayed and the user is not logged in	- Google Chrome 66.0.3359.139 - Internet Explorer version 11 11.431.16299.0	Windows 10
TC04 - Log in with empty email	Click on "Login" button at the header of the page Keep email field empty Set password field Click on the "Login!" button	Error message is displayed and the user is not able to log in	- Google Chrome 66.0.3359.139 - Internet Explorer version 11 11.431.16299.0	Windows 10
TC05 - Log in with empty password	Click on the "Login" button at the header of the page Keep the password field empty Fill in the email field Click on the "Login!" button	User is not able to log in	- Google Chrome 66.0.3359.139 - Internet Explorer version 11 11.431.16299.0	Windows 10
TC06 - Successful Login	Click on the "Login" button at the header of the page Fill in all the mandatory fields in their valid form Click on the "Login!" button	User is successfully authenticated	- Google Chrome 66.0.3359.139 - Internet Explorer version 11 11.431.16299.0	Windows 10

Figure 7-6. *Test cases for login and register functionality*

Of course, you can come up with several other scenarios to test. It is up to you how deep you want to go with testing. It also depends on nature of your business. If we deal with highly sensitive banking applications that can attract fraudsters and hackers, then you need to think of all possible scenarios and their combinations. If you are creating an application for your friends that doesn't deal with any sensible data, then you can be more relaxed.

Bug Report

While trying to follow the steps described in her scenarios, Natalia found that some of the cases where not behaving as expected. Particularly, she realized that there was no feedback when incorrect data had been provided. She marked those test cases as red in her test case sheet and created a simple **bug report** (Figure 7-7).

Bug # and title	Test Case #	Steps to reproduce	Expected Behavior	Actual Behavior	Operating system and browser
B01 - No error message on invalid email	TC03	- click on the login button on top of the page - fill in email field with invalid email format (e.g. test.com) - click on the "Login!" button	The error is displayed to the user and the user is not able to login	No feedback at all, the user remains on the same page	Windows 10 IE 11 and Chrome 66
B02 - No error message on empty email	TC04	- click on the login button on top of the page - leave the email field empty - fill in the password field - click on the "Login!" button	The error is displayed to the user and the user is not able to login	No feedback at all, the user remains on the same page	Windows 10 IE 11 and Chrome 66

Figure 7-7. *Simple bug report for the login functionality*

Of course, if you use a specific software designed for creating test cases and bug reports, everything will be linked together, and it will be a lot easier for developers and product managers to follow up with bugs and transforming them into tasks. Bugs can and should be prioritized and their priority to be fixed depends as well on their severity and impact. Some bugs can be considered showstoppers—without fixing them, the system is not able to function. Some bugs are considered such a low priority that they just end up in the bottom of the backlog forever, the backlog purgatory. Some bugs are considered... *features*! This is unexpected, right? Actually, this is one of the favorite jokes of programmers. When they are approached by a product owner or a tester pointing out some bug, they say, "It is not a bug, it is a feature!" Sometimes it turns out to be true. Some accidentally introduced functionality turns out to be so awesome that it becomes a new feature. However, these are rare and happy cases; in most cases, bugs are just somehow harmful to the system.

When thinking of bugs' severity, always think of your users. How likely will they suffer if this bug will not be fixed? How likely will they stop using your service?

For example, if I have an alarm clock application and the snooze functionality is broken, I will probably survive without it (actually, in some cases, we can consider this kind of bug an actual feature since it will make us on time for our appointments).

However, if the functionality of ringing will be broken at all, then I would stop using this app.

Unit Tests for the Frontend

You are already familiar with the concept of unit tests. Actually, you've seen them already—when you were reading the backend development chapter. Now we will take the code in the "before_frontend_tests" folder as the base and implement some unit tests on the frontend application. We will use mocha as a test runner and expect as an assertion library. All you have to do is install them using npm or yarn:

```
cd courses/frontend
npm install --save-dev mocha-webpack mocha expect

    // or

yarn add --dev mocha-webpack mocha expect
```

The next step is to add test script to our `package.json`:

```
// package.json
{
  <...>
  "scripts": {
    "dev": "nuxt",
    "build": "nuxt build",
    "start": "nuxt start",
    "generate": "nuxt generate",
    "test": "mocha-webpack --require tests/setup.js tests/unit/**/*.spec.js"
  },
  <...>
}
```

Now let's add the basic setup for tests and let's start adding them. Create a folder named tests and create a setup.js file:

```
// tests/setup.js
global.expect = require('expect')
```

Let's create a test example. Create a file called test.spec.js in the tests/unit folder. Add a fake test there:

```
describe('test', () => {
  it('should run test', () => {
    expect(1).toEqual(1)
  })
})
```

A lot of testing frameworks in JavaScript offer similar syntax. Use the function describe to specify a big test suite for some unit of code. Then use the function it that accepts the small test specification and the test function itself. The test function calls some parts of the unit being tested and asserts some results. Let's, for example, cover with unit tests the methods of the getters module of the Vuex store:

```
// store/getters.js
import { find } from 'lodash'

export default {
  courses: state => state.courses,
  isAuthenticated: state => !!state.token,
  auth: state => state.auth,
  user: state => state.user,
  course: state => find(state.courses, { id: state.courseId }) || {},
  userCourse: state => state.userCourse,
  userCourses: state => state.courses.filter(course => course.enrolled ===
  true)
}
```

These methods are easy to test because we can pass them the state object, and according to what we pass we can expect some specific result. For example, for the isAuthenticated method, if we pass the state object without a token, the method should return false, and if we pass the state object with the token then the method should return true:

```
// tests/unit/store/getters.spec.js
describe('isAuthenticated', () => {
  it('should return false if token doesnt exist', () => {
    expect(getters.isAuthenticated({})).toBeFalsy()
  })
  it('should return true if token exists', () => {
    expect(getters.isAuthenticated({token: 'asd'})).toBeTruthy()
  })
})
```

Check the code in the after_frontend_tests folder. We've covered almost all the methods of the Vuex getters. If we run the tests using npm test or yarn test, we will get the output on the console should in Figure 7-8.

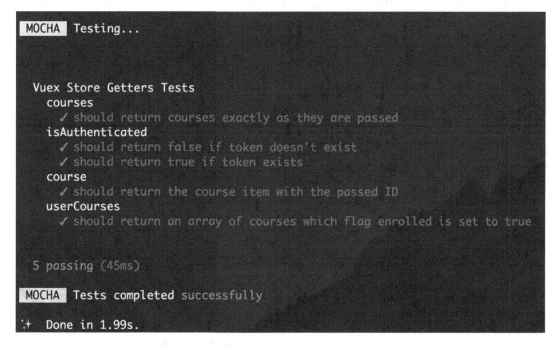

Figure 7-8. Running Vuex store getters unit tests

Isn't it nice to see those green check marks? Olga loves them!

Ideally, we should have written some end-to-end tests, but we will work on them after we have a more stable UI. You, however, are more than welcome to use Nightwatch or any other tool to define some UI tests.

Summary

In this chapter we have discussed how important it is to test our software, so our users are never frustrated with whatever we offer them. We discussed different types of testers out there and different kind of tests. We discussed about bugs, their severity, and their priority. We hope you do realize at this moment that there is no bug-free software in the world. All applications, systems, and products have some bugs. Some products have obvious bugs that prevent us from using them, some have hidden small bugs that we are not even aware about. The process of hunting bugs can be both challenging and fun. The process of finding the reason of the bug can be tedious and frustrating. Sometimes we spend a couple of days trying to figure out why some bug happens, and then we realize that it is just a stupid typo that can be fixed in seconds! Sometimes we know exactly why the bug is happening, but to fix it we would need a whole week. Every time we write code we potentially introduce new bugs. That is why it is so important to have testing processes in place and to have it as well-defined and automated as possible.

TEST YOURSELF

- What is a bug in the software development world?

  - An insect that bites computer cables

  - A small fly that bites programmers and prevents them from working

  - A malfunction in system that prevents it from working as expected

  - Actual behavior of the feature against the expected behavior

- You open a test case scenario and follow the steps that you have described before: you open a web page, click on the button that says, "join us!," fill in the form, click another button, and check that the next page displays a success message. You are:

  - a product owner

  - an automation tester

There is no correct answer for the second question. Of course, the described actions are usually performed by a manual tester, but if there is no manual tester in the team, it can be anyone! Even an automation tester.

The only correct answer for the third question is that the function should be covered by unit tests.

The fourth question is tricky, and it actually depends on many factors. Sometimes you have to be really strong to tell everyone, "IT SHALL NOT PASS!" Because if the system goes live with some critical bugs, in the end you will be responsible for it, because you've let it pass. However, sometimes due to some business goals, the bug can actually go to production and the user should be aware of it. So, all the answers except the one that says, "Who cares about Internet Explorer?" can be applied.

If you had similar thoughts during this test, then congratulations! You've successfully worn the hat of a software tester!

It's great that now we know how to test our software, but it would be even better if we could be relaxed and not even thinking about it. It would be great if every time we updated our product, the tests automagically would just run by themselves. It also would be great if instead of running our platform locally on our machines, we could see it in action by opening some nice URL. And what if on every change we could just push a button and then the page would be updated, live, and the tests would be run? Would it be magic? Actually, it would be a reality. We will learn in the next chapter how to build this reality. Chapter 8 is devoted to DevOps, infrastructure, continuous integration, and continuous delivery. You will learn how to go live with your product and how to automate the process of going live. Isn't it exciting? Let's go!

- a manual tester

- a developer

- Anyone from the above

- Anyone from the above, but less likely automation tester

- Your code has a function that sums up two numbers. This function is a perfect candidate to be:

  - Tested against SQL injection

  - Covered by unit tests

  - Tested against some performance benchmarks

  - Manually tested in the browser

- Today is a big day! We are releasing the final version of our product. The release has already been announced, and all the customers are looking forward to it. You are running the final stage of your regression tests suite. Everyone in your team—especially developers and product managers—are excited waiting for your green light, and all of a sudden you realize that the tests are failing on Internet Explorer. After digging a bit, you conclude that the login functionality is broken on IE. Your actions:

  - Create a bug report, stop the release process, tell product manager that the release cannot be shipped until the bug is fixed.

  - Who cares about Internet Explorer? This is not even a browser. Let's move forward with the release!

  - Check the share of IE users; if it's not too high, let's release. If it's more than 10%, let's fix the bug first.

  - Release it, but write in the release notes that there is a known bug in IE. Fix it as soon as possible and release a minor version.

The correct answer for the first question is "A malfunction in system," but actually the word bug appeared due to an insect that screwed up some circuits, therefore introducing a malfunctioning into the system.

CHAPTER 8

Let's Go Live!

In the previous chapter we discussed different testing techniques for our software product. We used different approaches to test our learning platform and we can tell now: ok, our product is implemented and tested, we're done. Just kidding.

First, our product is not yet ready, it still needs a lot of our attention and love, and second, it cannot be considered "ready" if we cannot show it to anyone. How do you show it? Right now, the only way you can show your work to your friends is by inviting them to your place, opening your webpage directly on your computer's browser, and making a small presentation of what you've done. For sure your friends will adore it! But... what if you want to make your work available for more than your friends who can come to your place? How do all these websites end up in the global network, and how can we access them just by typing some nice address in the browser's bar like "`www.google.com`"? If we manage to publish our product and then change something, how are these changes propagated? If we find some bug and fix it, how do we make the fix immediately available online? How do we guarantee that our tests pass before publishing the changes to the world? How do we know if our product is being used? How do we know if our product is up and running? If there is more than one person working on the source code of our software, how is its synchronization guaranteed?

These and many other questions will be answered in this chapter, which is devoted to the infrastructure and tools needed for keeping the code synchronized, tested, published, and up to date. We will also talk about the magicians who stand at the helm of these responsibilities. You will wear the hat of each of these characters and you will feel amazing and powerful.

© Olga Filipova and Rui Vilão 2018
O. Filipova and R. Vilão, *Software Development From A to Z*, https://doi.org/10.1007/978-1-4842-3945-2_8

How to Publish Your Software Project?

Now that you have implemented your web project, it is more than expected that you want to publish it. To make it available to the world, you have to run it somewhere and make it discoverable. You already know how to run the project, right? You have implemented a simple server and you are able to serve html pages with it. What does it mean to make it discoverable?

To be discoverable is to simply be accessible from any computer connected to the global network.

How do we make our pages accessible on the network? The machine on which you run your project has an address, just like your apartment or house. This address is called IP address, and this is how other machines connected to the network can find yours. Usually when you run your application, you have to specify a port to run it. The port is like a house number in building. In the case of our platform, the port is 8080. Now the full address of your application will be the IP address of your machine followed by the port—for example, 172.20.10.4:8080. If you give this address to your friends, they will be able to see your application from the outside.

Yeah, that's beautiful, but you don't want your computer to be on 24/7 just so your friends can access your application, do you? Also, what about the URL? Would you be able to remember and keep in mind the IP addresses of your favorite websites? Of course not, and besides the IP addresses change from time to time for private contracts! You want to give some meaningful name to your friends and you want to run your application on some other machine that is not yours!

Let's start by hosting your service somewhere that is not your personal computer. First, you can buy a dedicated machine and install it at your home. It will be your own *bare-metal server*.

A bare-metal server is a dedicated physical machine that serves the needs of one tenant only. The term has been introduced to distinguish physical machines used for hosting internet services from their virtual and cloud friends.

Keep in mind that if you want to run something on your own server, you have to have a really powerful internet connection that never fails. You have to be sure that the machine's IP address is fixed, and you have to be sure that you make an investment considering your needs. Remember that you might need your service to scale—with time you might need to have more space, more memory, or more power.

You might also host you service on cloud services. You have plenty of them; one of the most used is AWS (Amazon Web Services) —there you can pay for a virtual server, connect to it, and run your services there. You have Digital Ocean, Microsoft Azure, Google Cloud services, IBM cloud solutions, etc. Only lazy corporations don't offer cloud and virtual solutions nowadays.

After you decide where to host your service you can decide on how to name it. The top-level names to be used on the internet must be paid for and after you buy them you can easily connect them to the IP address where your application is running. The services that sell names for web services to be discovered on the global network are called DNS providers.

DNS means Domain Name System, and it is basically the system that maps meaningful names to IP addresses, making them discoverable and accessible in the global network.

DNS providers enable people to buy the names they want and map them to the services they need for business purposes as well as just private. The cost varies according to the name's simplicity, easiness to memorize, and top-level domain kind.

Top level domain is the last segment of the domain name (something that appears after the name: .com, .edu, .org, etc.)

There are different DNS providers out there. The one that we use is called GoDaddy (`https://www.godaddy.com`).

There are several other options: cloudflare (`https://www.cloudflare.com/dns`), ClouDNS (`https://www.cloudns.net/`), freeDNS (`https://freedns.afraid.org/`), namecheap (`https://www.namecheap.com/domains/freedns.aspx`), a free DNS provider called ... 1984 (`https://www.1984hosting.com/product/freedns/`), etc. The last one's name is a bit scary we must admit, but in the times we live in with easy data access—Facebook, Google, and others alike—at least this name seems accurate.

As we pointed out already, the prices of domain names can vary. Let's search, for example, for the domain name "**nice**" on GoDaddy (Figure 8-1).

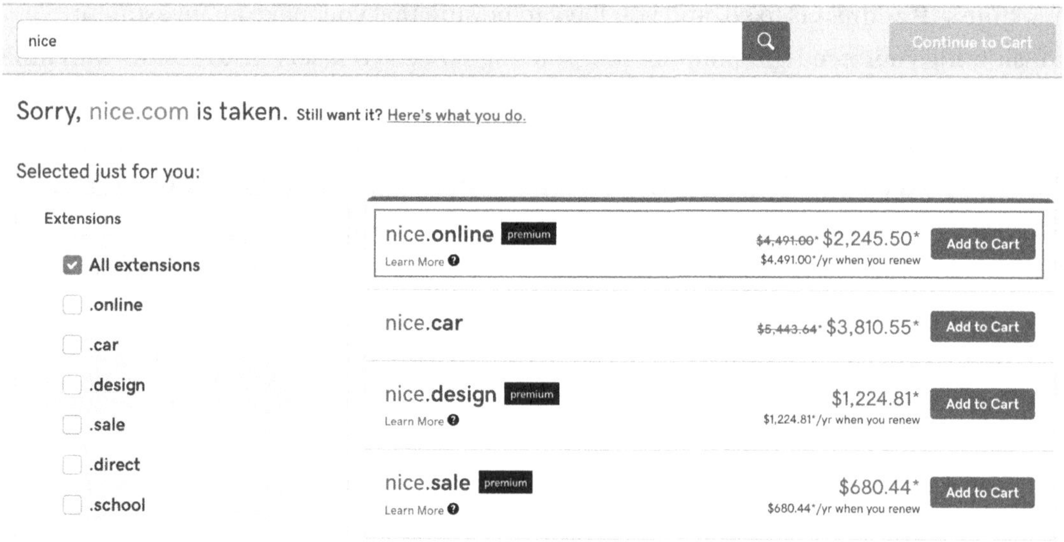

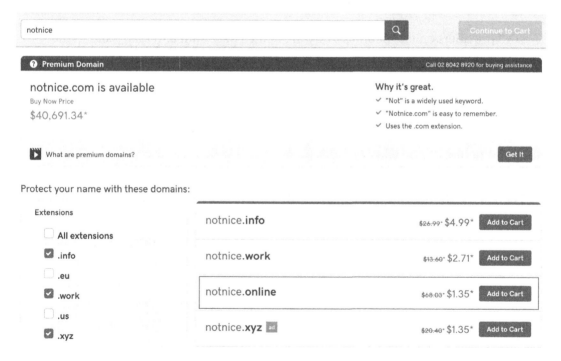

Figure 8-1. *The price for the domain nice.online*

As you can see, it's not very cheap.

Let's see what happens if we look for the domain "**notnice**" (Figure 8-2).

Figure 8-2. *The price for the domain notnice.online*

Wow, a bit cheaper, right?

If you decide to buy a domain for your web service, before discussing what names sound nice, check the availability and price on the DNS providers websites.

After you have bought your domain name, you have to connect it to the IP address of the host where you run your service. Both host and domain provider provide clear instructions on how to do that. Then just type the name in the browser and access your service!

If all of this sounds a bit complex to you, don't worry, there are plenty of services that can make your life easier.

For example, wix (`https://www.wix.com/`) offers you a journey from a simple drag-and-drop website creation to the domain registering. You build your website on the fly, you register it, and it becomes immediately available on the network.

Another similar service is squarespace (`https://www.squarespace.com/`). It also allows creating websites where you can choose from hundreds of stunning templates and immediate register your domain.

If you still want to build your service by yourself but would like to automate somehow the hosting part, so you don't have to manually copy and paste your files to the server every time you change them, you can use one of the automated solution like AWS (`https://aws.amazon.com/`), heroku (`https://www.heroku.com/`), Google cloud (`https://cloud.google.com/`), Google firebase (`https://firebase.google.com/`), etc. These services provide you with a simple command line interface that enables an easy way of deploying your service with just a set of few commands.

When Do We Start Thinking About Deployment?

If you were paying enough attention in the previous chapters and if you are good in drawing parallels, you might already know the answer to this question.

Of course, we have to start thinking about deployment at the very start of implementation. You need to know how your service will integrate with whatever deployment tool you'll be using. This means that you have to prepare the needed infrastructure in advance, so whenever your code is ready to be shipped, you can ship it on the click of a button.

Of course, when you start writing code, there is nothing to deploy. The first deployable version will probably take some time to be ready. So how can you prepare everything in advance? Simulate the environment; pretend everything is ready. You have an idea of your architecture and how things will interact with each other (e.g., the underlying database, backend and frontend). Create mocks of these things and put them online. Make sure it works. Improve the process of deployment until it is 100% or close to 100% automated. There are plenty of tools that can help you with this. Once you have your automated process of deployment, you are the king of your code. You know for sure that once you change your code, you can easily make it live.

However, you have to be sure that all the tests pass before deploying it. You have to also be sure that if you are not the only one working on the code, the code from multiple developers is easily integrated. This whole process should also be automated. The automated process of integrating multiple users code in the same codebase and running tests and other code checks before the deployment is called **Continuous Integration**.

Go one step further: besides the integration and automated tests, prepare your code to be shipped to production, and you will have **Continuous Delivery** in place. Deploy the result of your Continuous Delivery automatically to your hosting platform—voilà, you have your **Continuous Deployment** as well! If you want to be fancy, you can abbreviate all the continuous integration and continuous deployment process as **CI/CD** (if I had a rock band, I would probably call it that).

There are plenty of tools ready to help you to set up your continuous magic process, but before discussing them let's first think about the code itself. Where should we put it, so it can be easily checked, tested, deployed, and delivered? It is quite evident that just a folder on our computer is not enough for that job.

Where Do I Put My Code?

In the previous section we concluded that in order to be able to continuously run the automated process of software integration, building, and deployment, it's not enough for our code to live on our machine. There should be some centralized place where everyone who is involved in development can get the code at any time and where the code can be updated once it's changed.

Let's think. How should this place look? Maybe Dropbox or Google drive? Or some other cloud service, like iCloud? Well, it could be. It is centralized, you can share the access with relevant people, and you can access files, change them, delete them, and add new ones. That's true. Let's try to imagine the following scenario: you and your friend start working on some file at the same time. Both of you access your cloud, download the file, and start working. You're done with your changes first, so you upload the file. The file is replaced. After a while your friend is also done and also uploads the file, and the file is replaced again. This new version of the file will not contain your changes. Oops! Imagine another scenario—you work on your file alone. You introduce some changes, replace the file, introduce more changes, replace the file again, introduce more changes, and replace the file again. All of a sudden you realize that the system is broken. What exactly broke it? How do you revert the file? How do you check which of the three recent versions was working? Boromir has an answer to this question (Figure 8-3).

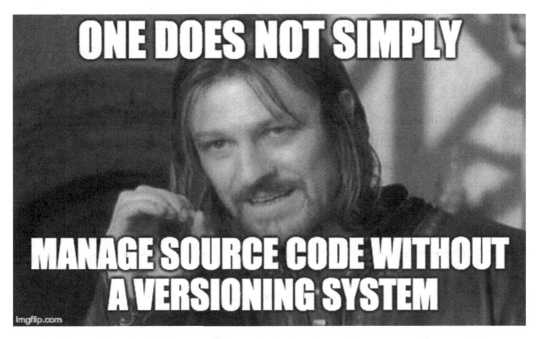

Figure 8-3. *One does not simply manage source code without a versioning system*

Boromir is right, as usual. To be able to control code versions, we need something more than just a centralized cloud system. We need a version control system. And they exist! They are called **SCM (Source Code Management** tools) or **VCS (Version Control Systems)**.

There are plenty of them: SVN (Apache Subversion; `https://subversion.apache.org/`), GIT (`https://git-scm.com/`), mercurial (`https://www.mercurial-scm.org/`), etc.

Among developers, GIT is the most popular one. It allows managing the source code using a set of simple yet powerful commands. For example, to create a git repository on a given folder, you would run "`git init`". To pull the recent changes, you run "`git pull`" command. To add new files, you would run "`git add`". Once you change some files and you are satisfied with those changes, you have to commit them; then you run "`git commit`", providing a meaningful commit message stating what you've changed. Once you are ready to share your committed changes with the rest of the team, you push them running "`git push`" command.

Every commit has an associated hash, and you can revert your code to any commit at any time. If your colleague is working on the same file, git will make sure that all the changes end up in the repository. If the changes are conflicting—imagine that you've changed the same line of code as someone else—git will warn you and ask you to solve those conflicts before the repository can be in a consistent state again.

You can use this visual tool to train your git practices: `http://git-school.github.io/visualizing-git/`.

Tip   Every time you work on a piece of code, make sure that you always work on the most updated version and that you commit and push your changes quite frequently. This will allow you to avoid conflicts.

Ok, running git commands sounds cool, but where exactly does the code live? There still should be some cloud service where the code resides so everyone is able to access it. That's true! There are lots of solutions for maintaining your git repositories.

Bitbucket (`https://bitbucket.org/`), gitlab (`https://about.gitlab.com/`), and github (`https://github.com/`) are among the most popular ones. We use github since it provides lots of useful tools and integrations for CI/CD.

GitLab is now gaining popularity as well, since it enables a set of features with the mindset on the DevOps side. All the CI/CD pipeline is already integrated in this tool, so you don't need to integrate it with anything else, and its frontend is written in Vue.js, of which Olga is a huge fan!

Continuous Integration and Automated Tests

We've already discussed how to continuously integrate our code with Git so you can be sure all your changes are carefully stored and versioned! Let's now talk about checking your code every time you push it. In the previous chapter, you've learned how to write different kinds of tests. Let's see now how we invoke those tests to run automatically when we push our code to our VSC.

Let's remember one thing: the tests usually run because we invoke some command, right? For example, in the previous chapter we wrote some unit tests for the backend, and to run them we would invoke the `mvn clean test -Ptest` command.

In the frontend app, we had unit tests that would run with the `npm test` command and end-to-end tests that would run with the `npm run e2e` command.

You can include other checks—for example, checks for code quality, test coverage, specific code guidelines like maximum number of lines of code per file etc.

You can configure thresholds for those checks and define commands to verify all of that (Figure 8-4).

Figure 8-4. *There are hundreds of code quality metrics that can be checked!*

Check all the things, but first identify those that are critical for your kind of business!

"*Ok, so I define some commands to check my critical things, now what?*" you might ask.

Now somehow you should tell your system to run these commands. When do you run them? It's up to you to decide. You can, for example, create a `pre-commit` hook that will run all the checks before you commit your changes. Or, it can be a `pre-push` hook. However, both `pre-commit` and `pre-push` hooks will run on your local machine, which will slow down your development process if there are many checks.

Usually, you locally run the most critical checks—for example, unit tests—and leave other quality checks for your continuous integration tool.

There are plenty of tools out there. They easily integrate with GitHub or any other Git hosting platform, detect new commits, run checks on them and get notified in case of failure.

One of the tools is Travis CI (`https://travis-ci.org/`). This is the one we are using for our courses platform. Basically, you connect to the TravisCI platform, use its interface to connect it to your GitHub repository, and create a configuration file for travis to know which commands should run to check your code's sanity.

Another good tool that easily integrates with GitHub is CircleCi (`https://circleci.com/`). It's very similar in its set up and configuration to TravisCI.

A very good old platform that has been used for ages by generations of developers is Jenkins (`https://jenkins.io/`). It is a bit ugly and cumbersome but really powerful, and there is no thing you can't do with it.

If you want to feel like a geek, you can use ConcourseCI (`https://concourse-ci.org/`). This tool is also configured using a yaml configuration file and provides you with a fancy visualization of the build pipelines.

It's up to you what to use. We prefer TravisCI or CircleCI because they easily integrate with GitHub and have a user-friendly interface. The learning curve for using these tools is minimal which allows you having a basic setup for your continuous integration in minutes.

Continuous Delivery and Deployment

We have already discussed that all the checks you run on each push together with the build and packaging for deployment define your continuous delivery. In the previous section, we discussed how to set up your CI tool in order to run all the checks; the only thing missing for having your continuous delivery in place is to tell the CI tool to prepare the code to be shipped to production.

Preparing the code to be shipped means different things, depending on the case. For example, if it's just a bunch of HTML, JavaScript, and CSS files that have to be copied over to some web server, then they are probably already production-ready.

However, if you use some frameworks or preprocessors, you might want to run some commands to transpile your code into a regular HTML+CSS+JS. For example, in our case we used Vue.js. In order to be ready for production, we have to transform all the Vue files into plain JavaScript files. Since our app was created using the Vue webpack boilerplate, which comes with a set of predefined commands, we can use the command "npm run dist" to prepare the code for distribution.

Therefore, we would have to tell to our CI/CD tool to run this command.

In case of a Java project, we know that we have to compile our server using the mvn clean install command. So, in order to cover the continuous delivery, we need to specify in our configuration file all the needed commands that will transform our code into runnable artifacts.

The only thing missing now is the deployment. Once you have built all your application files, you can deploy them. "*To deploy*" can also mean different things depending on which form of hosting your application uses. If it's just about copying your files over to some remote server, then you might tell your CI/CD tool to copy over SCP (secure copy protocol) the files generated by the build. In our case, since we are using Heroku, we don't need to copy anything, as Heroku provides also a building functionality. Thus, in our case, after Travis successfully verifies the tests so we can tell Heroku that the code can be built and deployed.

There are plenty of possible scenarios. You might delegate the building process to the hosting machine or service using the CI/CD tool just for triggering the process. For example, it is common to use Git for this purpose—the hosting machine has access to the Git repository and contains all the needed scripts to build and copy the files to where they should belong in order to run. Once the process is triggered, the hosting machine will pull the latest changes, build the files and copy them to the server's folders. This requires some manual work from you in order to set up everything correctly, but it works if you don't want to trust third-party services to do this job for you.

There are a lot of disputes about whether or not to deploy automatically once all the checks are passed. Some people prefer having a button to approve the pushing to production. We tend to agree with this approach. Sometimes it is too risky to have automated deploys on each push, especially when you have lots of users that rely on your service. Even with everything being automated and checked, we are still humans and we make mistakes! We don't want to accidentally roll something to production like this nice dung-beetle on telegram sticker (Figure 8-5).

Figure 8-5. *Telegram sticker that says "Rolled out to production"*

What is usually done is that you have a staging environment very similar to the production one. Then you tell your CI/CD tool to continuously deploy to this environment, and after you check manually that everything is nice and good, you push the button that will deploy to production. All the CI/CD tools enable somehow this approach. It is called "*promoting to production.*" This way it is not fully automated, but the effort of pushing to production equals a click of a button, which is perfectly acceptable.

Who Does What and How?

We discussed so many different things in the previous sections—setting up a CI/CD process, preparing the infrastructure to have multiple environments, writing scripts to run all the checks, pushing the button... Who is responsible for what? Who decides when to push which button? Who is responsible for defining a process?

Actually, everyone is responsible. On a good team everyone feels responsibility and takes ownership for the product and the process that helps ensure this product's quality.

When you start, most likely you can't afford to have special people for dealing with infrastructure and CI/CD processes, so the developers will have to implement the necessary steps to guarantee the automation of the delivery steps. Once your product is solid and the size of the development team is considerably big, you can think of having dedicated people to deal with all of those. These people can have different names—**DevOps** (development and operations engineers), **infrastructure team**, **security engineers**, **SRE (site reliability engineers**) —all these people are specialized in connecting *development* with the *operations* needed for maintaining your product in a healthy state and automating this process as much as possible.

We saw lots of different scenarios. For example, when we started working at Feedzai, we were a pretty small team. We didn't have CI/CD in place and our product was a standalone package that we would ship to our clients under a paid license. Therefore, we had 2-month release cycles, and in the end of each release we would ship executables for different platforms along with the release notes.

At Gymondo, where Rui works, we have both CI and CD, with automatic deployments for test and stage environments and ready to release to production with a set of simple manual steps to achieve zero downtime.

Where Olga works (OptioPay), we ship pretty often; once the feature code is reviewed, approved, and the tests are run, we click the button to promote it to production. Therefore, we don't have dedicated release dates, which we regret sometimes because we think that celebrating releases is healthy for the team spirit.

We think that the perfect scenario would be to ship fast and often but have some special "release" dates when you can say, "Hey, we've released this, this, and that. Let's celebrate!" And while you're deploying your new features to production, don't forget to play this song out loud: `https://soundcloud.com/the-avid-capitalz/the-avid-capitals-we-are`. This will give you a crazy happy mood.

Interview With DevOps

Of course, talking about DevOps guys without talking to one of them doesn't make much sense. That's why we have decided to have a conversation with a friend of ours named Anderson (Figure 8-6). He works for Zendesk, and he's a pretty good magician in his field. We had a Skype conversation with him and transcribed it for you. Enjoy!

Anderson Goulart • 2nd

Sr. Ops Engineer at Zendesk - CSM/ITIL

Ireland

Z Zendesk

m Universidade Federal de Minas Gerais

See contact info

500+ connections

From a mid-manager over 300 people, 500 apps and 5000 nodes, to a devops role within a small company and great engineers made me learn how we can change the business with simple steps, delivering better infrastructure, better customer experience and more time for everyone.

Plan, design, implement, scale, secure, monitor and automate infrastructure services to support portals, web and mobile applications, authentication systems, databases, clustered and distributed systems are the challenges that I look for my career. In essence, how can I help organizations to grow, enable faster innovation and manage costs through an automated process.

Figure 8-6. *Anderson's Linkedin profile (so you know he is a real person!)*

Olga: Hey Anderson, so I was told that you are a great DevOps professional. Can you tell us in a simple manner what are you doing and what it means to be a DevOps?

Anderson: There was a lot of struggling in the past between the developers and the operations guys. They could not talk to each other clearly and essentially to find a common ground. There is a lot of culture on how we can effectively develop a software and run this software in production with great efficiency, and that's all about DevOps—bringing developers and operations together and making sure we can create a pipeline doing the development until we get the software in production.

Olga: Ok, so it's basically to make the path from development to production easier. It means that it has an actual impact on the whole business, if something goes wrong the whole business might suffer...

Anderson: Yes, you are right. If something goes wrong in between... Imagine a factory and you are building a car and you have all these stages to build a car. You get the materials, you start building a car, and in the end, you have a car.

So, with software I think it is kind of the same, but it's a text that you write, so developers write a piece of text that must run in a computer or a set of computers.

So, while you are developing that software there are a lot of stages that need to be created and have quality gates to make sure that the software that goes into production meets the quality requirements.

We know perfect software doesn't exist in our world, most of the software have thousands of bugs, but at least you know that most of the bugs you face are not going to have an impact on our users.

So, the DevOps culture is to think how we can shift the feedback loop to the developers as fast as possible, because if something seems wrong and you can fix it straightaway, it's the easiest way and the one with the lowest cost as well. Finding a bug in production poses costs to any organization since it will impact our users.

So, we are talking about software delivery, delivering software faster, with faster feedback for developers, testers, or operations and thus reducing the number of bugs in production.

Olga: That sounds pretty important for the company to have professional people doing this. Could you describe us how did you become a DevOps? I am not sure if there are some courses specifically designed to be a DevOps engineer, so somehow people do some career path until they reach the DevOps role... How was yours?

Anderson: Nowadays there are some certifications for DevOps—for instance, *Amazon AWS* has a DevOps certification so you can even learn how to become a DevOps engineer. Answering your question, you mix a bit of **development** and **operations**, so I graduated in computer science, so I had all the background of software engineering but for the most part my experience was based on system administration, but I also have friends that came straight from software engineering.

So, you are a software developer and you start running your software in your computer, but you realize that your computer is not as complex as your production environment is, so people get interested on how they can deploy that software in production. My career started as a system administrator long time ago. Just like anyone else, I was a *Linux administrator*, I knew everything about operating systems, computer networks, managing all the servers, firewalls, proxies, web servers, application servers such as Apache nginx... So, a lot of technologies involved.

After a while I started realizing that operators just like me didn't use code to manage the infrastructure, so usually it was all manual or via a bunch of ad-hoc scripts, so if you need to set up a web server you need to SSH into a machine and type whatever command needed and make sure it works. The problem with that is that it doesn't scale, so I started learning more about software engineering, so I can create my own tools to support the deployment and strategy for the organization.

So, it's about *automating the entire process of provisioning an infrastructure and deploying applications that will run in that infrastructure*. So that is my career path, but to be honest you can become a DevOps engineer if you are a software engineer or if you are a system administrator. Of course, you might have more skills on one specific side of the dev or the ops so you naturally become a devops by learning and complementing the side you know less, so it's really important to have both sides on the table.

Olga: Imagine some of our readers or students decide to become a DevOps engineer but do not have a computer science background or have never done anything system administration-related. Is there anything they can do to become DevOps engineers, like courses and so on, or do you think they should just go and study hardcore computer science?

Anderson: You can be a DevOps engineer without a computer science degree— for example, if you want to follow a certification path, what Amazon suggests is that you have three fundamental certifications that include *development*, *operations*, and *architecture*. So, after you have those you can get the certification to become a DevOps professional.

Even though those certifications are based on their own AWS services, if you learn the principles of everything DevOps-related, I believe you can get there. AWS is not the only option on the market, but it is definitely a good start.

Olga: From your personal experience, can you tell us some major issue you had to work on, something that had a huge impact on the product or company and how you managed to solve it?

Anderson: This is actually what DevOps is addressing... Few years ago I was changing a machine in production, the machine was responsible for the entire authentication system of the university, so every teacher or any professor that had to access any resource they had to authenticate, and the authentication server, was managed by me.

So, I was happily upgrading the authentication system to a new machine; everything was going fine, but without any automation at all, changing all the configuration scripts and files manually in the machine using a terminal, and suddenly I realized I had a meeting with my boss and I was already late to the meeting, so I rushed to restart the server, and shutdown the old server, but instead I shutdown the new one.

So, the system went down, and with it the entire university for about an hour. Everyone was calling asking what was going on, why the system was down, and so on, and I was already at the meeting when another professor came in and asked what was happening; did we do some changes, maybe in the authentication system? I was like, "Oops..."

So, the moral of the story is that *if you don't have automation, you are more likely to make mistakes*. I had at that time maybe four terminals open with the configuration, and even though I knew what I was doing, if you type a command in the wrong window or something, you can run into problems.

So, by having a good automation mechanism, you don't touch any of the servers, you have a pipeline, an automated process that will go through all these steps and will execute all the tasks that need to be executed and will make sure that in the end you will get the expected result.

All these processes follow the DevOps pipeline, the same principles as any other software development mechanism, you have to check your code against a testing system similar to production, you have code reviews with your colleagues, you have to push this code to testing machines first, and only then you are able to push your code to production. I believe the biggest change from before came when they started to develop a concept called "*Software Defined Infrastructure*", so basically how can we as infrastructure guys define our infrastructure not only doing manual commands inside a router or a Linux machine but using software code. You write software to describe your entire infrastructure state and that state will be pushed to the infrastructure that you are trying to configure. And for that there are a lot of tools on the market.

Olga: Ok so now that we talked about some frustrating event that occurred to you, can you describe a big success that happened to you while being in DevOps role, something that you are really proud of for example?

Anderson: So, I was responsible for delivering the entire cloud infrastructure for the Brazilian government a few years ago. We used to have totally old bare-metal servers in an old way of provisioning, so we set up an entire new cloud infrastructure and not only that—we could actually provision infrastructure services for the entire Brazilian government.

So, I was not the technical guy at that time, but I was managing that project and I was really proud of that. Nowadays the company is still selling that solution to agencies in Brazil, and administration departments, so they are all using that solution and that was really really cool.

Olga: That is quite impressive...

Anderson: Yes, and it reduces the time of provisioning. Usually in our organization it took us about 3 months to provision a complex infrastructure, and with that cloud environment we could provision almost anything in about 5 minutes.

Olga: Wow... that is a huge difference! Maybe you also have a funny story to share as well...

Anderson: I was responsible for all the data centers in Brazil and once at 3 in the morning my phone rang. So, 3 in the morning I woke up, let's say not quite happy since I knew something was going on and really bad...

So, my manager there called me saying, "Ok, hey Anderson, we have an issue here... the fire alarm triggered in one of our data centers."

So, we don't know what was going on, and as I used to live two blocks away from that data center, I woke up my friend, who was staying with me at the time, and I said to him: "Hey man, wake up we need to go to the office...," and he replied, "Are you crazy? I am not going... it's 3 in the morning..." I said, "No man, wake up start calling the press because something really bad is going to happen..."

In the end we went there, and in the end it was a false alarm; the system itself failed, but when the alarm sets in the data center all machines are automatically shut down, so as you can imagine about *three to four hundred servers, storage systems, mainframes... everything went down.* So, we had 4 hours between 3 AM and 7 AM to turn on again the entire infrastructure, and some storage systems take around 1.5 hours to do all the checks to make sure data is not corrupted, but in the end we could do it.

So, in the end it was fun, I got to call every engineer; they were not really happy about it, but in the end, we got some pizzas and a lot of laughing and in the next day we went to celebrate.

Olga: That's really nice. What I feel is a lot of passion when you talk about what you are doing. So, it feels that you really love your job, and I believe this is really important, right?

Anderson: Yes, I think this is fundamental... If you don't love what you are doing, then I don't know why you are doing it. So, this is my basic philosophy for my life. I try to do only things that I love. Of course, there will be times you'll pick up that one simple task that might not be what you wanted, but that's ok! Sometimes you need to do those tasks as well, but in general I am passionate about technology and I cannot think of me doing anything else. I go to work happy every day; for me it's like a video game, I go there every day and play, but for me the video game is about coding and setting up infrastructures, new services. This is what I like to do.

Olga: That's great. I believe this could be a very good advice to our students and readers: Love what you do, and you will be happy and successful.

Anderson: I am pretty sure because if you don't love it just change please. Don't keep your life like that, **life is too short to not enjoy**.

Monitoring and Alerting

Well well well, we know now how to check if our code is production-ready, how to go live with it, and most importantly, how to automate this whole process. Is that enough?

Imagine you have a kid. You raise this kid, you prepare them to go to school, and one day, voilà—your kid is at school! Can you loosen the reins and just be sure that everything's right? Of course not, you have to control your kid's grades, you need to stay alert if something happens. You feel the need to be notified if your kid gets into some trouble in school or if they miss school.

That's right, we are talking about monitoring and alerting mechanisms. Your software is like your child—you create it, develop it, you love it, you open the path for it to face the real world, and of course you cannot leave it without being monitored. What if the system goes down at night while you are sleeping? What if lots of users start using your system and it's not prepared for that and it goes down?

It is a real scenario, by the way. At EdEra we run online courses. Our system has always used only one AWS instance, and it was always enough. We, actually, never thought about some extensive monitoring or controlling. For 3 years, it just worked. One day we launched a course for Ukrainian teachers. We told them that the course materials would be open in December 1st at 3 PM. It was an online course, so it would be available 24/7 but for Ukrainian teachers educated by a strict Soviet system, the words "December 1st at 3 PM"—it's like an order! So 100,000 teachers at the same time tried to register on the platform. Thus, on December 1st exactly at 3 PM, our system just went down. It was like a DDoS attack. After the website was down, we had e-mail and phone calls attack. All these teachers started calling and sending e-mails. During that night we answered around 1500 e-mails. We were not ready for that, but if we had monitoring and alerting systems in place, we would be at least warned in advance that the server's resources were going down.

Imagine that you open your task manager tool and just start staring at it detecting some anomalies and strange activities. This is what monitoring and alerting tools are about. Basically, you configure some benchmarks and alerting mechanisms (e.g., *"Send me an e-mail if the CPU goes above 80%"*) and these tools will do it for you.

Usually hosting providers also provide monitoring and alerting. You can also install and set up some dedicated tools for that—for example, **pagerduty** (`https://www.pagerduty.com/`). This tool will monitor the uptime of your service and alert via a specified channel (can be anything from a phone call to a slack message) if something goes wrong.

Pingdom (`https://www.pingdom.com/`) allows monitoring your website availability and performance and notifies you in case something goes beyond or below the specified benchmark.

For our learning platform, we use Heroku, which provides monitoring and alerting tools (you just have to pay for them).

If you use a cloud hosting provider and it's critical for you to stay alive, invest in a paid subscription to use the tools offered by this provider to keep a strong eye on your kid's health!

Analytics

In the previous section we discussed how important it is to stay notified in case your system goes down. What if it doesn't go down not because it's so good but just because no one's using it? How do we know if your software is being used at all? How do we know whether or not people like it? How can we know who are our users? Turns out, using analytics services on your system is as much important as monitoring it.

You have certainly heard about google analytics. This tool is present almost in every website you use nowadays. It allows web services' owners to know when and how their services are being used. It gives you a nice real-time overview dashboard that tells you how many active users are on the website, the regions the users come from, what are the most visited pages, how long the sessions last in average, etc. These are very important numbers, and it's good to have a data analyst to analyze that data and work closely with the team to find out the weakest spots of the system.

For example, just by carefully analyzing this kind of data at OptioPay allowed us to realize that on our user journey we were losing a lot of conversion on our landing page. Redesigning it and making it more attractive gave us a possibility to significantly increase the overall conversion rate.

There are a lot of tools besides Google analytics that provide you with means of getting important data of your services usage. *Mixpanel* (`https://mixpanel.com/`), for example, is a nice and easy to use platform. It also provides an API for creating custom events, so they can be analyzed afterward. It requires programming knowledge, but that is what we have our developers for, right?

Some analytics services even provide you with a heat map, meaning that you can actually see what parts of your web service are being used most. This will give you an insight on how to improve your UI/UX to engage users more.

Whatever you decide to use, don't forget about *privacy issues*. Nowadays technologies allow collecting so much data from users, but don't get too excited with that; otherwise it might have a negative impact on your business. Even if you think you know what you're doing, privacy issues can always affect you (let's not forget, e.g., about this case: `https://en.wikipedia.org/wiki/Facebook%E2%80%93Cambridge_Analytica_data_scandal`).

Hosting and Creating a CI/CD for Our Platform

Now that we got all that theory, it's time that we get our hands dirty. There are several options on the market for CI/CD and hosting applications. Some of them are paid, some are free, and some are hybrid. When we started writing this book, we internally decided that we would deploy our application in Heroku. Heroku offers a pretty good and easy way to deploy applications written in several programming languages. Moreover, it also offers integrated services such as databases, thus making integration easy. The services we are going to use in order to deploy our application in Heroku are all free, but irregardless, Heroku asks for your payment details. If you are afraid to provide your credit card details to Heroku, we advise you to at least continue with us as most of the steps are quite easy to understand even if you are not actually doing them.

Hosting

The first order of business is to create a Heroku account if you don't already have one. Go to `https://www.heroku.com/` and create an account. Download also the Heroku CLI (`https://devcenter.heroku.com/articles/heroku-cli#download-and-install`) and get the application code from the folder "`courses`". Download and set up git, create a github account if you don't have one, and create a repository for the source code you just downloaded and copy the repository URL. Then just clone the repository. For us it was like the following:

```
$ git clone git@github.com:rpvilao/courses-test.git
```

This will clone the empty repository you just created. Extract the source code into this new directory (`courses-test` in our case; yours might be different depending on the name you gave to the repository). What we will do now is add the files to the repository

```
$ git add .gitignore .travis.yml *
$ git commit -a -m "Init"
$ git push origin master
```

At this point our code is already on github and may be accessible to everyone (if you created a public repository). As you remember, Git is a version control system, meaning that you make changes to files and navigate in history and work properly with other collaborators of the project.

Congratulations, as you have just completed the very first step, yet an important one, to achieve continuous integration. Without a versioning control system, continuous integration wouldn't be possible... Well it would, but you cannot imagine how difficult and error-prone it would be, so let's assume that indeed it would be impossible for the nowadays standards. Now it's time to get back to Heroku. The first thing we need to do is to login and and create an application.

```
$ heroku login
$ heroku create
Creating app... done, ⬣ stark-headland-67097
https://stark-headland-67097.herokuapp.com/ | https://git.heroku.com/stark-
headland-67097.git
```

Since our application requires a database, let's create one. We decided to use `postgresql`. The application is already prepared to use it, so just run the following:

```
$ heroku addons:create heroku-postgresql:hobby-dev
creating heroku-postgresql:hobby-dev on ⬣ stark-headland-67097... free
Database has been created and is available
 ! This database is empty. If upgrading, you can transfer
 ! data from another database with pg:copy
Created postgresql-regular-72889 as DATABASE_URL
Use heroku addons:docs heroku-postgresql to view documentation
```

By running "heroku config" you will be able to see how to connect to this database. As our application is a Java application, we need to put the connection URL in the JDBC form. This step is not really obvious, but worry not, it's already good we created an application and a database with just a few commands! If you look at the connection string, you will notice you have something similar to

```
postgres://USERNAME:PASSWORD@ec2-XX-21-YYY-ZZZ.compute-1.amazonaws.
com:5432/DB_NAME
```

In order to make this a JDBC string, you need to match to the following:

```
jdbc:postgresql://ec2-XX-21-YYY-ZZZ.compute-1.amazonaws.com:5432/DB_NAME?ss
lmode=require&user=USERNAME&password=PASSWORD&currentSchema=public
```

This is the string you need to use to create bootstrap our database. Let's do that now using liquibase (we prepared a profile, so we can create our production database).

```
$ DATABASE_URL_JDBC="jdbc:postgresql://ec2-XX-21-YYY-ZZZ.compute-1.
amazonaws.com:5432/DB_NAME?sslmode=require&user=USERNAME&password=PASSWORD&
currentSchema=public" mvn liquibase:update -pl liquibase -Pheroku
```

We are almost ready, let's finally deploy the application

```
$ git push heroku master
```

Seriously, how cool is that? Things that you might be wondering right now: How does Heroku know how to run my application? The answer is in the Procfile in the project's root.

How does our application know how to connect to the database? Heroku exposes the database URL in an environment variable called DATABASE_URL and our application is already expecting that. You remember earlier, this variable was not in the JDBC form, so we read it, transformed it, and built the final string in the code.

Take a look at the PersistenceLayerConfig file in the persistence layer module.

Once the build is done and successful, just open the application using

```
$ heroku open
```

You might get an error at first since the application can take some time to load; just hit refresh if this happens.

Even though this seems pretty cool, how do we make sure the application is in a deployable state? Furthermore, imagine that you have a team of six people writing code on the application... It is very likely that at some point the code might not be deployable right? We are only humans... This is where **Continuous Integration** comes into play. We already stated that having a versioning control system is the first step to achieve CI, but now we will dive into the topic and set up a set of verifications where we assume that if they pass, our code is in a deployable state. Let's go!

Continuous Integration and Deployment

Just for a recap, Continuous Integration (CI) is a set of processes that allows people to work together and contribute for the same project without making it painful to integrate. Nowadays this literally means having a version control, an automated build, and a set of automated tests that run every time you make changes to the build. Our case is no different—we already created a version control repository in the previous exercise and you saw that our build runs automatically just by calling a command. Now it's time to take care of the part where we run a set of tests once we do some changes on a particular branch of the repository—in this case the master branch, the one that points to our current production version. Even though you can and should run the automated tests for every change on whatever branch, we are doing it only on the master for a matter of simplicity and to provide an example.

We could use Heroku as well to build our CI system; the problem is that we need to pay to use this feature. Luckily enough, there are more alternatives and even alternatives that can be integrated with Heroku. In this example, we will use TravisCI and integrate with GitHub and Heroku. The flow for our CI is the following: for every push on the master branch, Travis will receive a message from github saying that there was a change in the repository. Travis will then read the configuration and check what to do to perform the build. After the build finishes, if the change we just did applies to what's defined in the configuration file and in case it indeed applies, Travis will deploy the changes to our production environment on Heroku only if the tests passed and the build was successful.

Start by creating a Travis account (`https://travis-ci.org/`). Once you are in, connect your newly created Travis account to your github account and choose the repository for our project.

Now we need to allow Travis to be able to deploy the changes in Heroku if the build and the tests pass. For that we need to generate a token on the Heroku side, sign it with Travis and put it on our Travis configuration file.

```
$ heroku auth:token
 ›   Warning: token will expire 06/18/2019
 ›   Use heroku authorizations:create to generate a long-term token
258cfb90-XXXX-4720-XXX-9bfba5332254
```

So now we need to set this token in our Travis configuration file, so Travis can read it and make the call to Heroku. Hum... something seems off... isn't that a major security breach, exposing a token to the world—especially on a public repository? True, that's why Travis enables a way to encrypt this piece of text with a public key that can only be decrypted with a private key (only available in Travis and in your account); this is called asymmetric encryption—the same technique your browser uses to make secure calls over HTTP. Getting back to the topic, there's a small script in the root of the project called travis-encrypt.sh (https://gist.github.com/openscript) to get this job done. Replace "user/repo" with your username and repository on Travis and remember that the token is different for you!

```
$ ./travis-encrypt.sh -r user/repo -e 258cfb90-XXXX-4720-XXX-9bfba5332254
```

This will provide you with an encrypted string that you will need to place in a file called ".travis.yml". The file will look similar to

```
language: java
jdk:
  - openjdk8
script: mvn clean install -Ptest
cache:
  directories:
    - $HOME/.m2/
deploy:
  provider: heroku
  app: HEROKU-APP-NAME
  api_key:
    secure: YOUR-API-KEY
  run: "DATABASE_URL_JDBC=$DB_PROD mvn liquibase:update -pl liquibase
-Pheroku"
  on: master
```

Let's go through the file. We defined that the project is written in Java and that we want to use openjdk8 to run the build. Then we specify how we want to run the build by calling "maven install" with a profile named "test". In order to make the build faster, we are caching all the maven artifacts that our project uses; this means they will only be downloaded once and not every time the build runs (this speeds up the process in about 75% for the subsequent calls depending on the network of course). The final part is our Continuous Deployment, where we specify that if the build is successful and the branch is "master" we want to deploy it on Heroku along with running any necessary database migrations ("run" section).

We are almost done. In order for this to work, we just need to create an environment variable with the JDBC connection on Travis. Go to Travis, more options, settings, and just set an environment variable called DB_PROD with the JDBC connection string (jdbc:postgresql...) we defined earlier before in the CI section.

Ready to test it? Just commit your changes

```
$ git commit -a -m "Adding Travis' configuration"
```

and push them!

```
$ git push origin master
```

Refresh Travis' dashboard and check that your build is running. Once it's done, you should have the changes deployed in your application Heroku URL (if you don't remember it, just type "heroku open").

And just by that we created a simple CI/CD pipeline for our project. Was it worth it? Yes, it was! We have our application up and running on this address: https://eleplatform.herokuapp.com. Of course, in real scenarios, things are not that simple, but the same principles apply. It is very common that, for example, you have a staging version that is basically the same as the production but for testing purposes before you go live. This could be accomplished by creating another app and database on Heroku and configuring a deployment pipeline using Travis, where you state that if the branch is staging, then you deploy to the stage application and not the production one. Another thing you need to take into consideration is that in real scenarios, it is very unlikely that you will find backend applications to be deployed automatically to production on a push. Not only it is too risky, but also sometimes they need to have a certain order of execution in order to achieve a zero-downtime deployment with, for example, a blue green (also known as **canary**) deployment where the changes are rolled out on a phased approach. No matter what, it is a very good academic example for the purpose of this book, and now that you know how to do it, you can build a staging application and CI/CD pipeline for our courses application. Are you ready for that challenge?

Summary

In this chapter we successfully wore the hat of a DevOps professional. Or maybe you want to call it an infrastructure engineer, or Site Reliability Engineer... Call it whatever you want, the important part is that now you know what it means to "**go live.**" It is the same as "**deploying to production.**" You know how to automate this process. You also learned how important it is to ensure that basic checks pass before the deployment. We've seen how important it is to monitor your software in production and set up alerting tools for you to get notified in case something goes wrong. We've also discussed that it is important to have some analytics tools in place, so we know how our system is being used and can improve it based on this information.

Looks like... we're done? Not at all! With the first deployment, our journey has just started.

The application will be developed and improved over time. At this moment we have just deployed an MVP (Minimum Viable Product) and there is still work waiting for us. In the next chapter, we will describe what usually happens after the first deployment—besides the celebration, the work continues, the processes are going on, the product must still be maintained, evolved, probably refactored at some point of time, and someday even redesigned, because the time is moving on and the trends are always changing. So, let's move on to the next chapter and discover what is happening to the software after it gets deployed!!

CHAPTER 9

Maintaining and Improving Your Software

In the previous chapter we finally deployed our e-learning platform to production. Now we have it up and running on Heroku (`http://eleplatform.herokuapp.com/`).

However, the development process is not finished yet. Actually, our journey has just begun. It's like a baby. You plan it (or not), prepare for it, then you conceive it, then there is a long pregnancy period, during which you prepare your mind and buy all the things you need. You prepare the nursery, talk to the doctors, choose the right hospital, and make sure the world and environment around you are prepared for embracing a new human being. Then the baby is born. Yay! Excitement!

At some point you hold your baby and you slowly realize that everything that you've been doing during the last 9 months is actually nothing compared to what is actually waiting for you. You've just delivered a whole new human being into the world. It's not just a baby, it's a new life, a new journey, a new path, a new inspiration, and a new world. And the responsibility for all this is on you.

The software that you prepare for delivering to the world is no different. You also put a lot of love in its creation. You make sure that it's healthy and close to bug-free.

Once it's online you want to share it with the whole world because you are just so happy that you finally succeeded! Once it's up and running and accessible to the whole world, you know that its life has just started and that you are responsible for its quality and success. There's no time to relax. Now it's time for the real job; everything we've done before was just a slight preparation. Let's see what awaits us in this journey. On the way to its perfection you will be constantly involved in two activities: **maintaining** and **improving**.

© Olga Filipova and Rui Vilão 2018
O. Filipova and R. Vilão, *Software Development From A to Z*, https://doi.org/10.1007/978-1-4842-3945-2_9

Maintaining

You've certainly heard the term "maintaining." This is something that you will have to do with your baby—maintain it alive. Make sure your infrastructure allows you to keep your software in a solid state. Make sure that if you pay for your servers that all the payments are done on time. Otherwise you might end up in an embarrassing situation where your services are down due to some failed payment. Make sure no failure can destroy your business.

Backups

One of the pillars of maintainability is **backup**. Things happen. Your data can be accidentally destroyed for several reasons. The database can be compromised, hackers can attack you, your virtual server might go down and never be able to go up again. Some of the engineers might just accidentally run a "rm -rf" and everything is gone.

The command rm removes files. The flag -r does it recursively in the current folder and the flag -f forces removal, never prompting the user about deletion. This command is quite dangerous, since it will recursively remove everything without asking you any question!

Once I (Olga) accidentally created a folder called ~ on my Ubuntu machine. Once I realized that I decided to remove it. rm -rf ~. I was watching in slow motion how all my things disappeared, and my system just went away (~ in unix systems points to the user's home directory). Not super clever.

If you think that this dumb kind of thing will never happen to you, wait until the first time. An "rm -rf" incident is a quite popular reason among several that accidentally remove data. It even happened at Pixar with the whole movie **Toy Story 2**!

That is why it is very important to back up important data. When we are talking about complex systems, you might backup the whole system or just its data storage. Backing up means that once in a while all critical data is copied to another place, so if something happens the system can be recovered. You have to make sure that the files are easily retrievable from the backups, and once copied back again to the system, the system will work as usual. Pixar actually had a reserved copy of the Toy Story film, but it was corrupted (!!!); therefore it was impossible to restore the files from it.

If you use some cloud hosting service provider—for example, AWS—you might want to use the backup services offered by them. They are reliable and configurable. If your system is not changing that often, you might choose longer time gaps for backing up your data. If the data in your system is constantly changing and these changes are critical for the correct function, then you might want to choose more frequent backup intervals (e.g., every day whenever the application is being used less).

By the way, if you feel curious about the **Toy Story 2** film, the story had its happy ending. One of the employees that had to work from home because she had a small baby had a full copy of the film on her personal computer. This fact allowed Pixar to retrieve the files and successfully deliver the film to the audience.

Don't rely on such coincidence for your business though!

Replication

Sometimes data is so critical that every second matters. In this case, a simple backup is not enough. For this case, the data should be replicated and stored in multiple storage devices so that every time changes occur, they are propagated among all the replicas. **High-availability clusters** usually follow a **master-slave** scheme to achieve this effect.

Master-slave   is a scheme in which there is a main device or service that is doing all the work but also replicating all the operations to other nodes that are just awaiting to be picked up if, for some reason, the main one fails.

When some of the devices are down, the requests are sent to another device. The whole process should be totally transparent for the user. The process of switching to the redundant device is called **failover**. Cloud systems like AWS, MS Azure, Google Cloud, etc., offer replication and failover mechanisms among their services.

Natural Disasters and Cosmic Rays

It has been proven over the years that human errors are the most common reason for systems to fail.

However, there are rare cases that humans cannot control. Yes, we are talking about nature and its phenomena. You can heat up your house or make it colder using air conditioning devices, but you can't control the temperature outside.

Every year natural disasters take hundreds of human lives, and we can't do much about it.

Imagine that you have your system running on bare metal servers across the street. Imagine that there's an earthquake and the whole area gets destroyed. You lose everything you have been working on over the past years and your business is over. You can't do much about it. Just kidding. Of course, you can. There is even a term in computer science called **disaster recovery**.

> *Disaster recovery (DR) involves a set of policies, tools and procedures to enable the recovery or continuation of vital technology infrastructure and systems following a natural or human-induced disaster. <...>. Disaster recovery can be considered as a subset of business continuity.*
>
> —Wikipedia (`https://en.wikipedia.org/wiki/Disaster_recovery`)

Of course, if we are talking about a small project and a small set of data, your disaster recovery can be just an external hard drive hidden at your friend's place. But if it's a huge amount of critical data, then you should carefully think of a disaster recovery plan. Usually big cloud services provide those plans for you, and you can sleep peacefully. In any case, it is important to be aware of an existence of these things and be prepared for the worst and hope for the best.

Since we are talking about natural causes and their impact on software, we think it's quite interesting and fun to talk about cosmic rays. What? (Figure 9-1).

Figure 9-1. *Wait, what? Cosmic rays?*

Yes! Cosmic rays can result in errors in RAM (Random Access Memory). Long story short, cosmic rays can produce an effect in the atmosphere that can lead to potential changes in the running memory of a device, hence causing software errors. What is the probability of such errors to occur? Wikipedia cites a study conducted by IBM:

> *Studies by IBM in the 1990s suggest that computers typically experience about one cosmic-ray-induced error per 256 megabytes of RAM per month.*

> —Wikipedia: (https://en.wikipedia.org/wiki/Cosmic_
> ray#Effect_on_electronics

What should you do to protect yourself against cosmic rays? Maybe nothing. We just added this natural cause to spike your curiosity. Modern chips are mostly protected against these causes by implementing checksums, so it is highly unlikely that those can affect the system, but still possible. The same happens with radioactivity for example. Systems that are exposed to non-optimal conditions—for example, satellites—need to take this into consideration.

Improving

Your product, even well-maintained, needs to be constantly improved. Otherwise new trends and competition will destroy it in this crazy sea of technologies.

Imagine that the Windows operating system would look the same way it looked in its first versions. Would anyone use it? Consider any software or mobile application that you use—if it wouldn't constantly heat you up with updates and new features, how long would you use it? We are all humans—it is so easy for us to get distracted; it is so easy for us to be lazy; it is so difficult to be loyal to one specific trademark or product.

We want to try different things, and the world is constantly moving forward around us. At the same time, we are very suspicious regarding new things, and we would rather stick to an old technology than try a new one (because it requires time and effort), unless everyone starts talking about it and our natural curiosity wins.

If you correctly and constantly use these controversial human characteristics in your software development, you might win the market.

Thus, you need people who are good in **marketing**, you need good people in **sales**, you need a strong **R&D** (Research and Development) and **customer service** departments, and you need to build a strong vibe toward the users' empathy in your team. This is very important. It doesn't matter if you are B2B or B2C or B2B2C or whatever. There is always some end-user of your product, even though in some specific cases it is hard to reach this user due to a huge chain of B2B before the final customer. Think about this user, become this user, make everyone on the team feel this user, and be open to the new ideas even if they seem to be totally opposed to the initial direction of the product.

If everything is right, your customer base will grow. Make sure you have your scaling plan in place. Users will have questions; they will need a way to contact you and ask those questions. Make sure you have an easy way to collect users' feedback and provide them with an efficient customer service. The code base will grow, and at some point, it will need some refactoring or even rewriting. Make sure you allocate enough time for such things—they are important! Since the world will be constantly moving forward and new design trends will appear every day, the design of your product will have to adapt to those changes as well. Sometimes you will need to conduct a redesign process for your product. Be ready for that as well.

In general, always be ready for changes and for accepting those changes with a smile and positive energy. If you have read the book *Creativity, Inc.: Overcoming the Unseen Forces That Stand in the Way of True Inspiration* (`http://a.co/8kdojHA`), you know how the whole concept of Pixar animated cartoons could have changed after 1 year of working on it. Because they bet on quality and creativity, and everyone's voice counts.

Scaling

At EdEra, as we've already pointed out, we run an online courses platform. Since the very beginning, it has been using a single EC2 instance on AWS.

AWS EC2 is an Amazon Web Service that allows you to fire up general purpose instances that can easily match your computational needs.

Having one instance for it was totally fine for 3 years. In December 2017, we decided to launch a course for teachers. Luckily for us, this course was considered by the Ministry of Education as a required course for those teachers who would teach in the primary school during the school year 2018 to 2019. We are roughly talking about 20,000 teachers. Olga remembers when her brother Illia called in panic. He had attended the meeting at the Ministry and people were skeptical; they were wondering whether our servers would survive having 20,000 users. Illia told them that EdEra has the best engineers in the world, and nothing ever could possibly go wrong.

But he was in panic. He asked Olga whether or not it was possible that that number of teachers would bring EdEra servers down. Olga thought, "Well, the course is available 24/7, there will never be 20,000 users simultaneously on the platform." As Illia said at the meeting, nothing could possibly go wrong (Figure 9-2)!

Figure 9-2. *This picture was taken around 5 seconds before the kitten fell down*

Turns out that we didn't think about a very specific characteristic of our target audience. We are talking about teachers that were educated during the Soviet regime. We already spoke about this case earlier in this book, but let us remind you.

What happened is that the word "**required**" in combination with the specific start date and time of the course resulted in a call to action. All Ukrainian teachers thought that the course was required, not just the ones that were eligible to teach the primary school in the following year. Thus, December 1st, at that specific time, almost 100,000 teachers tried to register on our platform. Of course, our small instance went immediately down. We were not prepared for that. We had to come up with a scaling solution on the fly. We were lucky, because it is fairly easy to achieve if you use AWS. During that course we experienced huge slowdown on our servers during the days when new modules were being published and when the final test was out. We had a couple peaks when we had 50 instances simultaneously serving users requests. From 1 server to 50 without being prepared. Of course, it caused a lot of stress, nerves, and panic. Not only we were not prepared to handle that kind of load, we were also not prepared when it came to storage. Initially we were surviving with **50 gigabytes** storage only! Can you imagine that? Our phones have five times more than that!

Olga remembers being at a company event bowling, and all of a sudden, EdEra's server ran out of space and the server was down. Luckily for Olga, one of her colleagues had his laptop with him. She connected to our server and for 10 minutes, all of her colleagues were helping to free some space on the server—cleaning the logs, old backup files, etc. Needless to say, we had to increase this amount and put monitoring and alerting tools in place for this kind of occurrence.

We are writing all this not for you to laugh and think how dumb we were at the time; we are writing this for you to be aware of the importance of being prepared to scale. It is worth mentioning that how you design your architecture is of the utmost importance. At EdEra we are using a third-party open source system that is hard to scale. We had to put 50 servers to be able to handle the load. The same request load at Gymondo (where Rui works) is being handled by two instances only, because the application is designed in a way that it doesn't get stuck with the load. That is why it is important to run all kind of tests on your system, including heavy load testing.

If you use cloud hosting platforms, they usually provide the right tools for you to be able to scale according your load (**auto-scaling**) . Have a look at Google Kubernetes. This is an open-source system developed by Google that allows you to containerize your software and configure it for auto-deployment, auto-scaling, and management.

Getting back to our new learning platform, when we started developing it, we simplified several aspects of it. The current implementation cannot scale horizontally. This is partially true; in fact it can scale but not as we would wish. The problem is that our authentication mechanism is using an `in-memory database` to store the session information (access and refresh tokens). This means that if we are balancing the load between several application nodes, a user that hits the authentication node A and makes a subsequent request to the node B will not have the request satisfied, since the node B does not know about that authentication that was performed by node A. This can be easily solved by storing the authentication information in a place that can be accessed by all the nodes that are serving requests. This can be, for example, in a *relational database*, *elasticsearch*, or any other kind of storage, such as *memcached*.

If our strategy is to continue serving the website from the server nodes as well, it doesn't make sense that we are always serving the same static content and wasting computation time and resources. In this case, it is advisable that we put some caching mechanism in front of the application to serve this kind of content. In AWS this would be accomplished by creating a *cloudfront* distribution and specifying the cache behaviors based on the request paths—for example, - cache everything but not `/oauth*` and `/api*`. This way we will free the servers from computing unnecessary requests.

Don't get too enthusiastic with scaling though. Recently Olga had a conversation with a guy working as a CTO consultant. He is being invited by companies that get stuck in some architectural or in engineering management issues. Olga asked him what the most common technical problem in startups was. And it turns out that over-engineering sometimes becomes an issue. Engineers get overexcited with tools like Kubernetes and other containerization and cloud solutions and design the architecture that would scale for *billions of users*. Maintaining and developing for that kind of architecture becomes a cumbersome and complex process that slows down development and shipment. And, surprisingly, these companies had never reached the number of users for whom they'd been designing their complex architectures.

That is to say, be prepared for scaling, use monitoring and analytics tools to keep an eye on your users, but don't make it the only goal. The goal of your software is to solve your end-user's problem and make their life easier.

Handling Feedback

As we have already mentioned, your users will be willing to give feedback on your product and ask questions. Make sure you provide them with the right tools for doing so. Put a feedback form on your website, provide them with ways to contact you, and make those tools easily discoverable. Most important, have people monitoring the contact tools and answering your users. It is no good if you have an e-mail, phone number, or any other means of communication if you are not taking care of them and replying to your users.

Set up an automatic e-mail that will answer immediately something like, *"We have received your email; our team will get back to you in the next days."*

There will be, for sure, very similar requests. Some of them will be transformed into the new features; some of them you will just have to answer. Develop a template with the most common questions/answers to make your life easier.

Gather meetups and encounters talking about your product and its features, and organize a live testing with your potential target audience. Even if your product seems to be very clear and straightforward, you will be amazed with the amount of issues you can discover in such meetups.

Users' questions will bring you some UI/UX issues—for example, if the user cannot register because they cannot find the registration button, it is surely a problem in your user journey. Addressing them will improve your software. If you are a small team and everyone is doing everything, don't forget to add this kind of problem in your tasks' pipeline. If you have a product team and a customer service team in place, make sure the processes in the team are set up in a way that the customer service team works closely with the product team in order to include users' issues in the backlog.

If your software is open source, even better—the users can register issues directly in your GitHub repository.

Just keep in mind, whatever means for feedback you provide, make sure you have the means to address it!

Bug Fixing

In the previous section we've talked about addressing users' feedback. As you can imagine, the feedback is not about improving something **perfect**. In fact, there is no perfect software in the world. Any software contains bugs. Literally, every software in the world has bugs. If someone tells you that they can write bug-free software, you can burst out laughing right in their face!

Every line of code can potentially contain bugs. If you want to be a zero-bug programmer, don't code at all.

Having bugs in your software means that you have to fix them. Have a process in place to address this kind of issue. It doesn't have to be a complex process, but at least you should have bug-tracking tools and a way to prioritize bugs and categorize their severity. For example, if a bug prevents your users from registering on your platform, then it is a critical bug and it should be addressed immediately. On the other hand, if it is a small typo in the testimonials carousel, then it is a trivial bug that can be addressed at any time, and it shouldn't affect the current development.

Let's have a look at our learning platform, specifically at its registration page. Figure 9-3 shows how the registration form looks.

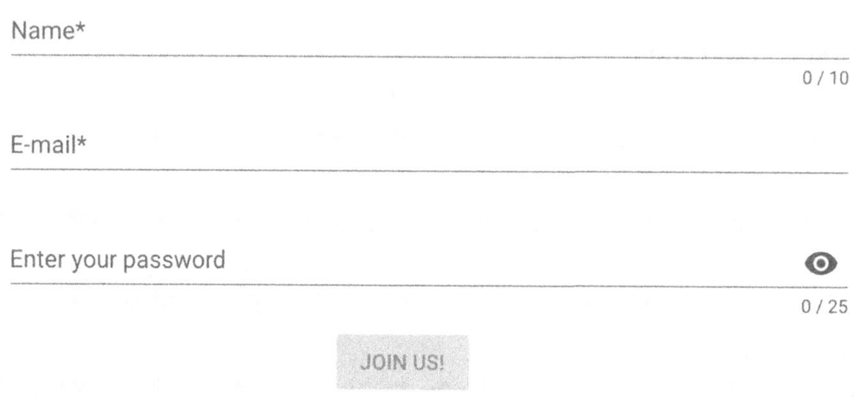

Figure 9-3. *Registration form*

What does it mean **0/10** on the name input field and **0/25** on the password input field? It seems obvious that it means the maximum number of allowed characters in the name and password, respectively. Ok, let's try to write something here (Figure 9-4).

Figure 9-4. *The form allows to type a name longer than 10 characters*

Hum, what? My name contains **13 out of 10** symbols? That's odd. And this is, obviously, a bug. The number that is used for the counter should be the same as the maximum allowed name length that we use in the form validation. If I were to work alone, I would just fix this bug, but if you have a team and processes in place, someone would have to file this bug. Figure 9-5 shows how a bug report for this specific issue would look.

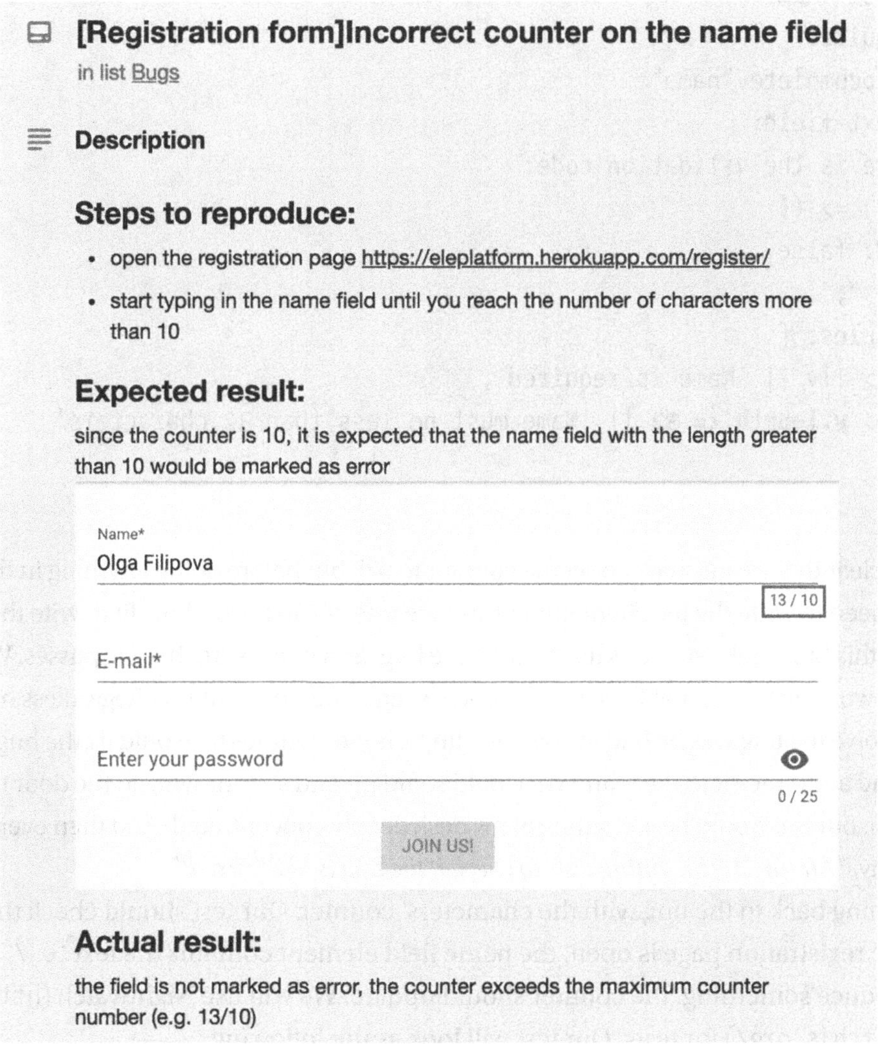

[Registration form]Incorrect counter on the name field

in list Bugs

Description

Steps to reproduce:

- open the registration page https://eleplatform.herokuapp.com/register/
- start typing in the name field until you reach the number of characters more than 10

Expected result:

since the counter is 10, it is expected that the name field with the length greater than 10 would be marked as error

Name*
Olga Filipova

13 / 10

E-mail*

Enter your password

0 / 25

JOIN US!

Actual result:

the field is not marked as error, the counter exceeds the maximum counter number (e.g. 13/10)

Figure 9-5. *Registered bug about the field name counter*

Let's have a look at the code to understand where the bug comes from. Here's the part of the form for the name field:

```
<v-text-field
    v-model="name"
    :rules="nameRules"
    :counter="10"
    label="Name"
    required
    autocomplete="name"
></v-text-field>
```

And here is the validation code:

```
data: () => ({
  valid: false,
  name: ",
  nameRules: [
    v => !!v || 'Name is required',
    v => v.length <= 32 || 'Name must be less than 32 characters'
  ],
}),
```

It is clear that we just have to set the counter to 32l, but before doing anything in the code, we first need to write the test! Remember this nice rule: if you have a bug, first write the test to cover this bug, make sure this test fails, fix the bug, and make sure this test passes. When we were working together at Feedzai, there was even a meme about Rui. Regardless of how easy to solve the bug was he had to cover it with tests. Sometimes he would fix the bug before lunch and announce it to the team. We would stand up and start moving to the door to go for lunch. But Rui would be still sitting at his desk deeply concentrated. And then everybody would say, *"Ah sure, he's running tests to check if the bug is really fixed!"*

Coming back to the bug with the characters' counter. Our test should check that once the registration page is open, the name field element contains the text "0 / 32". If we introduce something, the counter should update. We will use Nightwatch (http://nightwatchjs.org/) for tests. Our test will look as the following:

```
module.exports = {
  'Test Registration page': function (browser) {
    browser
      .url('http://localhost:3000/register')
```

```
    .waitForElementVisible('#app', 5000)
    .assert.containsText('.input-group__counter', '0 / 32')
    .setValue('input[autocomplete="name"]', '1234567890123')
    .assert.containsText('.input-group__counter', '13 / 32')
    .end()
  }
}
```

If I run this test now it will fail: Testing if element <.input-group__counter> contains text: "**0 / 32**". - expected "**0 / 32**" but got: "**0 / 10**".

Let's now fix the bug. As we already have mentioned, we have to change the counter number to 32. Or, even better, to avoid the amount of "*magic numbers*" through the code, let's add a constant value for the maximum name length and use it.

Magic numbers   are those numbers that appear in different places of code and whose meaning is hard to understand. Avoid using magic numbers; create constants with meaningful names instead.

Thus, after the fixing the code will look like this:

```
<script>
  import { mapActions, mapGetters } from 'vuex'
  const MAX_NAME_LENGTH = 32
  export default {
    middleware: 'notauthenticated',
    data: () => ({
      MAX_NAME_LENGTH,
      valid: false,
      name: ",
      nameRules: [
        v => !!v || 'Name is required',
        v => v.length <= MAX_NAME_LENGTH || `Name must be less than
        ${MAX_NAME_LENGTH} characters`
      ]
    })
  }
</script>
```

The markup for the name field will look as the following:

```
<v-text-field
    <...>
    :counter="MAX_NAME_LENGTH"
    <...>
></v-text-field>
```

And yay! The test passes! We can mark the issue as resolved.

The code for this part can be found in the folder `bugFixing` in two subfolders: `before` and `after`. Only the frontend code was changed. Take a look at the file `package.json` for added dependencies, `pages/register.vue` for the actual fix, and `tests/e2e` folder for the added test. File `README.md` contains steps for running end to end tests.

So, just keep in mind: you can't write bug-free code, but you can—and you should— write a clean, maintainable, and well-tested code. Then whatever bug that appears on your way will be cleaned in a matter of seconds!

Refactoring, Rewriting, and Technical Debt

No matter how clean your codebase is and how good its test coverage is, at some point you will look at the code and you will feel the need to re-organize it in a different way. Some classes might not make sense anymore, some files can be split in different modules, some functions can be divided into smaller subfunctions, some tests can be improved, and some documentation can be added. When you feel the urge to improve your code, to reorganize it and to make it better, it means that it is time for **refactoring**!

To refactor the code   means that the code is restructured, but its behavior and functionality remains the same. The more your code is covered by unit tests, the more you can be sure that no refactoring breaks its functionality.

For example, in the case of our frontend, we have a folder "`components`", which currently contains three components:

- CourseItem.vue

- CourseModule.vue

- UserCourseItem.vue

While it's only three components, it is fairly easy to understand the purpose of each of them. On the other hand, with the growth of the code base, the number of components will grow as well, and there will be a high possibility that we will have to restructure this folder into meaningful subfolders and maybe even think about renaming some files.

Regarding the architecture in general, as previously said, we are distributing the static website also from the `rest-api` node. In modern architectures this is a strong no-go, especially since nowadays everything is hosted in cloud providers that allow you to build a lot of the architecture using their services. One thing to refactor about our architecture is to split completely the backend from the frontend. The frontend can be served by dedicated web server nodes, or—even better—if it's simple enough and no crazy rules are needed, it can be served by a *S3 + Cloudfront* solution on Amazon AWS.

AWS enables you to host websites on their cloud storage (S3) and put a Cloudfront distribution in front of it and cache all the files in order to save money and make it even faster. Rui is an enthusiast of this solution, but it only works if you are just serving files plain and simple. It is also possible to enable some rewrite rules, but it will never be as good as any other specific web server on the market. Our example is a good match to be served by this solution, at least for now! It doesn't mean that in a near future, the product evolves in a way that this is no longer applicable. If or when that time comes, the migration will be smooth, so we don't have to worry much about that.

Sometimes it happens that we never stop to reflect on the quality and structure of our code. It happens when the sales team aggressively sells non-existing features and then the development team has to implement them with pretty harsh deadlines.

It happens when the product team keeps pushing new features to the backlog, when management wants to see new stuff on weekly demo-hours and the development team feels obligated to add that stuff no matter what. It might happen for lots of reasons. Where does it lead? It leads to the fact that 1 year later, we realize that our code base is a huge mess. We realize that our code is full of TODO statements.

Actually, when we leave a TODO statement in the code, we truly believe that we will do it soon! And we truly believe that at the moment we will do it, we will totally remember the context and the reason for this TODO. Believe me, never happens!

We feel terrified by the chaos in the code structure, by the monstrous number of modules, by the difference in the code style through the code base, and by the simple fact that we look at the code and we don't like it. In this case, we think that it will be easier to rewrite everything from scratch. We naively believe that if we start rewriting the whole code base from zero, it will be clean, nice, and perfect. Another case when we feel as we would rewrite the whole code base in a nice and perfect way is when we discover some new programming language or a new framework. We feel the urge of trying this great new stuff and we are totally sure that it is more applicable to our case than anything else. We want to rewrite everything (Figure 9-6)!

Figure 9-6.   *We truly believe that if we rewrite everything from scratch, it will be just perfect*

Please don't fall under illusion that it will happen with your code. You've probably heard about some success cases of the code rewriting, but usually it will not lead to what you expect. Netscape did it, and it took them 3 years, and they had to skip a version, going directly from version 4 to 6. This example is given in the article by Joel Spolsky, founder of stackoverflow (`https://bit.ly/2iF64Qm`).

The rewritten code will also have problems; after some time you will also hate to read it, and in the end, you will end up with two inefficient code bases.

However, if you decide that there is no other choice than full rewriting, make a nice plan for it, estimate in time how long will it take. Develop a strategy that will allow you to maintain the existing code while slowly but surely creating the new one.

Divide the code into strategically autonomous chunks; keep replacing them after the rewriting so you smoothly replace the whole code base. Make sure that the new code is clean, tested, and readable.

Nevertheless, keep in mind small refactoring is always better than huge rewriting. Thus, make sure that you always have room for addressing the **technical debt**.

Technical debt   consists of the issues with your code that might lead to refactoring. Inefficient test coverage, poor architectural decisions, lack of structure, incoherent code style—all of this can be considered as a technical debt. It is impossible to not have any technical debt, but it is possible to set up the processes in a way that it is not accumulated.

Talk to your team, make sure everyone is on the same page regarding the danger of accumulating technical debt. Make sure that whoever is responsible for the backlog includes technical debt tasks into it. Make sure that every sprint (or any other work unit that you use) addresses some of these issues. Make sure your code makes you feel proud and happy.

Redesigning and Rebranding

We have already mentioned in this chapter that while your product is being successfully used by your happy users, the trends in the design world change and new things become popular.

Flat buttons come to replace the three-dimensional buttons, gradients all of a sudden become a thing, clean grey patterns naturally come to replace blinking and colorful ornaments, etc.

Not to mention the invasion of mobile devices and the need to design the applications with the mobile-first mind in place.

Thus, your design team will constantly propose new solutions and your development team will have to implement it.

It is important to keep a good balance when it comes to a redesign. Don't run after all emerging trends—some of them are rather ephemeral and will probably die tomorrow. Keep an eye on those that might be beneficial for your product, bearing in mind the needs of your users.

Sometimes designers propose the redesigned mockups because they make a user research of the current design and find that it needs to be improved in some way. For example, while we were busy writing this book, our amazing designer, Alexandra Syrik, came up with the redesign of the login and registration page.

Just to remind you, Figure 9-7 shows how it was.

Figure 9-7. *Design of the login and registration page before*

And Figure 9-8 shows how it looks now.

Figure 9-8. *Redesigned version of the sign-in and sign-up pages*

256

Alexandra had also designed the landing page and completely redesigned the course dashboard pages. We like the new design a lot, and this means that we will have some work to do.

It is always good to occasionally redesign your product or its parts. Sometimes the redesign turns out to be a full **rebranding,** where the full identity is changed (logo, fonts, color scheme, etc.). Don't rebrand your product too often though, otherwise your users will stop recognizing it. However, sometimes it feels good and refreshing, especially when your business slightly or completely changes its direction. Branding has to do with your vision, mission, and values. Make sure they all combine.

Summary

In this chapter we have discussed lots of things that happen with software products during their lifetimes. We discussed many different processes starting from users' feedback, going through the code refactoring and rewriting and ending up with a redesign.

You know now how important it is to keep your product in a healthy state, how important it is to keep improving it, and how important it is to keep an eye on it that it never disappoints your users. It seems that you know what to do with your software being out there in the wild world. You are ready!

In principle, our journey is coming to an end. In the next chapter, we will give some tips and discuss some tricks from our own experience of being software engineers and managers for more than 10 years.

CHAPTER 10

Wrapping Up With Some Tips and Tricks

In the previous chapter we discussed everything that happens with the software after its first release. We concluded that the first release is just a start of a big journey that consists of lots of steps related to maintaining and improving your product. As with any other journey, this one can change its path. As with any other journey, it may end up in a corner with no apparent exit and you will have to go a step backward. It can also lead you into a tunnel where you'll be forced to move forward until you start seeing the light. However, it's an exciting journey; you will find beautiful sightseeing places and terrifying crashes, you will certainly meet new people and find yourself in strange situations and breathtaking adventures.

We've been through different journeys, working with different companies, different people, different products, and projects. We believe we can share some useful tips and tricks with you.

Development Tips

In this book we have discussed both frontend and backend development. Development consists of architectural decisions, coding, reviewing code, testing, pushing your code to production, working with the team, and constantly improving the code base so your software is easily maintainable and clean.

© Olga Filipova and Rui Vilão 2018
O. Filipova and R. Vilão, *Software Development From A to Z*, https://doi.org/10.1007/978-1-4842-3945-2_10

Choosing Programming Languages or Frameworks

When you start the development process, the question of what language to use will certainly arise. Developers will probably start fighting and presenting arguments for or against Java or Go, Python or Ruby, or even PHP. There will also be questions regarding the storage and search engines—SQL versus NoSQL, relational databases versus document stores, hipster tech versus classic solutions… What standards should you use? A REST old friend or modern GraphQL? What frontend framework should you choose? React and Redux, Vue.js? Or maybe, Elm? Or maybe, no framework at all?

Don't let these decisions evolve into holy wars. In the end it's not the tech that drives the product—it's the people who make it amazing. While choosing the right technology for your product remember, you shouldn't become a slave of that technology, it's the other way around—*the technology should serve your needs and the needs of your product.* **Make comparison tables**—write down the technical requirements of your software and depict the technology that corresponds better to it. Will your product have to perform complex combined queries that have to deliver results fast? Consider something like elasticsearch. Do you need near real-time synchronization between the data storage and your presentation layer? Have a look at the realtime databases. Must it solve complex tasks and have a high performance? Run some benchmarks on different programming languages.

If there is an endless discussion among the team members regarding this or that technology, ask each one to prepare a pitch deck and present it to the team and make a poll afterward. Establish strong deadlines for that decision. Tic tac clock is ticking, and you can't afford spending your whole time on this kind of discussion or your competition might overtake you.

In the end what really matters is that **everyone feels comfortable** with the chosen technology. If there is a lack of knowledge, provide the means for people to learn. Build your software in a **nice modular way** so if the technology proves to be a poor choice it can be easily **replaceable**.

Code Style Guidelines

Besides the holy wars over choosing the programming language or framework, there are other discussions among developers—what IDE is better, spaces over tabs, double quotes versus single quotes. Did you know that you can distract engineers from nearly any conversation by asking them whether they prefer vim or emacs? Once Olga was so bored by an endless "ski VS snowboard" discussion that she deviated everyone's attention just by saying that it's like a vim versus emacs discussion. Of course, then she was bored by the vim versus emacs discussion, but you get the point.

JavaScript developers will probably discuss whether or not they should put a semi-colon (;) after the statements—the latest trends are moving toward simplifying everything, so, no semi-colons. Overall people will probably argue regarding the maximum line width.

It might not seem important at all, and each person should probably code in their way, but there are several major problems with this:

- A code with mixed styling (e.g., double and single quotes in strings in the same file) looks incoherent and ugly.

- As soon as you start with code reviews, you will end up in a "request changes" hell. Imagine someone that has been coding using 2-spaces, and then another person makes changes in the same file and their editor applies a 4-spaces rule. The code review will be full of these changes, and important changes will be lost in this mess.

It is important that people have freedom to do things in their own way, but it is also important that your software doesn't suffer from it. Thus, we advise you to establish a **code style guideline** from the very beginning. This style guide should define all the important rules, regarding the line width, the naming conventions, colons, semicolons, quotes, complexity rules (e.g., no more than three nesting levels within cycles). Everyone should read and agree and then just comply with the established rules. Nowadays there are plenty of tools that format your code according to the given rules, so you can just port them to your favorite IDE and let it deal with the rules for you.

Code Reviews and Pair Programming

We have already mentioned code reviews in the previous section, and we mentioned how code reviews might suffer when people use different coding style. Actually, it works both ways—the **code review** process can help to achieve the uniformity and homogeneity in the code base.

This happens naturally because people start to read carefully each other's code, suggest improvements, and learn new patterns from each other. Thus, with time the code starts looking as it was one solid and beautiful piece. We felt this when we worked at

Feedzai when we introduced code reviews. In the beginning it was quite tedious, and we had a lot of discussions. Some code reviews had up to 20 iterations! However, in a couple of months we were not able to recognize our code. That was a piece of art—beautiful, readable, well-documented, tested, and coherent.

It is important to establish some rules for the code to be ready for code review—the so-called **definition of ready**. For example, the newly introduced code has to be covered by unit tests, the code must follow the style guide, there must be no more than N files changed per code review, etc. Note that establishing the maximum number of lines and/or files changed per code review is really important. As you can imagine, reviewing a small logical chunk of code is much easier than reviewing a huge piece of unrelated files that have been changed.

Some developers get enthusiastic with changes and start introducing small code refactors while working on a small feature. Then their code review might include over 40 changed files or a couple of thousands of lines of changed code. This is frustrating for the reviewers, and it can actually be considered disrespectful. To avoid this kind of frustration, make it clear in your definition of ready for the code reviews that there should not be more than, let's say, 1000 changed lines of code. Believe us, everything is possible to split into smaller logical chunks of work.

Another technique that is widely used among developers and that helps in achieving the homogeneity in the code base is **pair programming**. Pair programming is exactly what you just thought—two people sitting together and coding. Actually, only one developer codes at a time and the other one just looks and comments. The pair of developers can and should also brainstorm from time to time and discuss some solutions. After some time, the roles change—the "observer" moves to coding and the coder sits beside them and helps them to think. This technique helps to reach uniformity in the code for obvious reasons; people learn from each other and help each other to improve their coding style.

There is another advantage: the level of attention and concentration increases a lot. Think of any activity that you perform alone or when someone is watching you. When you are alone, you might allow yourself to be sloppy sometimes, you might allow yourself to procrastinate, and you easily forgive yourself for that.

When someone watches you, you want to show how great you are, how deeply concentrated on work you are, and the great results that can come out of your hard work. You will certainly ignore the new e-mail or social network notification.

Actually, the productivity achieved by pair programming, although one person seems to be idle, sometimes outperforms the productivity of two programmers coding at the same time.

Quality Assurance Tips

In the previous section we discussed some techniques that can be used to increase code uniformity. As you might imagine, the more homogeneous, well-documented, and covered with tests the code is, the higher its quality, and that's why we can say that code review and pair programming are the tools that help increase our product quality.

Besides that, there are other QA techniques and processes to which we have already devoted a whole chapter of this book. There are even dedicated people doing it.

When you start developing your product you probably don't have enough resources to allocate special people for securing the quality of the product, but don't underestimate this work. Once Olga tried to convince someone to hire a QA engineer and this person answered her the following, "Let's not worry about quality for now. Let's worry about having more users. When we have lots of users, we can afford to worry about quality."

You know what? This is the worst thing you can ever think or tell someone. With a premise like this, your product will never win! And be sure, your user base will never grow because no one likes unstable and buggy products. *The quality of your product defines you, your company values, the way you think*. Of course, mistakes happen and even the big players have problems. Sometimes AWS services are down, bringing down half of the internet. Sometimes Telegram's servers are under a huge load and its users are unable to communicate. No one is immune! But some will continuously run into these issues and still not learn from them, losing their customers' trust while others will have well-defined processes to help preventing the same mistake from happening twice.

That is why we advise you, even if you don't have dedicated people, establish from the very beginning some **quality control processes and thresholds**. For example, unit tests code coverage has to be no less than 80%. Have automated tests in place. **Set up a checklist of the most critical features** to check every time a new feature is being pushed to production, so you guarantee that new stuff hasn't broken the existing ones.

Make a list of browsers and/or devices that MUST run your software without any problems. Check them every time new things are being shipped. Even if you do it manually, if you have a well-defined checklists of regression test cases and browsers or devices, the testing process distributed among everyone in the team shouldn't take too long.

Invest in automation. You must have at least your happy path tested using automation mechanisms.

Just a reminder, the **happy path** is a defined set of user activities that lead them from the very beginning until a meaningful end. For example, in case of an e-commerce website, the happy path would be from the registration until an actual purchase is done.

A small but important tip for automation: don't get overexcited with it. Of course, it's good when your interface and everything that is possible to do with it is automated, but sometimes the tests are so complex, unpredictable, and difficult to implement that it turns out that it's easier and actually faster to check it manually before each release. **Automate only what is easy to predict**. Don't try to automate things like, for example, random pictures appearing in a carousel. Check it manually. Always try to keep a good balance between automation and manual checks.

Another tip on automation: make sure your frontend developers and whoever is doing automation are totally synchronized. When we introduced automated tests at Feedzai, it was a bit frustrating in the beginning since frontend developers would always change the CSS classes of the elements, thus breaking the automation that was relying on those classes. After a bit of struggling and blaming each other, we reached an agreement that we would use prefixed classes for automation and other classes for the actual styling. This decision helped us a lot to remove the dependencies between automated tests and development and decreased tension between developers and testers.

And last but not least, as soon as you have resources to **allocate dedicated people** for testing, do it! Not only it will increase the product quality, but it will also help in achieving the overall balance among the processes between different stakeholders.

DevOps Tips

In the previous section we've been discussing automated tests. You have probably figured out that in order to have nice automation in place, you need a nice infrastructure that allows having multiple environments and an automated process of continuous integration and delivery, thus enabling a smooth and transparent process of running tests.

Well, we are now talking about **DevOps processes** that must be in place if we want to achieve the harmony of continuous integration, testing, deployment, and delivery.

Again, as in the case of quality assurance, **don't underestimate the importance of your infrastructure**. You might think that in the beginning you can just build your files locally and copy them manually to the production server and that someday you will improve this process. Doesn't work like that. Well, it might work, because sooner or later you will be terrified by the hell of dependencies and the amount of manual work you need to do to perform deployments. The more your codebase and number of dependencies grow, the harder it is to establish a right and smooth pipeline to push all of those into testing or production.

It is a lot easier to **define your CI/CD pipeline from the very beginning**, making it really simple and small, and then with time adapt it accordingly to your code base and dependencies growth.

Once Olga worked at an online advertisement measurement company. Their script was running on web pages and measuring the success of ad campaigns of their clients. In order to make it work, all campaigns had an ID, and this ID would have to match the ID defined in the script. There was a semi-automated process that would build the script along with the configuration file per campaign in order to embed the ID into the script. Once Olga was fixing some bug, and in order to make her testing easier, she hardcoded this ID in the script, thus overriding any possible configuration. Then she manually pushed this script to the staging server. At least she thought it was the staging server. In fact, she committed a terrible mistake and pushed it to the production server. For half a day they ran the script with the hardcoded ID for each and every client of theirs. Imagine what it means for the advertisement industry, where each minute might cost millions, to not measure the impact of your ad for half a day. After that epic fail, Olga setup a CI process that started running all the needed checks for the project and campaign ID enforcing that no one would ever push to production manually.

We don't want for you to pay for this kind of learnings. Someone has already learned, and you can just use this knowledge. Set up your automated processes and invest in the right people who enjoy working with infrastructure, servers, and scripts from the very beginning!

What About My Idea?

You probably start questioning, "Why do I read tips on development and quality assurance if I barely know what am I going to do? How do I know that my product will win? What should my product look like? Give me some tips on product ideas!"

The most important tip about your product is the following: **Love it**! This is not even a tip, this is a fundamental base for your success. If you don't feel an unconditional passion about what you're doing, you might succeed if you are professional, well-organized, and structured. But love for what you do creates an unbeatable determination, faith, and confidence.

You don't need to be the first one. Turns out that it is not enough to be innovative in order to be successful. Turns out, the **quality of your product,** even if there are plenty of alternatives, defines its success. Find your niche, define key success points, make them perfect. For example, Olga's father's company, Elvatech (`http://elvatech.com/`), produces equipment for spectrometric analysis. What is important for this kind of equipment? Of course, it is important how it looks; it is also important that the software is easy to use; it is also important that the equipment is made of light-weight materials to be easily transported. But the most important characteristic is the *precision of measurement*. What's the point in a beautiful design and awesome software if your spectrometric analysis' result will show that there is 50% of gold in a piece of jewelry containing 75% gold? The Elvatech's team worked hard to increase the accuracy of the algorithm to such precision that the error is close to 0—that is what defines the success of the company that has already existed for 25 years and continues to grow.

At EdEra we do what lots of people do—we create online courses. Nothing really revolutionary here, but people keep coming asking us to create courses for them. We position ourselves as a *bridge between those who possess the knowledge and those who need it*. We realized that each kind of content requires its own form to be better delivered to the final consumer. We realized that we can find this form if we work closely with the experts of the content and study this content thoroughly and passionately. Usually the creation of online courses consists of some video-making process, production, post-production, tests definition, and content management. At EdEra, all of this takes less than the preparation part—the part when we talk a lot with the experts and define the best way to deliver their content to people. Every course, every educational project is unique. We love what we do, and this defines us as the best online education studio in Ukraine (for now).

If it happens to you that you are the first one on the market with your idea, **work hard** not to let anyone beat you. If you have an idea and find out that you are not the first one, see it as an advantage—**you can learn** with the pioneers' mistakes. A nice example of being the first versus being the best happened a couple of days ago here in Berlin near a metro station. Imagine a metro station and the crosswalk leading to its entrance. It happened that it had been raining a lot and a huge puddle was formed between the crosswalk and the entrance to the metro (Figure 10-1).

Figure 10-1. *The puddle between the crosswalk and the metro station entrance*

People had to go and zigzag a little in order to bypass the puddle and to be able to move from the crosswalk to the station and vice versa. Then there was a beautiful soul who threw a brick in the puddle (Figure 10-2).

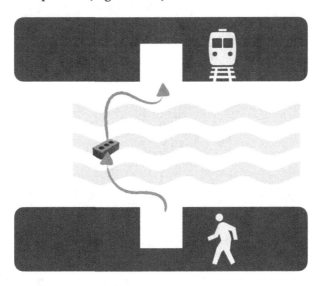

Figure 10-2. *The puddle with the brick in it*

So, people started jumping on the brick and then on the dry surface, but it was still not optimal, making people do a small zigzag. But the idea was great! Everyone at our work using the metro noticed that. People even took pictures (Figure 10-3) and sent them to our team chat, commenting, "I wonder who built this lifehack."

Figure 10-3. *Brick in the puddle lifehack—picture taken by OptioPay's amazing head of HR, Maria Kopp*

So people were happily using the brick bridge, when the very next day someone threw a huge stone right in the middle of the puddle (Figure 10-4).

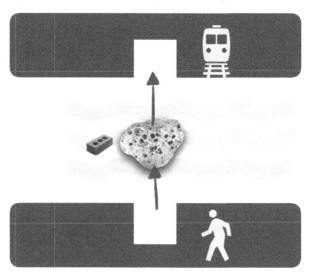

Figure 10-4. *Improved version of the brick-bridge: huge stone in the middle of the puddle*

As you can probably imagine, the brick was immediately forgotten, and the stone became the hero. It just required two short jumps to cross between the crosswalk and the metro station. This example is a very good example of how the pioneer had a short success while the second idea, which was based on the first one and slightly improved, clearly won.

Project and Product Management Tips

If you happen to be a product or a project manager, then your task is to guarantee the product delivery on time and in its highest quality while keeping the good mood of the team and business goals all aligned together. In this section we discuss some very simple and trivial tips for the success of the product management.

- **Keep focus!** This is not even a tip, this is a rule of thumb. Don't forget why you are doing this and keep reminding your team. Everyone on the team should know the goal of the project and how the current unit of work (sprint or set of tasks or whatever you're using) is impacting this goal. If everyone on your team is focused and knows the impact caused by their work, then your product development will run nicely and smoothly. A very good technique that has been used at Slack, for example, consists in having *goal lunches*. Once in a while (e.g., each month), gather a lunch with your team where you talk about the goals for this month and explain their alignment with the overall business goals and needs. It is a nice team-building event that helps the team to feel accountable and responsible for the product.

- **It's ok to change the goal.** Sometimes we try to keep such a deep focus on some goal that we cannot even imagine that this goal might suffer some change. Our main goal becomes to protect this goal and to align everything we do with it. However, the world around us changes, so do the business requirements and the users. Some unexpected turnaround might change the whole concept of our product, and you shouldn't be afraid of that! Change the goal, communicate it to the team, keep working hard to achieve the new goal. Of course, if you start changing goals every day, you will lose the trust of your team, it will be impossible to keep focus, and the product will never reach any purpose. Anyway, sometimes changes in the direction are good and refreshing. Embrace them with a smile and confidence. You are the captain; your crew will go after you if you smile.

- **Don't micromanage.** There are several books on management that talk about micromanagement and how poisonous it can be for the team. We believe that if you are already or going to be a product or a project manager, you are certainly familiar with this topic.

Nevertheless, it is never too late to remind yourself one more time: you can't keep an eye on everyone and everything. Your team is here because you trust each and every member of it. Trust your developers, don't try to understand every technical detail; they know what they're doing. Just make the expectations clear—for example, "our goal is to deliver this feature until the end of this month" and provide your team with a nice working environment to achieve the expectation. For example, if you are responsible for describing the tasks for the team, make sure that the acceptance criteria are as clear as a mountain stream. If there are some dependencies (e.g., the task for the frontend team requires the mockups from designers), make sure that they are all there. Put your energy in the right direction, and you will see how everyone wins. Control everything but don't micromanage—this is a balance that is hard but possible to achieve. When you reach a state at which you know everything that is going on without sneaking around and making everyone feel uncomfortable, you can consider yourself a successful manager!

- **Transparency over all**. Make sure everyone at all times knows everything. Sometimes we tend to report "from bottom to top"—that is, we make sure we know what exactly the team is doing to be able to deliver this information to the upper management. However, it must work the other way around as well. If your sales team had an important meeting with a customer and soon the requirements will change, you must communicate it to the developers' team. If your CEO failed to get another financial round and the deadlines should tighten up, you must explain it to the team. You are the bridge, and you should establish the communication chain in a way that no one at any point feels excluded. We talked about the impact, which is very important for each team member to feel. It will be hardly possible if people feel that they are not trusted with some piece of information. Use the whiteboard for it, for example. Divide it into some sections— for example, long running goals, shortcoming goals, sprint goals, important updates, action points, etc. Keep it up to date. Make everyone feeling the ownership, responsibility, and accountability.

- **Celebrate!** This is very important. Celebrate everything! Sprint goal achieved? Celebrate! New feature is released? Celebrate!

Everything is "*celebrateable*"—new client acquisition, the increasing number of active users, the achievement of some important threshold in quality metrics, etc. Celebrations help to feel the impact and importance of what we do. Not to mention that they are great for the team spirit!

Time Management Tips

Being able to manage your time is an important feature of project management. A very important thing to understand here is that you cannot actually manage time, but you can manage yourself in order to use your time in a great way to achieve the best possible result. Turns out it is not easy at all! We are humans, we love to procrastinate, we love to be lazy, and we have all the tools in the world that help us to be unproductive—Netflix, Online shopping, social networks... Have you ever caught yourself on Facebook's or Instagram's infinite scroll? We have! Happens every day! However, despite all this deconcentrating power that surrounds us, it is still possible to make the best of your time.

Define your goals. This one is the most difficult, but once you're done with it, everything else just needs to be adjusted. Define what you want to achieve during your life, in 10 years, in 1 month, in 1 week, tomorrow, today. Write down your goals somewhere where you are always able to see them. Adjust them periodically. Try to do the "backward" exercise—that means, imagine that you've already achieved your goal. Go one step backward. How does it look? One more, one again, until you reach the current state. Now you have the set of steps to reach your goal. Just do it.

Define your big three. Your daily routine is composed of some activities. Write them down and figure out those three that actually help you in achieving your goals. Work on improving them and making them perfect. Consider everything else as distractors, and try to delegate those things or spend less time on them.

Revise Vilfredo Pareto law. Vilfredo Pareto law, or 80/20 law, applied to the time management topic, states that 80% of what we do is accountable for 20% of results, and vice versa—20% of our daily activities are responsible for 80% of results! Define this important 20% of what you do (actually it is aligned with your big three) and work on them carefully.

Track time. Tracking the time you spend on your daily activities is a powerful and scary exercise. Try to track every 15 minutes of your life. At the end of the day, check it.

You will be amazed and horrified by the amount of time you spend on some crazy stupid things. If you think that tracking time every 15 minutes will steal a lot of time of yours, just try it. You will see that not only does it not steal any of your time, but it makes you more focused and productive, because every time you feel a need to be distracted you will think twice before acting on the distraction. For example, I just got an e-mail. I feel an urge to open and read it, but I know myself—after I read the e-mail, I will probably open Facebook, then I will check my phone, and after 15 minutes are over, and I have to track something, what will that look like? No, I'd rather continue writing this section and check my e-mails and other stuff after I'm done with it.

Use tools. There are plenty of techniques that help you to keep focused. The simplest one is the Pomodoro timer (`https://en.wikipedia.org/wiki/Pomodoro_Technique`). There are several applications that use this technique as a base. Basically, you stay focused for 20 minutes and then you have a 5-minute break to check your e-mails or social media or do whatever you want. Olga has implemented a web app that offers you a small workout at the end of each Pomodoro iteration, so you stay fit even if you work in the office. Here it is: `https://profitorolife.com/`.

Celebrate. Celebrate each and every achievement of yours. Define your celebration ways for each of the achievements. Olga does it all the time. For example, after she finishes this section, she will eat some strawberries with ice cream. After she's done with the chapter, she will watch her favorite TV series. After we finish the book, we will gather a small party with our close friends. Look forward to your celebrations, and don't let any of them skip any of your achievements. There are no small or big ones—all of them matter for your goals.

Check Olga's presentation on Time Management on Slideshare (`https://bit.ly/2NzPVao`). In the description you will also find a link to the video of Olga giving this presentation at OptioPay.

Team Management Tips

It was Olga's birthday a month ago. She was at home, in Berlin, planning a small family dinner. A friend of hers called asking if he could drop by after work. Since our place is right in the middle between his work and his home, Olga didn't find it suspicious at all and said, "Yes sure." Around 7 PM he rang on the door bell. Olga opened the door, he gave her a hug, and he looked behind him and said, "Come in!" And all of a sudden, Olga's brother and around 10 people from EdEra filled our living room with their happy and noisy presence, laughter, flowers, and congratulations (Figure 10-5).

Figure 10-5. *EdEra team coming as a surprise from Ukraine to Berlin for Olga's birthday*

They made a 2-day trip from Ukraine through Poland to catch a low-cost plane from Wroclaw just to appear as a surprise on Olga's birthday. It is hard to describe the palette of emotions she had, and these are the moments when you realize that you work with the best team in the world. Wouldn't you like to be surrounded by people like that?

You've certainly heard this pretentious phrase that states that "**people are your greatest asset.**" This phrase became such a cliché that we might pronounce it without even thinking about the whole meaning of these words. We invite you to close your eyes, write down these words in your mind, and think for a while about their meaning. What does it mean for the relationship you have with your team members? What does it mean for you as a manager? What does it mean for you as for someone who is being managed? What value do you give to the greatest asset you have around you? What do you know about them? What do you know about their family, thoughts, problems, dreams, successes, and failures? If some of them express an opinion you don't agree with, how will you behave? If one of them is in trouble, what will you do? What does it mean personally for you to be the greatest asset?

In this section, we want to discuss some situations or practices we've seen and participated in that improve the teamwork and team relationships.

Trust

Do you trust your team members? To answer this question, first we need to understand what we mean by trust when applied to the people you work with.

Usually we associate trust with deep secrets and thoughts—if I can share them with someone, it means I trust this person.

Does it mean that in order to establish the relationship of trust at a workplace, we have to take all our deep and dark secrets out of the farthest corner of our soul and just put them naked on the table beyond our colleagues? Sounds a bit creepy and scary, doesn't it? But it almost has to be like that. How many hours do you spend with your teammates? Most of the time, it's more than with our family! That is why it is so important to feel comfortable at our workplace, both physically and emotionally.

Ideally you don't even have the feeling of "*going to work.*" You just do what you love among people whose company you enjoy a lot. This kind of nirvana is not easy to reach. Actually, one thing complements another. If you really enjoy working with your team, some boring activities can be transformed into a funny piece of work—for example, meetings. I am pretty sure some readers are making a facial expression as though they are eating an entire lemon. Do you know that developers usually find all the meetings boring and useless? But bring a bit of conflict to the meeting to create some human interaction, and you'll see how people change.

What does it mean to trust? It means that you can *talk about your weaknesses openly without feeling any discomfort.* Our weaknesses are so deep inside us that sometimes we are even afraid to confess them to ourselves! For example, imagine you are afraid to hire a very good professional because you think he might take over your position. Would you admit this fact to your team? Would you admit it to yourself, or would you rather make yourself believe that the person is overqualified, or this person will destabilize the working environment, or this person too expensive, etc.?

If you are able to confess your weaknesses to your team and you feel that your team is there to give you support, you may consider yourself happy.

What can you do to increase the level of trust within the team? There are different kinds of team-building events and exercises that can help you in this—for example, *retreats* where everyone talks about their childhood, exercises in which people talk about what they hate and what they love, or simply gathering and cooking together!

At OptioPay we have the so-called "*user manuals*"; everyone has a public document where they describe themselves answering different questions. An example of such a user manual can be seen at Figure 10-6.

My style at work
- Honest direct communication
- Love to laugh
- Active learner
- People-oriented
What I value at work
- Honesty
- Immediate feedback
- Coaching and mentoring style of management
- Caring about people
What I don't have patience for
- People being late for meetings - I take it really personally and think that people don't respect my time
- Hierarchy and bureaucracy
- Unnecessary stress and pressure
How best to communicate with me or give me feedback
- Slack
- Face to face
- Telegram
How to help me
- Talk to me
- If you're late to our meeting, please let me know in advance
- If you're willing to cancel our meeting please do it as early as possible so I can replan my day
- If somehow our discussion made me upset/angry/sad and I become silent, don't push me for answering you immediately, that won't help. Just give me one minute and a glass of water.
- I love hanging out with cool people, if we go for a beer, it will be a great help!
- Let me know if you think I could communicate in a better way. I would love to reach the level of a perfect communicator, without your feedback this is impossible.
What people misunderstand about me
- Sometimes people find me aggressive when I just try to be direct. If you ever feel it, please let me know. (see "how to help me")
- I am not a "wow! a female in a men's field". I am a software engineer.

***Figure 10-6.** Olga's "user manual"*

We have also introduced user manuals at EdEra, and we've gone a bit further besides just having them publicly. We gathered a meeting where everyone could show their user manual on the whiteboard and talk a bit about themselves. The team also had a couple of minutes for comments or questions. It was pretty late when we finished but we felt an incredible bond. It seemed like we used to go to the same college and all of a sudden decided to go to a first date all together. It was an amazing feeling.

Another trust-building technique that we use at EdEra, we call *"the hot chair of self-awareness."* Once a month the team gathers, and each team member sits on a chair and talks about what they think they could have improved in themselves in order to be better professionals. After their confession, the team has the right to comment on the pronounced issue. At this point it is important to understand that the one sitting on the chair must not take the comments personally and try to defend themselves. The comments are there to help.

So, after the comments session, the team discusses the means of improvement and sets a feasible checkpoint date.

For example, one of the team members was telling that he was feeling like a terrible communicator. After he admitted that, everyone started giving examples on how his bad communication affected their work in one or another way.

After this discussion the moderator found a couple of online courses and a book on communication skills. The person made a commitment for learning, reading, and establishing a date to deliver the results of his findings through a presentation for all the team. I should say, this person is now one of the most diplomatic team members and is responsible for the communication with a large number of our clients.

Another important topic related to trust is conflicts. **Don't be afraid of conflicts**! Do not ever avoid them. Conflicts are actually a very healthy and efficient tool for trust and bond creation if you detect them early, admit them, confront them, openly talk about them, and learn from them.

For example, once two developers independently told me on our 1:1 session that they were frustrated with each other's way of pair programming. One was upset because he felt that another one was treating him like he was dumb, while the other one was feeling that the first was a great professional that was not acting as a such due to a lack of confidence, which made him angry and disappointed.

That was a clear conflict situation. What I told both of them is that they should have spoken with each other and expressed exactly how they felt. Both were scared to death of having to confront each other, but in the end, they felt great after the conversation, they learned a lot about themselves, and they became the most efficient pair of programmers doing a pair programming session.

Don't confuse healthy conflicts with a *poisonous environment*. Some people just like to create conflicts out of nothing just to be the center of attention. This kind of behavior requires a "hot chair of self-awareness" or at least a couple of one-on-ones with people who can directly talk with this team member. Assuming that everyone does what they do for the best of the company, the person will admit their problem and try to do everything to improve.

Working on trust issues within the team lies on a very complex, tricky, and never-ending path but it is a rewarding and satisfactory activity. Don't stop doing it.

Appreciate

There are a lot of articles on different kinds of incentives for people to get motivated to do what they do. A lot of research and studies are being done to figure out a perfect recipe of people's motivation. The companies are competing in creating different incentives to make people love their workplace: unlimited holidays, ski trips, retreats, flexible hours, bonuses, high salaries, equities, shares, office dogs...

Of course, all of this is important. It is important that the office is a comfortable place to work. It is important that your mind isn't occupied with "where to get the money from" or "how to wisely spend my vacation days." The feeling of ownership of a person who gets company shares is important as well, but there is something more.

Turns out, we are just humans, and despite our complex nature, it is pretty easy to make us happy. What would you appreciate the most—an expensive present for your birthday or a totally unexpected small surprise organized by your best friend? What would make your eyes to start tearing—when your loved one buys you a piece of expensive clothes or tells you that their life makes no sense without you? How would you feel more appreciated at work—if you got a huge bonus as a transfer to your banking account or a smaller bonus given you in an envelope personally by your manager with some words of appreciation on how important your effort is for the future of the company?

Turns out that simple words like *"thank you," "you are awesome," "your work means a lot to me,"* and *"it wouldn't be possible to achieve this result without you"* are in fact more valuable for us than anything else. And it's the easiest way to show the people their value! Don't forget to appreciate your colleagues. Don't be shy in expressing your kind opinion. There are several things you can do.

Public appreciations. At OptioPay we have weekly family lunches: it's the time when we all gather as a team, discuss some important updates, and in the end tell the appreciation stories about each other. For example, someone organized a successful event that everyone loved. Why not thank this person in public and tell them how awesome they are? Or maybe your team member spent the whole day helping you to fix that awful bug. They certainly deserve appreciation. Or maybe it's just a great person next to you who you admire. Why not tell everyone how great this person is? It feels good!

We also do appreciation celebrations at EdEra during the weekly all-hands meetings: every team member has a couple of minutes to tell about some update and say thank you to another team member.

At Gymondo, where Rui works, they also have appreciations but in a different way. They have a special *appreciation token* that changes its owner every week. Every week the person who possesses the token has to choose the successor and tell the appreciation story while passing the token to this person. Are you interested in knowing what that token is? Well, it's a life-size cardboard figure of... Queen Elizabeth!

"Thank you cards." It's not always easy to publicly appreciate someone. Sometimes we feel that it has to be an intimate one-on-one act. As we already pointed out, it's never too much to come to the person and thank them. Or, you can go further and write a thank you card! Olga has a pile of thank you cards in her drawer and has a rule of using them at least once per week. There are always people who deserve your "thank you card". It feels so good to write them. It feels even better to give them to people. And it feels awesome knowing how good people feel when they receive these cards. And it is so easy to do!

Inspirational post-its. When Olga worked at Meetrics, she once had to spend a weekend in the office finishing some work. At some point she had this crazy idea, grabbed a pile of post-its, and wrote a bunch of inspirational messages like, "Have a great and sunny day!", "You are awesome and let your days be awesome for you!", "There is nothing you can't do!", etc. It took around half an hour to write all those post-its and then put them on each team member's desk. She knew people would like it, what she didn't expect was that some people put those post-its on the most visible place of their workstations and kept them forever. It really means something!

You can be creative and find your own way of appreciating people you work with. It's up to you!

Invest in Education

If you are walking down the street and you stop, you will remain at the point where you stopped. Here you have quite a useless piece of information from Captain Obvious. Despite its obviousness, this rule doesn't apply to any kind of movement. If you stop while swimming, you will not remain at the same point, you will drown. If you had wings and stopped using them while flying, you would inevitably fall down. If you stop talking in the middle of a sentence, the thought will go away and you will not be able to continue afterward.

Our brain is built in a way that when we stop learning, our knowledge doesn't remain at the same level where it was at the moment we stopped; it will gradually drop down until it reaches something close to zero. That is why it is so important to be in the constant movement of learning and studying. That is why it is crucial for companies to invest in education for their teams.

When we talk about investment, it is not only about money. Of course, it's great to provide people with some learning budget to be spent on conferences, books, meetups, etc. (we do have that at OptioPay). Time is also a great investment, and people should know that they can and should use their time for studying. For example, at Meetrics we had a half-an-hour-in-the-morning rule, which meant that you could spent your first half an hour doing some online course. At EdEra, we have 2 hours per week for studying. At OptioPay we have each second Friday for working on whatever you want. The same concept exists at Gymondo, where Rui works: once per month they have a "Innovation and learning day." This day is announced, and everyone spends this day learning something new or developing some interesting project that contributes to their learning.

Encourage the culture of knowledge sharing at the company. At OptioPay we organize *internal meetups and academies.* Internal meetups are engineering events where engineers share their knowledge with each other regarding technical topics. OptioPay academies are about broad topics that are being shared by anyone in the company. For example, our CFO gave us a presentation on financial topics like profit and loss, income and expenses, debit versus credit, etc. Our sales team made a workshop on how to sell nearly anything.

Every person has some knowledge that is valuable for the company and for the growth of your team members. Use it!

At EdEra we invite external experts to share their experience and provide us with workshops on different topics—communication, fundraising, cognitivism, scribing, scenic skills, and even makeup skills (it is important for us to learn how to use makeup wisely, so people appear nice on camera).

The thing is, people love learning new stuff. Give them the means for keeping their knowledge on a good level and they will never leave you! People learn even more while teaching other people. Foster the culture of knowledge-sharing, and you will have the best team in the world!

Be the Best to Hire the Best

It is no secret that it's very hard to hire good professionals. Even if the person is available, how do you convince them that your company is the best company for them to be? You have to be the best and tell your story everywhere, so everyone knows that you are the best.

Actually, if your team is happy, they will do 90% of the recruitment work. People that are happy within the company where they work share their happiness everywhere. Sooner or later the happiness of your team will become your company's visit card. Until very recently we didn't have a jobs page on the EdEra's website; however, every week we would receive e-mails of people that wanted to work with us.

The process of hiring might differ from company to company, but one thing is very important: **involve all the team** in this process. Everyone should be able to express their opinion. Remember, you are not hiring an employee, you are hiring a team member. It is like marriage, or even bigger than that, because in marriage there is only one person dealing with another (we are keeping polygamy apart in this statement), whereas all the members of your team will have to cope with the newly hired member.

Be persistent in your hiring process, and **don't easily take "no" for an answer**. Once we were hiring a frontend developer. There was an amazing candidate that everyone on the team loved. Everyone was looking forward to working with this guy. We went through a full hiring process, and right at the end of it the candidate said he won't proceed with us because he preferred other option over us. Our HR manager and I considered that answer as a final "no." Our CEO, however, was not satisfied. He truly believes that our company is the best company to work with (and that is how it should be!). So, he called the candidate and told him how much he would appreciate working with him, how sad he was regarding his decision, and asked if there was anything he could do. The guy told the CEO that actually yes, there was something. He shared that the other company that he chose over us was also amazing like ours, but they offered a slightly higher salary and that was the only reason. Thus, we covered the offer and we got a great team member and a frontend engineer. Don't let good people slip away from your team; be open with them, show your trust. This makes the process of hiring an exciting and rewarding part of your culture.

Don't make people wait. A friend of Olga's who was a very good QA engineer was going through a hiring process at a very nice company. The thing is, after completing the technical challenge that everyone loved, and going through a process of interviews that also went pretty well, she had to wait for nearly a month for an answer. She was so frustrated about it that even though she loved the idea of working in that company, she was about to give up and send an e-mail explaining that she had reconsidered her options and didn't want to work there anymore. Luckily for the company, there was a person that she knew inside the company who told her that the head of HR was on vacation and there was no one else that could maintain feedback communication. That piece of information calmed down a storm of emotions for this friend. In the end, she got this job and both the company and she are really happy.

At OptioPay we have a system of warnings that would let us know if the candidate hasn't got any feedback during the previous 3 days. Then some of us would send an e-mail to the candidate sharing how important they are for us and that we need a couple more days to give an answer. Yes, this is a semi-automated process, yes, there is a template for such an answer, but in any case, our candidates never feel themselves abandoned. They feel that they are needed. And this is true, we really need good people, and so do you!

Reflect on Everything

Reflection is a very good practice not only for self-discipline but also for the teams and the companies. Post mortems for things that don't go well, retrospective meetings at the end of working cycles—all these processes were designed to reflect on how things went and why they went like that and what to do to improve them.

It happens a lot that we organize a lot of post mortem and retrospective meetings for things that don't go well because we want to prevent the failures from happening in the future.

What we do forget is to reflect on things that go great. We just take it for granted. And this is a big human mistake. Things don't just end up being successful because it's in their intrinsic nature to be like that. They end up being successful because someone did something extraordinary for them to be like this. There was a team effort, there was some chain of events, there was something that made things go this way and not another. It is crucially important to reflect on success. How did that happen? What lessons should we retrieve out of this success to make it happen more and more in the future?

At EdEra we started using this reflection on success in our one-on-one and all-hands meetings. There is a kind of template for these meetings, with a couple of questions like the following:

- What happened last week?

- How did it go?

- What failed and why?

- What was great and why?

Although it seems as a bit of formality, it makes every team member reflect on both failures and successes and develop a mindset that allows them to tune into success in the future.

Create YOUR Thing

What defines your team? Do you have some stupid jokes no one else would understand? Do you have some strange ritual that only applies to your team? What is so special that you have only within your team and nowhere else?

It is nice to have this kind of thing. Don't force them—they will appear naturally, just don't oppose them, and let them evolve. These small things make your team play well together for success. We will give a couple of examples.

At Gymondo, where Rui works, every Friday the team plays skribbl (`https://skribbl.io/`)—an online game where someone has to draw a given word and while they draw everyone else has to guess the word. It's a funny game that makes people know each other better and brings the team spirit up!

At Meetris, every Friday we would try to send the "Friday" music of Rebecca Black to the team. It was not easy, because if you just send the YouTube URL, everyone would understand what it was and would not open it. So, we had to be creative! We would include the links to the code reviews and ask people to review them, we would create some web pages, QR codes—whatever we could to mask that URL. It was so geeky and funny at the same time!

At OptioPay we have a "Friday beer syncs". This is like a standup, but in the afternoon and only talk about positive moments is allowed. Also, after each team member speaks some positive moment, they are required to make a toast. The toast should be in some language that hasn't been spoken at the table before, and it should be creative, not just some "Hey, cheers." So, we've learned a number of ways of cheering with the beer in different languages—French, Iranian, Ukrainian, German…

It is really funny to have these special things with your team, and it is great for the team bond. It would be great to hear back from you about some things you have within your teams. You can write us to chudaol@gmail.com or rpvilao@gmail.com.

Summary

In this chapter we discussed some tips and tricks that we took from our own experience regarding the development process, quality assurance, DevOps, and product, project, and team management. It felt really good to share our experiences with you. We hope that what we have learned through the years of our experience will help you in building your products, teams, and companies.

We haven't forgotten about our product—our learning platform. Actually, you are more than invited to be the first ones to use it! Please open it at `http://eleplatform.herokuapp.com/`, register, and enroll in the "Software Development from A to Z" course. There you will find only one lecture—a small video we have recorded for you, and a couple of questions regarding this video.

Welcome to the first online course on the platform we've been building together on our journey throughout this book!

Thank you for being with us.

Yours truly, Olga and Rui.

Index

A

Acceptance testing, 186
Access token, 117
Amazon Web Services (AWS), 75, 211
Animation design, 73
Application stack, 119
Asynchronous JavaScript and
    XML (Ajax), 170
Authentication, 115
Authorization Code Grant, 116
Automated tests, Feedzai, 264
Automation QA tester
    login functionality, 191
    manual to, 191–193
    regression testing, 190
    Selenium, 191

B

Backend applications
    definition, 102
Backend development
    database module, 120
    persistence layer, 120
    registration implementation, 121
    REST API, 121
    service API, 120
    service layer, 120
    transformation layer, 121
Backups, 238–239

Bare-metal server, 210
Big bang testing, 184
Bitbucket, 216
Black-box testing, 185
Block elements, 146
Bootstrapping, 103–104, 158
Box model, CSS, 154
Brainstorming, 90–91
Browserstack, 198
Bug fixing, 247–252
Bug report, 202–203
Build automation tool, 104
Business owner, 17
Business-to-business (B2B), 17
Business-to-consumer model (B2C), 17

C

Cascading style sheets (CSS)
    box model, 154
    change color, 161
    colors, 152
    definition, 137
    font-related properties, 152–153
    grid layout, 156
    LESS tool, 160
    rules, 149–150
    Sass tool, 160
    selectors, 151
    sizes, 152
    styling, 138